ON FULL AUTOMATIC

SURVIVING 13 MONTHS IN VIETNAM

WILLIAM V. TAYLOR JR.

On Full Automatic: Surviving 13 Months in Vietnam
Published by Deep Water Press
Dyer, Indiana

This book is a memoir. It is the author's story and to the best of the author's knowledge, the events shared in this book are as they occurred. Many of the people in the book are named, and a few of the names have been changed to maintain their privacy. The conversations in the book all come from the author's recollections, though they are not written to represent word-for-word transcripts. Rather, the author has retold them in a way that evokes the feeling and meaning of what was said, and in all instances, the essence of the dialogue is accurate. The author most humbly apologizes for any mistakes that may remain.

Publisher's Cataloging-in-Publication data

Names: Taylor, William V., Jr., author.
Title: On full automatic : surviving 13 months in Vietnam / William V. Taylor Jr.
Description: Dyer, IN: Deep Water Press, 2021.
Identifiers: ISBN: 978-1-7366216-0-8 (paperback)
Subjects: LCSH Taylor, William V., Jr. | Vietnam War, 1961-1975–Personal narratives, American. | BISAC BIOGRAPHY & AUTOBIOGRAPHY / Personal Memoirs | BIOGRAPHY & AUTOBIOGRAPHY / Military Classification: LCC DS559.5 .T39 2021 | DDC 959.704/3373/092–dc23

Cover and Interior Design by Victoria Wolf, wolfdesignandmarketing.com
Cover Photo by: Bruce Axelrod
Map Illustration by: Kelli Green

QUANTITY PURCHASES: Schools, companies, professional groups, clubs, and other organizations may qualify for special terms when ordering quantities of this title. For information, contact the author at: williamvtaylor.com/contact.

DEEPWATER
PRESS

To Jeannie,
for shouldering the burden of my tears and
for filling the darkness with the light of your love.

CONTENTS

PREFACE AND ACKNOWLEDGMENTS

THIS BOOK IS A MEMOIR. It reflects my present recollections of experiences that occurred more than fifty years ago. As such, some names have been created because I cannot remember the actual names of the people they represent. However, all characters portrayed in this book reflect real individuals.

To portray my experiences as realistically as possible, I found it necessary to use dialogue. It is impossible, of course, to remember the exact words people said more than fifty years ago, but I've done my best to reflect what was probable and realistic. In some scenes, I have used dialogue to reveal important details. I've done this only to tell the story in the most natural way possible. While the actual, specific words spoken by any given character may not always be historically exact, they always reflect truth.

Throughout this book, I've used the word "gook" to describe the enemy—the North Vietnamese Army and the Viet Cong. I realize this is a derogatory term, but in 1967-1968, we used the term as a way of dehumanizing the enemy. To accurately reflect the reality of the period and the way we talked, I found it necessary to use the term frequently. I apologize to those who find it offensive.

Though most of this book is derived from my own personal experiences, I have included some elements that were shared by other Marine veterans from my unit. I have included their stories when they are directly or closely related to my own. Some of their stories were revealed to me during our tour of duty, but many were told years after the war—during Third Marine Division Association reunions, for example.

In addition to the help I've gotten from my fellow Marines, I've received tremendous support from several others. When I set out to write this book, I had no idea how hard it would be to get the job done. Had it not been for a multitude of people who came to my aid, this would have been a different book.

To Cody Burleson, for the years spent helping me understand and respect writing as craft, for adding magical touches of literary genius, and for helping me find better words and ways to tell this story, I will forever be in your debt.

I've always felt it was a miracle that I survived Vietnam and that there were angels looking out for me, perhaps for this very purpose—to tell this story, to honor the men I served with, and to honor the families who shared in their sacrifice. I believe I have been continually graced by spiritual forces that have pushed this book forward. Among those forces are the Carmelite Sisters of Des Plaines, Illinois, who have blessed me with the power of their prayers and who have given me the spiritual strength to complete and publish this work.

I must thank Bruce Axelrod, a Marine combat photographer from my unit, for snapping the incredible photo that appears on the cover of this book and for his permission to use it.

I must also thank those who took the time to review early versions of this memoir and then provided encouragement and constructive feedback: Pastor Bayo Arowolo, Bruce Axelrod, Monica Baber, Roger and Ellie Bacon, Bishop Robert Barron, Don Bumgarner, Kenneth Burkett, Loretta Caravette, Kat Canfield, Ryan Donovan, Arnold and Kathy Ewings, Lisa Fieldhouse, Linda Futral, Spencer Framke, Stacy Lyn Harris, Tom Harrison, Terry Hiestand, Candace Kil, Tom Laberda, Edward Little, John Matuska, Maureen McKenna, Brendan and Siobhan McKinney, Edward Niederberger, John W. and Pat O'Brien, Robert J. and Rita O'Brien, Robert J. O'Brien III, Kealah Parkinson, Doug Peacock, Wayne Pilgreen, Aaron Rasala, Colonel Gerald Reczek (USMC Ret.), Terry Roberson, Michael Smylie, Dan Sullivan, James F. Sullivan, Jeannine O. Taylor, Melanie Taylor, Lieutenant Colonel Curt Bruce (USMC Ret.), Captain Ron Sutton (USMC Ret.), and Beverly Tucker. I tried to remember everyone who helped me, but if I forgot someone, I apologize.

Others who encouraged and supported me were Laurie Bauer, Brian and Danielle Rossi, Nancy Smylie Kehoe, and Matt and Nancy Taylor.

I'd like to express my special gratitude to Robert J. O'Brien, Sr. (Poppy) for being my inspiration in life since I was a young boy.

I'm especially thankful to my kids, who were my original inspiration for writing this book: William V. Taylor III, Kelli Green, Danielle Rossi and Lisa Rasala.

Finally, I must acknowledge the families and friends of all Marines who gave their lives in service of their country during the Vietnam War. While I realize that my descriptions of the violence of war may invoke painful memories, my intent has been only to honor those men for their sacrifices—that they may never be forgotten.

PROLOGUE

ON MEMORIAL DAY 2017, Colonel Gerald F. Reczek wrote this letter to the survivors of Charlie Company, First Battalion, Third Marine Regiment, who along with Alpha, Bravo, and Delta Companies, a helicopter squadron, and Navy elements, were the Special Landing Force Alpha in Vietnam from February 1967 to November 1967.

Monday, May 29, 2017

Fifty years ago now, and as Memorial Day approaches, each of you lived and demonstrated what the current values of the Marine Corps are all about: Honor, Courage and Commitment.

Your actions on the battlefield reflected those values when the First Battalion, Third Marine Regiment took the fight to the Viet Cong and NVA base areas in the Republic of South Vietnam.

Over the years, you have heard or read about the battle of the Ia Drang Valley with the Seventh Cavalry in March 1965 or saw the movie, *We Were Soldiers.*

Over the years, you have heard or read about the New Year Tet Offensive in February 1968, of the battle for Saigon, and the battle to retake the city of Hue, the Citadel and the Imperial Palace from the NVA and VC.

Over the years, you have heard or read about the Siege of Khe Sanh in February/March 1968 and also the battle of Dai Do along the Cua Viet River.

The courage and commitment of the American and South Vietnamese fighting men prevailed in all of these battles and defeated the NVA and VC.

The Special Landing Force concept of operations was put into action in 1967 as part of General Westmoreland's new strategy to take US offensive action into the base areas of the NVA and VC. Little did the Marines of First Battalion, Third Marines know that they would become a key player of that strategy when they conducted a tactical retrograde from Khe Sanh in February 1967 where they were defending the combat base while it was being built up to become a military and political target for the NVA and their Government.

First Battalion, Third Marines redeployed to Okinawa to re-equip, rehab and train to become the Ground Combat Element of Special Landing Force Alpha as part of the Ninth Marine Amphibious Brigade (9thMAB).

The Aviation Combat Element was a squadron of UH-34 helicopters from HMM-263 nicknamed the Thunder Eagles. That squadron and their pilots were magnificent! They flew from the USS *Okinawa* in all kinds of conditions, day or night, to support our Marines on the ground.

Their first priority was to do whatever it took to answer

the call from First Battalion, Third Marines in the battle on the ground.

As an example, one of their birds brought a resupply of ammo and off-loaded the ammo in the middle of Charlie Co. on May 10th. They stayed there on the ground, at our request, so we could load seriously wounded casualties aboard. We found out later, after the operation, that when the bird landed on the *Okinawa* with our casualties, the crew counted thirty-four holes in the fuselage. We can never give them enough kudos for what they did for us. Thank you, Thunder Eagles!

SLF Alpha, with 1/3 Marines and the rest of the Battalion Landing Team and the Amphibious Ready Group (ARG) that made up the Special Landing Force, had the mobility, combat capability and combat support to respond to Third Marine Amphibious Force (3rdMAF) operations in I Corps, which was commanded by Lt. General Lewis Walt, USMC.

1/3 Marines answered the call, time after time engaging VC and NVA forces in search-and-destroy operations throughout all of I Corps. From the Ben Hai River bordering North Vietnam and south to Chu Lai, and west to the border of Laos at Hiep Duc and places in between, such as the Que Son, Hoi An, Go Noi Island, the Street Without Joy, Quang Tri, the DMZ, and the Market Place.

During the approximate six months or so as SLF Alpha, BLT 1/3 was awarded two Presidential Unit Citations: one by the First Marine Division, and one by the Third Marine Division. Each of you was no small part of those operations. You distinguished yourselves and were recognized by being awarded the highest combat unit distinguishing citation by the US Marine Corps. Well done BLT 1/3 Marines and Sailors!

We can never forget the cost and sacrifices of our buddies and comrades-in-arms that we lost in battle. They were lost, but never forgotten. Their names are etched on THE WALL, but still live on in our memories all the days of our lives. May God rest their souls and grant them eternal peace, and comfort to their families. They died defending freedom and fighting for us so that we could be successful in battle and life.

We salute them and recognize their sacrifice on this Memorial Day.

Each of you has your own stories to tell on this Memorial Day. Tell your stories in whatever forum that you have available to you. Your families, friends, and your communities need to hear them.

Semper Fidelis,
Gerald F. Reczek
COL USMC, Ret
Charlie Six

I'm Bill Taylor, a Marine from Charlie Company, First Battalion, Third Marines. I was there and served with Special Landing Force Alpha in 1967, during the height of the Vietnam War. This is my story.

CHAPTER

ONE

WE WERE SPEEDING TOWARD the coast of Vietnam when our convoy of ships ran directly into Typhoon Violet, packing 115 mph winds. There were specific orders against going to the carrier's flight deck, but I needed to get away from the putrid smells of the seasick Marines confined within the ship. Desperate for fresh air, I snuck my way to the deck and opened the steel door. Extreme wind and cool, wet spray hit my face. I took a long, deep breath of the sea-salted air and was immediately refreshed. I was then entranced by what I saw next to us in the colossal wave.

The USS *Duluth*, a transport ship that carried the fleet's amtracs, had just ridden up the side of a fifty-foot swell. The bow came completely out of the water, exposing the entire front end of the ship. Then, like a forty-story building turned sideways, she drove through the crest of the wave. The stern rose high, and I could see propellers churning out of the water. With all its weight rushing forward, the front end burst through the incoming wave with an explosion of spray that went as high and as far as the bridge where the crew steered the great ship. Then, she pointed skyward again, riding up to repeat the process over and over.

Beyond the USS *Duluth*, miles and miles across the violent sea, I searched for some steady line of horizon—for some sense of the earth beneath us. I was an eighteen-year-old Marine who, like so many before me, had embarked across the vastness of the sea to serve my country and to stop our enemies where they stood. I wanted to prove myself to the other Marines and to prove myself worthy of the title, but truth be told, I was still just a young man— unsure of myself and afraid of whatever fate awaited us on the other side of the storm.

I found no horizon out there—only an ocean swelling and spitting cold spray into a gray sky. I tasted salt on my lips and felt the sting of it in my eyes, like sweat, as I steadied myself. I couldn't help but think of John Basilone, a great Marine who crossed the very same sea, fought heroically in the Battle of Guadalcanal, and then later died on the first day of Iwo Jima. The thought occurred to me that giving one's life is the ultimate sacrifice and that I could soon be among those called to make it. I held some pride in the fact that, as a Marine, I had promised to do my duty for my country. I had passed the point of no return; the fleet would not be turning around for me. Whatever was going to happen was going to happen, but dammit, I had no intention of dying. I wanted to survive my thirteen months, the tour of duty for a Marine, and then come home to marry Kathy. I could live with my head held high, knowing that, like those who served before me, I answered the call.

After two days of battling the storm, the ship resumed her course heading for the coast of Vietnam. On April 26, 1967, we arrived thirty miles south of Da Nang City. That afternoon we were called to the hangar deck where helicopters are stored, just below the flight deck. Marines streamed in from all directions and gathered in groups. My unit, Charlie Company, gathered at the rear of the ship where some mechanics were working on one of the choppers. First, Second, and Third platoons, along with the Weapons Platoon, were positioned left, center, and right, respectively. Our company commander, Captain Reczek, looked totally squared away as he walked toward us with a complement of four platoon lieutenants at his side. Two hundred Marines jumped up as someone yelled, "Attention!"

"At ease," Captain Reczek said. "Sit, Marines!"

Everyone looked around and began sitting where they could.

"Four battalions of Marines, plus three ARVN battalions, are closing in on what we think could be a full regiment of NVA troops in the foothills south of Da Nang. There have been reports of significant enemy movements, and we should assume the locals in the area are sympathetic to the VC and NVA," Captain Reczek said.

I considered the scope of what he was saying. Four battalions would have been as many as 4,500 Marines. With the ARVN (Army of the Republic of Vietnam) battalions, there would have been as many as 3,000 more men out there. Against a regiment of NVA (North Vietnamese Army), I liked the odds, but still the sheer numbers were frightening.

"This area is called the Que Son Valley," Reczek continued. "They have controlled it since the beginning of the war because it's been a big source for rice and for rations, so we're going in to take control of the valley and stop them."

"Semper Fi!" one of the Marines yelled.

"The valley extends into the foothills directly west of where we'll be landing," he said. "After we land, we're going to move up the center of the valley until we hit the foothills. The Marines and ARVN out there should be sweeping south of us and north of us, which means that if those NVA are out there we are going to find them in the valley and corner them on all sides. Men, it will be our job to trap and eliminate the enemy.

"Only God knows what lies ahead of us, but I do know one thing for sure: you will take care of each other. I have confidence that we will accomplish this mission and be successful. Gentlemen, we take off at 0630 in the morning."

"*Dismissed*!" someone yelled. I looked at the men's faces. Some appeared to be inspired by Reczek's talk and excited about the thought of going into combat for the first time. They wore eager smiles, chewed on their gum more vigorously, and kidded around. Still, others were clearly worried. They stared off in the distance, as if looking into an abyss. As for me, I wasn't sure how to feel.

Our first operation was to be called Operation Beaver Cage. God only knows who came up with the name, but this was it. We were going to do what we had trained to do—find and kill the enemy.

I followed the group that gravitated to where our bunks and letter gear resided. I wanted to send letters to all my friends and family. The letters could be, I knew, the last words they might ever hear from me.

WE WOKE UP BEFORE dawn, 4:30 a.m. One in ten men started to stir right away. I wasn't one of them. I had stayed up late writing letters—twelve in all, plus a very long one to my high school sweetheart, Kathy. I lay there for a time, clinging to the safety of my bunk and the comfort of sleep as half-naked Marines headed for the shower—the last that any of them would have for a long time. Someone screamed from the snap of a wet towel. The grab-ass had begun.

Everyone wanted that last gratifying meal before flying off to battle, so we headed to the chow hall and filled ourselves with runny scrambled eggs, half-cooked bacon, and greasy linked sausage. After breakfast, I spread everything I was taking into combat on the floor at my feet. There was no way I was going to fit everything in my pack. It became truly hectic. What do you take into combat? The hard decisions had to be made. Do I take more ammo to fight off the enemy? On the other side, I certainly didn't want to run out of food. The other supporting gear was important too. I needed my letter-writing gear, extra socks to keep my feet dry, soap, toothbrush, and a camera and plenty of film to record my experiences, just to mention a few of the items.

With gear and food all over the floor and with fifty anxious Marines crammed together like sardines, tension was high and tempers started to flare. One of the Marines stood up from his bunk and bumped his pack into another Marine, who then fell over his gear. A small fight ensued. There was plenty of yelling and screaming, but the fight was quickly broken up.

I made a last check of all my gear. My cartridge belt was worn around my waist. It held two canteens of fresh, clean water, one on each side. I had a small medical kit located at the back of my belt, which contained a heavy-duty rubber band that acted as a tourniquet, gauze wrappings, Band-Aids, and various tubes of salves. All the Marines purchased a unique combat knife called the KA-BAR. I had one of these sharp knives on the right side of my belt and a bayonet on the other. My rifle needed a magazine to hold the ammunition. Each magazine contained twenty rounds. So I added four magazine pouches to my belt. Each pouch held two magazines. It was obvious I was going to need more ammo, so I picked up two seven-pocket bandoliers. A bandolier has a cloth strap that connects to seven pockets sewn together. Each pocket is large enough to hold one magazine. Both bandoliers would then give me fourteen extra magazines. They were draped from my left shoulder to under my right arm. In all, this gave me twenty-two magazines. It seemed like more than enough ammo to take into combat, at the time.

I had had to dye my underwear green so I wouldn't make myself a target when relieving myself. We were issued two long, green jungle jackets. The jackets had large saddle pockets where I kept my extra grenades. Each jacket had two chest pockets where most of the guys kept their cigs. Being a nonsmoker, I kept my bug spray in there. The loose-fitting jungle pants had four pockets: two normal slit pockets and two long button pockets down the outside of my thighs. Our dog tags were shiny as hell, so Jones, the squad leader, gave us black electrical tape to secure them, solving two problems: keeping the glare down and stopping the clanging when they were free-flowing. My helmet had a jungle montage of green leaves imprinted on the cloth cover. The helmet liner secured the cloth into place, and there were little slits in the cloth to slip in live small branches for a realistic camouflage effect. Some of us were going into battle without the new jungle boots that were promised. I, of course, was one of the unlucky guys. Apparently, someone in the rear neglected to do his job, and we ran short of my size, 11. I was looking forward to those boots, too. They were unique because of the thin metal strips in the soles to deflect the dreaded punji sticks. Another good feature was that the sides of the boot were made of a porous green cloth that would evaporate moisture around the feet and cut down on jungle rot.

With my pack filled to capacity, I strapped my shovel and poncho to the back and was now ready for combat. I waited in the squad bay with Second Platoon until we heard the call to move out.

"Head 'em up, move 'em out!" someone yelled—words from the theme song to the TV series *Rawhide*.

I finished the jingle. "Rollin', rollin', rollin', keep them doggies rollin'," I sang. "*Rawhide!*"

Someone laughed; he must have also watched the show. We moved down the hallway and up three precipitous, steel, almost-vertical stairways. As we emerged from the depths of the ship to the hangar deck, we picked up hand grenades from boxes on the deck. The ship's PA system kicked in.

Now hear this:
BATTLE STATIONS! BATTLE STATIONS!

Excitement raged inside me at this point. It was like the first time I stood in line for the roller-coaster at the Riverview Amusement Park in Chicago. I was seven years old, standing in a long line with my sister, Bev, waiting for our turn on the infamous "Bobs." The advertising for the Bobs said, "One of the fastest roller-coasters in the world—150 miles per hour and lots of crazy drops." I remember feeling like I wanted to get out of the line because it seemed too scary. I didn't get out of line, and all went well, though. I wasn't going to be able to get out of this line, either.

Our platoon moved in a long line to the front of the hangar deck. No one talked, just followed the person in front of him to a steep stairway and to a hallway that led to the flight deck. The closer we got, the louder the sounds from the choppers warming their engines became. I got to the doorway of the flight deck. Five men in front of me were escorted to a chopper. Each time a flight deck member arrived at the door, he took the next five to their respective chopper. Now it was my group's turn. Five of us ran to the center of the flight deck and jumped aboard our chopper, as we had practiced in training. I sat on the floor next to the door gunner, who wore a green, full-bodied flight suit and a war-worn aviation helmet. He gave us a thumbs-up sign. I smiled and passed the sign back.

The others in my group, Mac, Ski, Smitty, and Pilgreen, had the same look of quiet apprehension on their faces. No one had anything to say until finally, Ski thrust his M16 out in front of himself and yelled, "Geronimo!" Everyone smiled.

It was 6:45 a.m., and the go-ahead sign must have been given, because our chopper's engine started to rev up. The exhaust pipes protruding from the front nose section spewed plumes of diesel-smelling fumes. The speed of the turning blades increased, and the downdraft began to dissipate the fumes. As the engine reached full throttle, the chopper began to shake with such violence that it seemed the machine could rip apart at any second.

We could feel the chopper lifting off the deck. As soon as we were airborne, the ride became smoother. The nose of the chopper dipped, the tail lifted, and we moved forward and up over the sea. As we continued to lift, I could see many choppers converging for the attack. Looking out the open door, I noticed the hospital ship, USS *Sanctuary*, entirely painted in pristine white with large red crosses on the sides of the ship. It was eerie and comforting at the same time.

As we continued to climb, the sound of the engine diminished because our ears had plugged from the changes in atmospheric pressure. I yawned to relieve the pressure, and a flood of sound rushed back into my ears. Off we went into the morning sky. The choppers behind us caught up, and we were flying in a close formation. I felt the anticipation of my situation in my stomach and wanted to see where we were. Being next to the door gunner, I was able to lean forward as far as I could and see the shoreline below. It stretched for miles—sandy beaches all up and down the coast. A short distance from the shoreline, I felt as if we were slowly descending. Square rice paddies and fields of corn became visible as we neared the ground. I was shocked to see an old farmer running for his life and poking his water buffalo in the hind quarters to make it move faster. I'm sure he was terrified as twelve helicopters were now landing in his backyard.

Smitty, my team leader, said, "Lock and load," and we all put a round in the chamber of our M16s. The chopper was losing altitude fast. The ground came closer, and our ears felt the pressure of the descent. As we neared one of the paddy fields, I felt a rush of adrenaline surging through my body and I began to shake inside. The pilot raced the engine to counteract the gravity pulling at the fast-descending chopper. He lifted the front end slightly to allow the single back wheel to touch first and, in one smooth maneuver, the two front wheels touched a second later. I jumped out of the open door and found myself on hard ground moving forward and on line with the other Marines.

We looked intently for any signs of the enemy. There were no incoming rounds. The choppers' engines began accelerating with an ear-shattering roar. The tail of our chopper lifted, and the spinning blades threw debris in all directions as it moved away. We had landed at 7:11 a.m. In a matter of a couple of minutes we had sixty men down and ready to fight. On the other side of the coin, we were alone and the choppers had left the area, returning to the sea where the next group of Marines was waiting. Lieutenant Francis was on the radio, and orders started coming in from Captain Reczek to widen the landing zone because more choppers were coming in with more Marines.

Jones, my squad leader, yelled, "Spread out and move forward!"

We secured the area around us and continued to spread out. It was still early morning, and the temperature was about eighty-five degrees. Because of the heat and high humidity, our foreheads and bodies dripped with sweat. Vietnam was a lot hotter than Okinawa, where we had trained for the Special Landing Force (SLF). It felt like we were in a humid oven. Our packs and gear weighed between forty and fifty pounds. My platoon staff sergeant, Malloy, spotted one of the Marines downing water.

"Tell your men to conserve their water," he yelled at the squad leaders. "We have to be out here three days before our next resupply."

We didn't receive any fire on our first landing, and we were relieved that no one was hurt. Most of the Marines were digging small fighting holes, but not nearly as deep as we should have. It was just too hot, and besides, the area appeared to be tranquil.

The next group of choppers came in exactly where we had landed, and after about an hour and a half, Charlie Company was on the ground. The other companies, Alpha, Bravo, and Delta, were landing in other locations.

"Pack 'em up and get ready to move out," Sergeant Jones commanded. "The chopper pilots landed us too close to the ocean. We're over three miles from the LZ where we were supposed to land. Our new orders are to move out and sweep down the valley toward the foothills."

Pilgreen looked at me, shaking his head in disbelief. With a disgusted look on his face, he said in his Southern drawl, "This shit ain't gettin' it, is it?"

I had to agree with him. I sure wasn't looking forward to a long hike, with the weight of all my gear in such horrible heat.

We started to move out with First Platoon on our left flank, my platoon in the middle, and Third Platoon on the right. We were always told in training that you spread out so that no mortar round kills more than one Marine. Each platoon had a pair of M60 machine guns attached to them from Weapons Platoon. Weapons Platoon, which consisted of Marines armed with M60 heavy-duty machine guns, rockets, and mortars, could be called upon from any platoon for support.

We started moving slowly toward the hills to our west and away from the ocean. The ground was made up of ninety percent pure white sand and ten percent dirt. Short, thin stalks of weeds protruded everywhere. We had to cross a lot of real estate between us and the hills. After about three hours of struggling with the sandy ground, we came upon an area that was rich in jungle growth.

As we entered the tangle of weeds and trees, enemy machine-gun fire erupted from our front. I was near Third Platoon when the firing commenced. It sounded like several AK-47 machine guns. Second and Third Platoons became mixed in the thicket as everyone ran for cover. I dove forward toward a downed tree and lay in the prone position. Using the tree as cover, I fired an entire magazine of twenty rounds toward the sound of the enemy fire. The enemy was well-hidden, and I was unable to see them because the jungle growth was too thick.

Dan Varner from Third Platoon was next to me. "Screw this shit!" he said. He sat up with his legs crossed Indian style and aimed directly at something. I yelled for him to get under cover.

He looked at me for a second and said in a nonchalant way, "You can't hit what you can't see!" Bullets were dancing around him. It was a miracle he didn't get hit. He was the bravest person I had ever actually seen, in true esprit de corps. The gooks, as we began to call the enemy, must have been able to see him but apparently couldn't shoot worth a shit.

The fire stopped as abruptly as it began, and the enemy disappeared. We were soon to find out that this was a delaying tactic they would use on us repeatedly. It worked, too. We didn't move for another hour while a few Marines cleared the area ahead.

No one had been hit, but it was my first contact. The act of training for that scenario was much different than experiencing it firsthand. People were actually using bullets from machine guns, and they were trying to kill me. I felt helpless as I lay trapped on the ground, and an uncertain feeling came over me. *What did I get myself into?*

The order came down, and we continued our march. The guys complained about the extreme heat as we approached the foothills.

I heard a *bloop* sound in the distance. Then, I heard another and another.

"*Hit the deck*!" someone yelled.

The new guys, like me, watched as the old salts all hit the ground. Then I heard a whistling whoosh go over my head and many more after that. Explosions hit to my rear. We were getting hit by mortar rounds. I would recognize that sound for the rest of the war. All we could do was take cover. They exploded like the hand grenades we used at the range. We couldn't see any movement from the location where the sounds were coming from, but we kept hearing *bloop, bloop* in the distance in front of us, just over a hill. The next set of rounds hit closer to us as the enemy adjusted their fire. I recognized that they were zeroing in on us, and it really became frightening. They must have had a spotter on top of the hill passing adjusted fire instructions to their mortarmen. Don Bumgarner, our own mortarman, was instructed to return fire. He sent his rounds toward the enemy positions, which suppressed the enemy fire.

I began wondering about our ability to fight a large battle. They had hit us, but we hadn't even seen them yet. I realized that we had encountered a small unit, but they had been in control of the battle and were able to stop an entire company of Marines. Captain Reczek was cautious not to overreact and do something stupid, which I could appreciate, but I still wondered what would happen if thousands attacked us? After all, Captain Reczek had said there was believed to be a full regiment of NVA troops in the area. It wasn't a game; I knew we were playing for keeps. It was time to be more alert because anything could happen at any moment.

After about three more hours of walking, we stopped to wait for a medevac chopper. Six Marines had heat exhaustion and were unable to continue. That was another hour of not moving. The temperature had to be over one hundred ten degrees. Our heavily laden packs and a shortage of water didn't make life any easier.

We ended up moving out and continued to sweep until 6:00 p.m., when we finally stopped for the evening. Charlie Company set in on the west side of the valley near a small village. First Platoon was sent into the village to check it out thoroughly. One of the Marines discovered a bunker loaded with three thousand pounds of rice. It was thought to be for the NVA and VC units in the area, so the Marines were told to destroy it and then return to the lines. Engineers were called on the radio to blow up the contraband.

"Fire in the hole!" someone yelled.

There was a huge explosion, and then an enormous amount of smoke billowed up from the center of the village. The rice was totally destroyed.

FIRST PLATOON RETURNED TO stand watch on the lines for the evening with the rest of us. The best protection for a company of Marines for the night was to use the old circling-the-wagons routine like in the Old West. We all set up our fighting holes next to each other. One fighting hole connected to another until we had a complete circle. Jones came around with someone from Weapons Platoon to set up the fields of fire.

It was extremely hot, but for my platoon, the evening was otherwise uneventful. I had started the operation with two canteens of water and went through one and a quarter on the first day. I was dying of thirst, but at the same time, I realized, I had to conserve. Most of the other Marines were completely out.

One of the lieutenants from Alpha Company sent two squads (thirty men) out of the lines and down into a ravine where there was known to be a small stream. Their mission was to bring back as much water as they could, using extra canteens gathered from Alpha Company. When they arrived at the stream, the anxious, thirsty, mostly eighteen- and nineteen-year-olds dropped their rifles and gear to fill canteens. The Marines knelt down to unscrew canteen caps and, as they plunged the canteens under the water, they scanned their surroundings apprehensively.

The men worked quickly and quietly. Though there was no sign of the enemy, some could undoubtedly sense a presence—the invisible eyes of some predator staring them down. A couple of the Marines noticed large rocks and quietly edged themselves toward the cover. Just then, a well-placed machine gun in a haystack, plus other automatic weapons from as many as sixty to seventy NVA, opened up on the ill-fated Marines. Twenty were hit immediately. The two squads tried to return fire, but the enemy's firepower was overwhelming. Of the twenty Marines, fourteen were killed outright. Nine ended up wounded but were able to escape back to the lines to be medevaced out to the USS *Okinawa* and the USS *Sanctuary*. Artillery was called in on the enemy position, and Alpha Company was able to recover its dead using the artillery barrage for cover.

The officer who ordered the water run told the company commander he had sent out a patrol and not a water run. The official record states that a patrol went out and was ambushed. There was talk that the officer lied to save his reputation.

At dawn, we were told to move out about a hundred yards near a large, dry rice paddy. We were being airlifted to a location called LZ Buzzard. As the choppers approached our position, Shoeships, an American Indian Marine from our Second Fire Team, said, "Someone call for a limo?"

Ski, a short, thin, five-foot, one-inch Marine said, "I did! I also ordered some cocktails and suntan lotion."

It felt great to laugh again.

Once on board, we were told to remove our flak jackets and leave them on the choppers. With all the heat casualties, they were just too hot to wear.

After a short ride, we landed at LZ Buzzard and marched closer toward the foothills, where a Marine recon unit had reported many enemy positions. We ended up on a long, hot, sweaty walk that was much farther than it looked. Training did help us push ourselves, humping one foot after the other. The heat was so brutal and intense that even without the flak jackets, men were still dropping like flies. Our company commander called for ten medevac choppers. Sixty-five men had come down with severe heat stroke, and it took a long time to get them all medevaced. Some of the Marines' eyes were starting to roll back into their heads, which is never a good sign. I found out later that, at the same time, Captain Reczek was being reprimanded on the radio because the company was not close to where we were supposed to be. He was ordered to send as many men as he could to the top of the first foothill and secure it, "*Now!*"

Reczek immediately got the lieutenant from Third Platoon and sent him with a squad on a forced march to the top of the hill. Exhausted upon getting to the high ground, they spotted a VC in black pajamas in the valley below. He was down on one knee watching our company's progress as we moved up the valley—definitely an enemy scout. The lieutenants set up an M60 machine gun and opened fire at the lone soldier. The rounds danced around him, and he leaped headfirst into the brush of a tree line. The man in the black pajamas disappeared into the foliage.

The lieutenant set up a defensive position at the top of the hill until the rest of the company arrived. My platoon commander, Lieutenant Francis, and my squad leader, Sergeant Jones, had us walk up the side of a hill a little south of the command post (CP). Our hill was loaded with a heavy weed growth, three to four feet high. We struggled in the heat to get to the top and, once there, we secured the hill. Our location was right in the middle of the company. The command post and Third Platoon were at our right flank and exposed to enemy fire. The CP was getting creamed by mortar rounds fired from the hills in the distance. The enemy position was well-concealed and protected by huge boulders.

The accuracy of the bombardment was such that the North Vietnamese must have set up the coordinates prior to our arrival. The initial mortar rounds hit right on target. They must have had some indication we were coming, because they had us zeroed in like hunters shooting ducks in a pond.

From the CP, Reczek had our forward observer (FO) call in an air strike on the enemy positions. Two F-4 Phantom jets came in, and each dropped two 500-pound bombs on the surrounding hills. At the same time, 105 mm cannons from one of our bases sent huge rounds into the rocks where the enemy fire had been coming from. Enormous explosions erupted in front of our positions.

Our platoon was receiving sniper and machine-gun fire from closer, hidden positions in front of us, not far from a village in the valley. The enemy couldn't get a good read on us because of the heavy weeds we had settled into. I had hated those weeds going up the hill, but now they'd become our savior. The gunfire became more of a harassing fire, just keeping us pinned down for the time being.

Bravo Company to our left was given orders to sweep the hills and flank the enemy in front of us. As they moved around, they ended up in the same situation in which we found ourselves. Bravo Company got pinned down and was getting mortared as large groups of NVA shot machine-gun fire into their positions. Bravo Company was receiving more casualties than we were.

At this juncture, hundreds of North Vietnamese moved forward toward our positions as mortars began to fall all around us. Machine-gun fire was hitting us from the large rocks to our front. Several Marines were severely wounded from the attack. Dave Hart, First Squad, and Ed Kalwara, attached to our platoon as a machine gunner, were right next to each other laying down fire on the enemy. They were no more than ten inches apart looking at the hills in front of them, when a bullet whizzed directly into Hart's chest and sent him backward to the ground. Kalwara reacted with the speed of a jackrabbit and hit the ground alongside him. Kalwara told me that he crawled to Hart, thinking there might be something he could do, but it was obvious that Hart was already gone. He told me that he could have been the one lying there dead; the bullet that struck Hart had been only inches away from him as well.

Corpsmen moved bravely into the oncoming fire to help patch up the wounded and move them to the landing zone. With some hesitation in the continuing fire, Captain Reczek called in the medevac choppers. For those critically wounded, every second was vital.

We watched as the choppers landed. They took fire mostly from the front. We saw the enemy in the distance, moving from their positions to our right flank to get a better shot. They didn't have the big packs we had and were not heavily laden with gear. All we could see was a glimpse of men in black pajamas as they carried their AK-47s. They were fast and stealthy.

The choppers kept landing while the crew kicked off extra ammo and helped the wounded aboard. I saw one of the choppers take numerous rounds as it landed and then receive more fire as it took off with the wounded inside. How it kept flying I will never know. I looked up to the sky because I heard the jets above. They came roaring in and targeted the area in front of us. I was happy as they dumped their loads of two 500-pound bombs on the entrenched enemy.

Another pair of jets came in and unloaded large canisters of flaming napalm in the densely wooded hills. It was awesome to see our firepower in action, saving the day. The sniper fire stopped immediately. The enemy must have either left the area or gone underground. It seemed like the logical thing to do. Other Marine battalions were in the vicinity, and we could see the jets and Hueys in the distance on our left and right flanks, shooting rockets into the hills. I saw the great coordination of firepower we had over the NVA, but even as a well-trained Marine, I was still terrified at what could be lurking out there waiting for me in the coming night.

After the artillery and air strikes came to an end, it appeared the enemy had retreated for the time being. With the enemy guns now quiet, the company moved cautiously forward.

AT DUSK, CAPTAIN RECZEK called for the company to stop and dig in for the night. He decided to use a B-52 crater for cover. Without any warning, mortar rounds and sniper fire erupted again and began hitting the exposed point men. Four Marines were wounded and trapped thirty yards out. Roger Bacon and a couple of other Marines who were with Captain Reczek in the crater jumped up from the cover and ran to a trench just behind the fallen men. The Marines who followed Bacon gave suppressing fire as Bacon jumped out and dragged each man, one at a time, into the safety of the trench.

John Steiner and I heard the firing to our front and right. We were setting in for the night, and we thought it would be best to dig our fighting hole a little deeper for a better defense. The ground was hard as cement, and it took us quite a while to get an extra couple of feet. We took turns digging in the horrible heat. The weeds that protected us from the snipers became a disadvantage again. With night approaching, I imagined how the enemy could slowly and quietly creep up on us, using the weeds as cover. To make matters worse, there was no moon this evening. I could see it was going to be a long night.

Steiner and I waited for darkness before carefully crawling out of our positions. We had to push the brush down directly in front of us for fifteen yards. Sergeant Jones crawled along the lines to make sure Second Platoon was ready for the possible onslaught before us. He came over to the hole where Steiner and I were.

"Be prepared and stay awake, because we're expecting to get overrun this evening," Jones said. "There are thousands of gooks out there, so just stay alert. You know those F-4 Phantom jets that were hitting the gooks to our west?"

"Yeah, I saw them," I said.

Jones added, "One of our FOs saw movement in the hills. There weren't supposed to be any friendlies in the area, and an air strike was called in. The jets sent eight rockets directly on the movement. It turns out it was another outfit sweeping the hills, and they were not on our radio frequency. Our jets killed five and wounded twenty-four of our own Marines."

I shook my head. It was enough to worry about getting killed by the enemy, but now I'd be looking over my shoulder wondering if the good guys had me in their sights.

"Anyway," he sighed, shaking his head, "no smoking and only cold food tonight."

"It's too bad about Hart," I said. "Did anyone else get it?"

"Second Platoon got some wounded, but Hart was the only one who didn't make it," Jones said.

He then crawled off to the next firing position out of our sight. Hart was the first man to die from our platoon, but he wasn't going to be the last.

The sun had set, and the night came with a cloak of darkness so total that I couldn't see my hand in front of my face. Around 11:30 p.m., random explosions started up and down the lines; they were enemy mortars. It was a harassing fire, a somewhat chaotic plan, hoping they would get lucky or draw fire to give away our positions. Their mortarmen sent rounds everywhere, and hot shrapnel zinged in all directions. The explosions became much more powerful, and we knew they must have been using recoilless rifles.

Recoilless rifles are actually small artillery pieces. A large shell is placed inside a portable tube that is attached to a tripod and fired. The NVA's larger units carried them and were using them on us. Steiner and I sunk into our fighting hole, glad we had dug it deeper.

About an hour later, we heard artillery rounds coming in from our backs, going over our heads toward the enemy. There were huge explosions in the valley and then on the hills in front of us. I realized then that the artillery was called in to suppress the enemy's recoilless rifles. Small firefights arose in the valley from listening posts and Marine reconnaissance units. The North Vietnamese had come out to kill Americans and were probing for any weakness. They were out there in force. Both Steiner and I were frozen in place, waiting to see or hear anything. If only there had been a little light, we would have felt more secure.

Our senses now played an important role in staying alive. The only thing we could do was to sit and wait for anything out of the ordinary. Our minds started playing tricks on us as it got later in the evening.

"You hear that?" Steiner would ask.

Listening intently, I would say, "No, I didn't."

A few minutes would pass, and we would do it all over again, several times.

I grabbed my canteen and drank the last vestiges of water from it. I was too scared to worry about the water at this point because I was just trying to stay alive.

Small firefights broke out again in the valley about 1:00 a.m. when I heard a faint sound of an airplane, first from a distance, and then louder as it began to fly above us. The plane dropped a flare that drifted down slowly. It lit up the entire area like daylight for two whole minutes. We felt a few moments of relief and confidence, as long as it stayed lit. But, of course, the light would burn out and, again, there was nothing Steiner or I could see in our field of fire.

Out of the darkened sky, a brilliant stream of red light shot like a laser from the plane and flowed all the way to the ground. A loud, fast, roaring and whining sound followed just a few seconds later—the delayed sound from the airplane's miniguns. We had heard about "Spooky," but none of us had ever seen him. The old salts talked about a plane that could put a bullet in every square inch of a football field in one minute. There was another name for "Spooky." It was "Puff," as in "Puff the Magic Dragon." The stream of light was actually thousands of tracer rounds giving the effect of a dragon's breath spewing death and destruction from above. Every fifth round fired was a tracer round.

A tracer is like a Star Wars laser. It's a bullet that glows with red-hot phosphorus and provides a visual aid for better aiming. There were so many tracers that they gave the illusion of a single ray of red light. One minigun shoots one hundred rounds per second, and there were three firing at the same time. We had heard the plane carried infrared detection and could see heat signatures from the enemy on the ground. Our fire-breathing dragon had to be terrifying to the enemy.

"Puff" stayed with us for several hours, disappearing and then returning, dropping its large flares to light up the area and breathe its showers of machine-gun bullets from above. God, I was glad he was on our side! I can't imagine how many enemy combatants

Spooky killed or wounded. Between Spooky, the artillery, and a fear of being attacked, we didn't get much sleep that night. Any plans the enemy might have had to overrun us were thwarted after Spooky appeared, but we stayed on high alert throughout the night. Charlie was still out there.

By morning, the enemy was quiet. Those who survived our dragon's breath had disappeared into the night. Charlie Company went on the hunt once more, but other than occasional harassing and delaying sniper fire, our search demonstrated the enemy's illusive strategy. They would choose the time and place to confront us again.

A COUPLE OF DAYS later, we were on line sweeping in hilly terrain toward a large reservoir in a beautiful grassy valley. As we approached, we could see the reservoir stretched far and wide, three quarters of a mile all the way up to some scattered rock formations in the distance. We were at the top of a hill looking down into the valley, and the lack of cover was obvious. Captain Reczek sensed danger and gave the order to halt and take a break while he figured a plan to move through the open valley.

Bacon took off the heavy radio he was carrying for Lieutenant Sutton. The break wasn't very long, as heavy machine-gun fire and mortars opened up and began concentrating on some exposed Marines at the front of the column. Bacon was on top of the hill looking down with some semblance of cover. A mortar round hit down in the valley and a little to the left of his position. The next one was in the middle of the hill.

"Where is the fire coming from?" someone yelled.

Bacon raised his torso to take a look and said, "I think it's ..." and before he could say another word, a mortar round hit directly in front of him, knocking him unconscious. He was thrown backward as the shrapnel blasted his body, along with four other Marines. One of the other Marines who was closer to the blast died immediately. He may have sheltered Bacon from the full force of the blast.

Doc Eastman was called. He and a couple of others helped Bacon and the other wounded to the LZ.

It was May 10. All the battalions were sweeping the same area looking for "Charlie," which was another name we called the enemy. In the distance, we could see our jets hitting positions in the hills. A unit must have spotted movement and called in for the air strikes. We continued sweeping and chasing small units, and they would retreat farther, toward cover. Little did I realize they were leading us into a trap.

The battalion was spread far to the left and right, sweeping toward a magnificent hill, when the *bloop* sounds started. Machine-gun fire erupted from the hills. Mortars rained like hail from above, and explosions hit the ground with tremendous accuracy. Charlie had our command group zeroed in. The rounds were hitting in and around Captain Reczek and his entire command. I saw Lieutenant Sutton, our executive officer (second in command, or XO), running toward Captain Reczek. Mortar rounds started raining down on all of them. Sutton dove down between Lieutenant Richard Chapa and another Marine. The rounds seemed to stop. Sutton got up to proceed toward Reczek when a mortar round exploded, blowing another man in half and throwing Sutton from the blast as if he were a rag doll.

Several Marines ran over to the wounded men. Lieutenant Chapa had been protected from the discharge because Lieutenant Sutton and the other Marine absorbed most of the blast.

Bumgarner and his crew were ordered to return suppressing mortar fire. Dead Marines were everywhere. Both Sutton and the other Marine were taken to the location where we laid our dead. The wounded were taken immediately to a hastily established LZ where they were sent back to the LPH *Okinawa* emergency room or, in more severe cases, the hospital ship, *Sanctuary*.

The choppers flew in, and Charlie erupted with machine-gun and mortar fire again. We were inspired by the bravery of our chopper pilots. They kept coming and removing the wounded. Our mortar rounds hit the gooks hard, and they went silent once again.

Lieutenant Chapa asked a corpsman about his friend, Lieutenant Sutton.

"Sutton's over there with the dead," the corpsman said, pointing to the line of poncho-covered corpses. "He's second from the last."

Lieutenant Chapa went over to his old friend to pay his last respects. He lifted the dark green poncho back. The entire left side of Sutton's face and body were fully covered in blood. Lieutenant Chapa said a quick prayer and gave one last parting glance. He looked again and felt like something was amiss. Lieutenant Chapa saw there was a glitter of moisture in the slit of Sutton's right eye. It was a tear. He bent forward and looked even closer at Sutton's face and saw that Sutton had been looking at him through the smallest slit under his eyelid. Chapa then noticed fresh blood dripping from Sutton's wounds.

"My God!" he yelled back to the corpsman. "He's still alive! Sutton's still alive!"

Sutton had been lying there with the dead, alive and aware, but not able to say a word. Several Marines came over to assist him, and another medevac was called in. Doc Eastman bandaged him up as best he could. The chopper came in but was under heavy fire. Regardless, four Marines grabbed each of Sutton's limbs and carried him to the chopper. Once he was on the floor, one of the Marines aboard immediately began pushing hard and fast on Sutton's chest. The engine roared, and debris flew everywhere from the rotating blades. AK-47 bullets punched through the skin of the chopper as it rose. The door gunner's M60 machine gun exploded with flames of bullets as he fired into the enemy positions. With Sutton aboard, the chopper disappeared in the distance on its way to the USS *Sanctuary*.

The next orders were to sweep the hills along the perimeter of the valley, and that is when the enemy mortars resumed. They were right on us again, and the explosions walked directly toward me. I got down, sure that I would end up like Sutton. Then, as if the sounds of my own defiant voice could assert my right to live or drown out the explosions and the desperate cries of my fellow Marines, I screamed.

MY INCOHERENT SCREAMING ALWAYS wakes me up. As the ceiling comes into focus in the darkness above, I begin to feel the wetness in the bed beneath my seventy-year-old body, soaked from sweat. I sit up on the side of the bed and stare into the carpet for a minute. My wife and I no longer sleep together because of these nightmares.

In the bathroom, I see some old stranger in the mirror. The feeling of being that boy back in Vietnam with my platoon has not yet left me. I splash cold water on my face and keep my hands pressed there, pressing my fingers hard against my eyelids. It's not the first time I've relived the battle, and even now, fifty-two years later, I know it won't be the last.

I return to bed and lie back on the dry side, but I won't be sleeping again tonight. Instead, I stare into the darkness and think about how I ended up in that war and in the Special Landing Force. I think about how I survived it and how so many of my friends, like Hart, did not. I think about that innocent and invincible young boy who stepped on a jet airplane for the very first time in his life. If I could go back in time and meet him on that tarmac, I wouldn't tell him about the day he almost died, but I also wouldn't stop him.

CHAPTER

TWO

ON FEBRUARY 18, 1967, I found myself on a Continental Airlines jet traveling at 500 mph, heading for a refueling stop in Hawaii. Once refueled, I was heading to the Orient and the Naha Airport on the island of Okinawa, off the coast of Japan. My orders were vague, but the insinuation was apparent. I was going to Vietnam. My suspicion was that Okinawa was another refueling spot along the way.

There were others like me on this flight: eighteen-year-olds, fresh out of high school. Our hair was cut short and tight, up against the scalp, as it had been since our first day of boot camp. There were twenty-five names imprinted on my orders. I smiled and felt less alone when I recognized one of the names on the list—Dan Varner, a guy I had met in California during basic infantry training. Dan stood six feet, four inches tall and was so big he looked like he could take on three guys at a time. He was soft-spoken though—easy-going, like me.

Once, during basic, Dan and I took a weekend leave together in San Diego. We were walking down the street toward the business district, minding our own business, when three Navy guys began to taunt us from the other side of the street. We didn't do anything at first, but the humiliation became too much. With three against two, the odds were on their side, but we were up for the challenge. We had to prove ourselves, so we ran across the street and became confident and aggressive in our talk and demeanor. Neither Dan nor I would have even thought of doing this before joining the Marines. I remember thinking, just before the imminent fight, *I hope we can pull this off.* Sure enough, we did. They ended up running away before anyone could throw a punch, just proving that courage and belief in oneself can accomplish anything.

We arrived at the airport in Okinawa and exited the plane. There, on the other side of the world, it was a pleasant seventy-six degrees, and I thought the weather wasn't so bad. I was expecting it to be a lot hotter, similar to what I had heard about Vietnam's heat. We all filed off the plane to an open-air staging area where the service personnel directed us to our duty stations.

I walked up to a lance corporal who was sifting through several files of expected Marines. He directed all twenty-six of us to a military-looking bus to be transported to Camp Schwab for jungle training. I was assigned to the First Battalion, Third Marine Regiment, Charlie Company's Second Platoon. All of us were to be in the same battalion, but in different companies and platoons.

As soon as we had all boarded and sat down, the Marine driver slammed the door shut and stepped on the gas. My head jerked back from the acceleration. He wanted to beat the oncoming traffic at the exit of the airport, so he ignored the stop sign and drove recklessly onto the highway. The bus nearly tipped over. We all felt like we were going to die for sure. A thought passed through my head ... I could see my father receiving a telegram: "We are sorry to inform you that your son died, not on some battlefield in Vietnam but on a random bus ride on the island of Okinawa."

The driver peered into the rearview mirror and laughed as if he were doing it on purpose, as some kind of initiation to Okinawa. He continued down the paved, winding road through a beautiful rural area, still smiling and driving like he was on the Illiana Motor Speedway in Schererville, Indiana. Those of us in the back of the bus bounced in our seats like we were bronco busting in Denver, Colorado. I wanted to check out the scenery, so I just settled in and accepted that I was in for one hell of a ride to the base.

There were many typical Okinawan homes along the way. They were mostly square structures with small, but beautifully crafted wooden porches that stretched around the entire home. Red clay shingle roofs extended over their porches and accented the local style. There were many variations. Some were simplistic and naturally beautiful. Others were unpainted, unkempt, and dilapidated. Around each home, old stone walls still stood as ancient perimeter guards from another culture and era. After about half an hour, we passed through an area of straw huts, which I suspected belonged to the farmers of the region who led a simpler lifestyle. We were away from the city now and passing fertile rice fields. About thirty minutes later, we saw a scenic view of the ocean, mountains covered with dense jungle, and many beautiful valleys.

The Okinawan drivers were just as crazy as the bus driver. Small cars and motorcycles zipped past us doing 50 mph around two-lane curves. They passed on curves and jumped brazenly in and out of the lanes, just missing oncoming traffic. Unlike back home, there were no posted speed limit signs anywhere, nor guardrails to keep vehicles from tumbling fatally down the hillsides.

We passed many villages, but one in particular stood out from all the others. The driver had slowed down to peer at the local beauties. There were several very young Asian ladies walking on the side of the road. They wore the typical conical hats known as Asian rice hats. The white silk, full-length dresses they wore fit so tight against their slim figures that any man would be moved to look. All the Marines ran to one side of the bus. We were a bunch of teenaged boys full of testosterone and vivid memories of the girlfriends we left behind. Of course we had to look.

"What the hell, guys. Haven't you ever seen a woman before?" the bus driver yelled. "Sit down!"

We reached Camp Schwab at the end of the paved road. We were all instructed to get off the bus and file into a large, two-story brick building. Next on the agenda: hurry up and wait. So, for the next hour, I waited and wondered what was next for us in Okinawa. Another bus pulled in with more troops, right behind us. As my turn in line got shorter, the Marines in front of me peeled off and went to their respective units. Finally, it was my turn.

The clerk told me I was in BLT-26 (Battalion Landing Team 26) for assignment to Special Landing Force Alpha. The clerk said my barracks was on the right side of the road and I was to report to building number three. He stamped my papers three times so hard that a few of the items on his desk moved. I took my papers and proceeded to building three.

There were many long and narrow one-story buildings in a row. All of them were on the right side of the road and up a slight hill. I found building number three and walked up the few stairs to the entranceway. Upon entering the barracks, I expected to have a positive feeling seeing my new unit for the first time, but not everything was as expected.

The old-salt Marines of my new platoon had just arrived from Vietnam. They'd been stationed in Khe Sanh, a base near the Laotian border. This base was last in a long line of bases that ran along the DMZ from the ocean to our farthest outpost in the west. All the bases were valuable because they were the high ground overlooking the DMZ and the infamous Ho Chi Minh Trail. Charlie Company had run patrols toward the Laotian border and around the surrounding area but met little contact. One of the problems with Khe Sanh was the huge rats that foraged in large numbers at the dump. The Marines told us the rats would leave the dump at night and run over their bodies while they slept. The rats were looking for scraps in empty C-ration cans the Marines had discarded.

Many of the old salt Marines also talked about a bear they killed while on patrol one day. They talked at length about how big it was. Some said it was six feet tall, while others said it was nine. It basically depended on who was telling the story. Lieutenant Francis, who was in charge of a reconnaissance patrol, was walking along a creek bed in a ravine. PFC Donald Smith was in the center of the squad and was shocked when he saw a huge black bear running down the hill toward the squad. The animal got within a few yards and reared up with his arms and claws outstretched. Smith saw the huge, white teeth as the bear growled, dripping saliva from its huge mouth. It took another few steps toward the men, and that is when the entire column opened fire at the beast. It appeared as if nothing was going to stop him. PFC McCarthy pointed his M14 at the bear and pulled the trigger, and all he heard was a click. His rifle misfired, and he thought his number was up. PFC Robert

Manning fired full automatic into its chest. Round after round hit the bear, but nothing seemed to be able to stop it. Pilgreen was a few feet away and was in the process of climbing over a fallen tree in the stream. He tried to take a shot from behind the tree, but Hart jumped up in front of him and opened fire on the bear. The bear finally fell with a thud.

Pilgreen yelled to Hart, "Hey man, I almost killed you!"

Hart wasn't concerned. The bear fell just a few feet from the squad, and he wanted to see the incredible beast. The entire squad was totally out of order and Ski, the radioman, told Francis that the commanding officer wanted to know what all the firing was about. Were they under fire, and if so, did they get any KIAs (killed in action)?

"Yes, Sir!" Francis told him. "We got one KIA. We bagged a black bear."

The guys surrounded the dead bear to get souvenirs. One guy went for a tooth to hang around his neck, while another worked at a claw. The only one who had success was Flick. He cut off the bear's hairy ear, which came off pretty easily with his razor-sharp KA-BAR knife. The ear eventually became fetid and stunk for weeks until they, thankfully, disposed of it.

Lieutenant Francis had to restore order, and everyone hated him for it. He yelled for everyone to get back on the trail.

These were just some of the stories they bragged about. Of course, Lieutenant Francis was right to get order, but the men felt that Vietnam was miserable enough without someone always ragging on their ass.

Not a single old salt welcomed any one of us into the unit. The grunts seemed indifferent to the extra new men. You might say that I felt more like a nuisance than a brother Marine. As far as they were concerned, we were the FNGs (fucking new guys), and we would have to prove ourselves to them. While the old salts ignored our existence, the new guys stuck together—each assimilating into his own respective clique.

OUR TRAINING STARTED THE following day, which was a Monday. Staff Sergeant Malloy, the platoon sergeant, came into the squad bay with his three squad leaders. First Squad was assigned to Sergeant Pike. Pike was about six feet, two inches tall and very lanky. He had blond, almost-white hair that was cut tight on the sides but a little longer on the top. He was from Danville, Kentucky.

The leader of my squad, Second Squad, was Sergeant Jones. Jones was from Nashville, Tennessee and stood about five feet, ten inches tall. He had the body of a weightlifter, but it wasn't overdone. Rather, it gave him the wide-shoulders look. Jones wore a buzz cut, making him almost bald. The buzz cut also gave him the appearance of an extreme Marine. He had the look of authority—of being a lifer and a leader. Whatever he said or did, I was certainly not going to be the one to question it.

Corporal Muller was in charge of Third Squad. Muller's look was that of an average older-looking Marine. He was twenty or maybe closer to twenty-one. This was old for our platoon. Most of the guys in the platoon were just over nineteen.

Our platoon sergeant, John Malloy, was actually a staff sergeant and not a big guy at all. He was maybe five feet, eight inches tall, and an older man, who I would later learn had a lot of common sense. He was all Marine and a lifer who hailed from Great Barrington, Massachusetts. All the squad leaders and the old salts looked up to the "Old Sarge" because he was totally concerned about their welfare. I noticed they spoke of him with respect, and I could tell they all trusted that he was smart enough to get them through Nam.

This wasn't Malloy's first go-round either. It was his second tour in Nam, and he didn't take any shit from anyone, especially some boot lieutenant. Malloy knew exactly what to do, and even his superior, Lieutenant Francis, knew it.

Francis was the new platoon commander. He was a "butter bar," a second lieutenant. A butter bar was the lowest rank of officer. Yes, Francis was trying to make his mark on the world and was totally gung ho. He wanted to make a name for himself and couldn't be bothered with anything else. He was tall and thin, with a tight flattop haircut. He didn't have an ounce of fat on his body. He had obviously been working out a lot. His pants had creases in them, and his blouse didn't have a single wrinkle on it. We called that "squared away." Francis talked in short, curt commands but as soon as Malloy walked into a room, Francis was silenced by the cool command presence that Malloy carried. Malloy talked as if Francis wasn't even in the room. Sure, Malloy was outranked, but he was way too valuable for Francis to reprimand. The butter bar would have to take second fiddle for now. You could tell he didn't like it.

"Today," Malloy said, "we're starting our training for the SLF. We will be out in the field on compass marches for the next five days. You will be making forced marches in the night and in the jungle. We'll cross many rivers and devise routes through the steep ravines. This platoon will go to the rifle range for target practice and to set the sights on your weapons. You will be tested at recognizing booby traps and mines. Then we will go through camouflage training and learn to cross various types of rope bridges. Mike Boat, landing craft, and amtrac assault training will be toward the end of our training. At the very end of the training, you'll have to get used to helicopters because that will be our primary mode of transportation in and out of Nam from now on."

And that's exactly what we did day after day until the weekend. On weekends, we had liberty unless someone messed up and had to stay on base for KP (kitchen police) duty, peeling potatoes for the entire day. Kin Ville (village) was not far outside our base and the easiest place for Marines to spend their money. The locals made their living on the Marines. There were lots of bars and small businesses on the main street in the town. Several of these businesses thrived as houses of ill repute where a lot of Marines lost their virginity, if they had any to lose.

We didn't have to be twenty-one to drink like we did back in the States. In Kin Ville, we just had to be old enough to put money on the bar.

Then Monday came and we started the training all over again.

For six weeks straight, we trained in the NTA (Northern Training Area) at the Counter Guerrilla Warfare School. We attended demolition and land mine training. In Booby Trap School, we studied how the enemy would use low-tech devices to injure or maim Marines. The VC would sharpen pieces of bamboo into spears and place them into a hole on a path, facing upwards. We called them punji pits.

Lieutenant Francis kept challenging Malloy for control of the platoon. Some of the other officers in the company thought Francis was on the stuck-up side. I was sweeping our barracks and was shocked when I overheard Malloy saying to one of the squad leaders that Francis was the kind of officer who would get people killed trying to get the Medal of Honor and still use it as an opportunity for higher rank and advancement in the Corps.

After six brutal weeks of jungle training, we started the second phase of training: helicopter and amphibious assault exercises. That was going to be more fun than humping through the jungle.

Before we began, we were introduced to our new company commander and his newly appointed XO. Charlie Company stood at attention when Captain Reczek and Lieutenant Sutton appeared. Our company commander, Captain Reczek, seemed really old. He had to be at least twenty-nine, and Lieutenant Sutton seemed almost as old, maybe twenty-eight. Reczek looked squared away and was all business. There was no smiling, just assertive concern. Lieutenant Sutton followed him around because he knew Reczek was in charge. Sutton, a tall, thin, dark-haired, physically fit individual, seemed a lot friendlier, with an occasional smile for the troops. Reczek spoke in a loud and assertive voice.

"*Okay*, Marines," he said. "I'm Captain Reczek, and this is Lieutenant Sutton, my XO. A lot of you Marines who came from Khe Sanh will recognize Lieutenant Sutton because he was the platoon commander of Third Platoon. I'm the new commanding officer of Charlie Company. I imagine you have a lot of questions about the extra training. Well, I'll fill you in on what's happened so far and what's about to happen. The Marines who came from Khe Sanh needed a face-lift. While in Nam, every squad had depleted in numbers by almost half, and we were in need of new equipment. That is why you were brought here to Okinawa. You new men are here to boost the battalion to full strength and, at the same time, train to use new tactics to defeat the enemy. This is why the First Battalion, Third Marine Regiment came here to Okinawa to train and regroup. We have been chosen to be a fast-reaction task force—a battalion of Marines that can be called on in a moment's notice. We are called, 'SLF Alpha.' Yes, get those initials clear. We have been selected to be, SLF Alpha. What does SLF stand for, you may ask? We are a 'Special Landing Force' with a full Reactionary Battalion of 1,750 men and 68 officers.

"We will be different from any other Marine unit. Our rear area will be in Quang Tri, but the fighting force will be on a helicopter ship, the USS *Okinawa*. Our designation is a Reactionary Battalion! If any Marine unit catches shit, we can be called at a moment's notice to give them support. We will also be executing search-and-destroy operations. Today we will be the first Marine unit to receive the new M16 rifles. The heavier M14 is no longer going to be our weapon of choice. The M16 is lighter, but it has the same stopping power of the M14. The new rifle is made of a resilient plastic with metal moving parts. It has a large spring inside the stock to absorb the recoil, making it more accurate and easier to shoot. You will be able to carry twice the ammunition because the rounds are half the size. We will be at the rifle range most of the day today and tomorrow getting used to these new weapons. Wednesday and Thursday we will train with amtracs. Friday we meet our helicopter squadron and practice takeoffs and landings. All next week, we will continue working the bugs out of our training. This will also help the Navy get their act together. The helicopter pilots, amtrac personnel, as well as the ship's crews need this training as much as we do. Everything has to be coordinated to work perfectly, or men will die."

WEDNESDAY MORNING, WE BOARDED trucks that took us to the harbor where we then boarded LCMs (landing craft mechanized). They are a much larger landing craft than the ones used in World War II. As we stood there waiting for the ramp to come down, it looked like the entire fleet was in the harbor. All sorts of ships were anchored: supply ships, destroyers, corvettes, and a helicopter ship looming in the distance.

We were going to practice rope climbing on the USS *Duluth*, LPD (landing platform dock) like we had practiced on land with wooden structures. In order for Marines to speedily get on or off a ship, the Navy used cargo nets. The larger ship sends down nets, creating a rope ladder. The ladder could hold three Marines across, climbing up or down at the same time. The key to climbing a rope ladder is that you never put your hands on the horizontal part. Someone can always step on your hand and down you go with a sore hand and maybe worse. The larger ship is usually steadier because of its size, where the LCM holds one hundred men and moves rapidly up and down with the waves of the ocean. We had to hop on the rope ladder when the LCM was at the top of the wave. We were told that many Marines had been crushed between the two boats because they didn't time the jump just right. It didn't take us long to learn how to board, with only a couple of close calls.

Once aboard, we were led into the depths of the *Duluth*. The LPD has a huge door that encompasses the entire back end of the ship and that is hinged to the bottom of the ship. The top part of the door lowers downward, creating a ramp that stops at wave level and leads to open water. Whatever is in the huge cavern can exit easily through the door.

As we boarded the LPD, we were instructed to go through a bunch of passageways leading downward. There was a roaring sound coming at us from deep inside the ship that got louder as we moved closer to the ship's center. Our unit entered the cavern of the ship where there were amtracs lined up from front to back with all engines roaring.

An amtrac looks exactly like a small tank with tracks for wheels but without the big gun turret on top. Attached to the front of the amtrac is a watertight ramp that opens up the same way as the LPD, from top to bottom. The tracks of the amtrac rotate in the water and create forward movement. When the front door opens, men and equipment can be loaded and off-loaded. The seven-ton amtrac is designed to float. That's the theory anyway.

My entire platoon walked down steel ladders attached to the side of the bulkhead wall. The sounds of the engines were deafening. Carbon monoxide and white clouds of gas filled the huge cavity of the ship. Once we arrived on the bottom floor, Staff Sergeant Malloy assigned eight Marines to each amtrac. We entered the steel tank and, with the sound of heavy hydraulics, the door closed and sealed behind us. I wondered if the damn thing could possibly float. It brought back memories of riding "Shoot the Chutes" at the River View Amusement Park.

Standing in a crowded line at the age of seven years, I was both excited and afraid for my life. The anticipation to get to the elevator was part of the excitement, but once we reached the top, my adrenaline really began to flow. I was so small I had difficulty entering the open-aired barge. It had several rows of long seats, and the seats accommodated up to five people across. Once we were fastened in by the safety crew, they released the gravity-fed boat and it slid downward through a long chute. When it hit the pool at the bottom, it threw gallons of water on the riders. The thrill was mind-blowing. Boarding the amtrac felt the same way as boarding the Chutes.

A loud horn sounded, blaring on and off. The *Duluth's* huge back door started its way down to the ramp position. As the door lowered in the down position and locked, another horn sounded and the front amtracs took off, full throttle, exiting the ship. One by one, the seven-ton vehicles went onto the ramp and then dove into the water nose first and started sinking as if they were rocks. When our amtrac went under the water, saltwater poured in from various non-watertight places, and I felt a sense of doom. Next thing I knew, the roaring amtrac started to float and move briskly forward toward the shore. It's incredible that damn thing floated with eight men, full packs, and ammo. In no time at all, we rolled out of the water and onto a nearby beach. The front ramp opened, and the sun's rays almost blinded us.

From there, we all climbed aboard trucks that were waiting to take us back to Camp Schwab. Pilgreen and I had been sitting next to each other during the entire amtrac trip. He was a country boy and a realist. He always seemed to look at everything with a critical eye. I, on the other hand, just rolled along for the ride and didn't contemplate the meaning or the whys. Just follow orders, no matter what they are.

Pilgreen said in his Alabama drawl, "Y'all suppose we are going to be riding a lot in the portable caskets?"

"What?" I said, as I laughed.

"Did y'all think when you were under the water the amtrac thingy would just keep going down to the bottom?"

"Oh, hell yes," I said. "But it didn't."

"Did y'all try and figure out why we are fighting this Vietnam War?" Pilgreen asked.

"Sure!" I said. "We're here to stop communism from spreading any further. Stopping it here, dead in its tracks."

Pilgreen looked at me with a cocky smile on his face and said, "I know that's what they said. I was just wondering what you thought about it."

He wanted me to think about it. He said it like he knew something I didn't. I blew it off, and we rode in the back of the open-air trucks to Camp Schwab, laughing and joking the whole way. I didn't realize it at the time, but Pilgreen had taken a liking to me and was taking me under his wing. One of the old salts was human after all.

ON APRIL 3, WE packed up our gear and headed for our new home, the USS *Okinawa* (LPH). She was a huge ship anchored in the middle of the harbor. The entire battalion was dropped off at the harbor ramp where an LCM landing craft was coming to pick us up. We had all our gear with us, packs filled with most of the items we would take out into the field, and a cartridge belt. We also brought our sea bags filled with our military clothes and personal belongings.

A very large landing craft approached our position. The numbers "1582" were displayed in bold italic numbers on the driver's cabin. As the boat arrived, it slowly moved ashore. The ramp was already in the lowered position and began to grind against the shore as it pushed onto dry land. The sounds of small rocks and shells meeting the underside were like fingernails on a chalkboard. The LCM eventually stopped, and the entire platoon of fifty men boarded. The ramp went up, and the diesel engines roared with enough power to transport a tank. The boat had no problem backing out and turning around. As we cruised briskly toward the great helicopter ship, the USS *Okinawa*, the adrenaline rose inside me.

The *Okinawa* was the largest ship I had ever seen. It was like approaching a skyscraper floating sideways on the water. Seven UH-34 choppers were secured at the very front of the ship and pointed in the direction the ship would be going. The chopper's blades had all been folded back to the rear of each chopper. I didn't know they could be altered like that.

The LCM had six huge, rimless truck tires hanging off its sides. When the LCM nudged up to the side of the *Okinawa*, the tires acted as cushions, preventing the two ships from damaging each other. Permanent steel ladders were attached to the side of the *Okinawa* to make it easier for personnel to get on and off the great ship. The bottom ladder, which was adjustable, was lowered into the LCM.

The harbor was protected from the rolling waves of the ocean, and both ships connected very nicely. We all followed in a line carrying our gear up the ladders and then into the innards of the ship. We ended up in the massive hangar deck where twenty-five helicopters were stored.

Continuing our trek, we walked all the way through the hangar deck to the other bulkhead, then through a door passage that led to ladders that went down into the depths of the ship. I felt like one of the third-class passengers of the RMS Titanic.

We were guided through several passageways going deeper into the ship. In the passageways, huge pipes the same color as the hallways ran lengthwise along the ceiling. Everything was painted with a waterproof, light gray, semigloss paint. We entered a passageway that led us to our accommodations. It was a tight fit for fifty men to live and sleep. There were two-by-two footlockers for each of us where personal items could be stored. They were stacked four high throughout our quarters.

The bunk beds were stacked four high, and only twenty-two inches separated them. Each bunk was made of a sturdy stretched canvas, and attached to the sides of the canvas were ropes holding the canvas to heavy-duty aluminum pipes. We were issued a small thin mattress, a pillow, and bedding. That was it.

The passageways between bunks were very narrow, just large enough for two men to squeeze past each other. Of course, the grab-ass started immediately. The old salts bunked close to each other, and all the new guys did the same. The next thing was to get used to the ship and locate the bathrooms, showers, and chow hall. Every unit had its complainers. When we had to squeeze around them, Drust and Szuminski made it known they were none too happy with the tight accommodations.

It took us a couple of days to get accustomed to the ship. Word came down that we were going on a trial run, attacking with choppers. We were going to assault Kin Ville, where we took our liberty, and Camp Hansen, another military base near Camp Schwab. So, on April 4, the day before we were going to assault the two areas, we met in platoon groups on the hangar deck. With the extra training and leadership, we felt confident about the task ahead. Staff Sergeant Malloy and Lieutenant Francis led the discussion about what we were going to do in the morning.

"Gentlemen, we will be taking off at 0800 tomorrow morning," Malloy said. "Our objective is to experience what it's going to be like to attack a village. Twenty-five helicopters will be taking off from the deck of the *Okinawa*. Once we land, you will spread out and set up the perimeter so more choppers can come in. We'll expand the perimeter and then move on to the ville in a sweep toward our objective, the barracks of Camp Hansen. We will then eat chow at Camp Hansen and afterward return to the original landing site where we'll board the choppers and head back to the ship. Then, we'll do the same thing again tomorrow to work out the bugs."

APRIL 5 CAME, AND we carried all our combat gear just as if we were in Vietnam. The gear we carried was heavy, but we were ready for anything the enemy could throw at us. The extra forty to fifty pounds seemed necessary at the time.

We all congregated in the hangar deck in our platoon groups of forty-five to fifty men. We had four platoons in Charlie Company: First, Second, and Third Infantry Platoons, plus a Weapons Platoon. I casually met some of the men from the Weapons Platoon that had been attached to us. There was Don Bumgarner (we just called him "Bum"), a mortarman from Missouri. Burkitt, in Rockets, was from Southern Illinois. He carried the 3.5-inch rocket launcher commonly known as a bazooka. His assistant carried six high-explosive rounds. Bacon, the radioman for the XO, was from Ohio. Eight o'clock came fast that morning, and we had to make our way to the front of the hangar bay. The ship's PA system blared.

Now hear this:
BATTLE STATIONS! BATTLE STATIONS!

We climbed up steel ladders attached to the side of the wall inside the ship's hangar deck. At the top of the ladder there was a hallway that led to a door. As we got closer to the flight deck, we could hear the choppers warming up and, once through the door, we were on the flight deck. The sounds became magnified, and the wind hit my face. I could feel lightness in my stomach. You know that funny feeling that warns you of impending danger and excitement at the same time? Each Marine had to stay focused on the man in front of him at all times. We were sent out in groups of five. One of the flight personnel ran with the first five men to the first chopper. There was another person standing at the door yelling for us to follow the white line. Still another guy yelled for us to keep our heads down when boarding.

I approached the door to the flight deck and followed the Marine in front of me to the third chopper from the back of the ship. Each group of five Marines ran in single file to the roaring helicopters. The choppers had practiced this maneuver before, but this time they were carrying combat-ready Marines. The ship was moving at about thirty miles an hour, and all the choppers were facing into the wind.

I sat there on the floor of the chopper as the engines idled for what seemed to be at least fifteen minutes. Then the sound of the choppers' engines became deafening. I felt alarmed, as the chopper seemed to be out of control. It shook as if it would fall apart or explode. We could hear the choppers in front of us moving out. Ours started to lift off, and its tail moved to the side instead of forward. The lack of control lasted for only a couple of seconds. Once it was off the deck, the machine rose into the air. The nose tipped down and the chopper moved forward. Just like that, we were moving away from the ship and following the choppers that had already taken off. Still more choppers followed behind us. It was to be our last training exercise. The real test was about to begin.

CHAPTER

THREE

AFTER WE WERE MORTARED in the Que Son Valley and Lieutenant Sutton had been flown to the USS *Sanctuary*, our first operation, Beaver Cage, was coming to an end. There were three more days of light contact, and then our battalion walked twenty miles to an extraction point where we were airlifted back to the USS *Okinawa*. We had lost only one Marine from my platoon, but several were wounded. In the whole battalion, 55 of our men were killed and 151 wounded. For us, it had been bad, but worse for the enemy. We were told that we'd killed more than 800 and captured 37.

The NVA sacrificed hundreds dead and an equal or greater number wounded. They retreated to their hidden caves in the hills to lick their wounds because they couldn't continue in the onslaught they were receiving. I realized the NVA were unyielding to a point, then flexible enough to fall back when they became overwhelmed by our superior firepower. Marines would be able to regroup in their rear areas, or like our own battalion, use helicopters to return to the safety of the ship.

It was going to be a long, hot walk to the extraction point, mostly through dried-out rice paddies and villages of the very old and the very young. I walked down a path that led to a hooch where an old woman and a little five-year-old boy lived. The child looked poorer than any child I had ever seen in my life. All he wore was a pair of tattered shorts. His bare belly stuck out as if he were pregnant. I figured he had some kind of dysentery or worms. There was a huge scab on his forehead, and I wanted to see if there was anything I could do for him. I approached the little boy and reached out toward his scalp and the scab. As soon as my hand got close to his head, about forty flies scurried away. The scab I saw was not a scab at all, but rather flies eating away on his head. I was repulsed at the sight of it. I took the little boy by the hand and approached the old lady. From my pack, I retrieved my only bar of soap and handed it to the mama-san, pointing to the little boy's head. She nodded with no emotion at all.

I wished I could do more to help the poor people of South Vietnam. I thought by destroying the North Vietnamese Army and the Viet Cong, we were supposed to be doing that. But something about the way that old mama-san accepted the soap gave me the impression that those old farmers didn't want us there any more than they wanted the NVA or VC. She didn't smile. She didn't show an ounce of gratitude. It was almost as if I'd forced her to take the soap at gunpoint or that the offer was an insult. Either way, I felt that she didn't know why we were there anymore than why the North was her enemy. They were just rural farmers who wanted nothing to do with the lot of us. They just wanted to be left alone.

We continued through the ville and then spread out as we exited into another rice paddy. Today my path headed toward a semidried pond that looked traversable. The top part of the ground was hard but as I stepped, my foot sunk into a moist muck and I became bogged down. It seemed that the more I struggled, the farther my boot sunk into the quagmire. I was way beyond my calf in the muck. I tried to pull my right leg up, but it felt like I was sinking deeper and getting even more stuck. Pilgreen held out his hand and I grabbed it. We both struggled to lift my right leg, and to my surprise, it came right out. My boot came out all right, but the sole was gone. The jungle had eaten all the threads holding it to the shoe. I struggled to lift the other leg and the same thing happened. Unlike everyone else, I had not been issued the jungle boots, and I had literally walked completely out of my boots in a single month. I unlaced my now completely worthless boots and took them off. I complained to Jones and Muller about the boots, and neither showed sympathy.

"You'll just have to wait until the next chopper comes in tomorrow," Jones said.

I was barefoot and was going to have to deal with it. After taking off what was left of my boots, I continued my trek. It was painful to step on prickly pieces of dried, hardened shrubs and sticks, dried-out grass shoots, and hot rocks. Next to the extreme thirst I had experienced in the days prior, this was the most physically painful day I had experienced in the war so far. For hours I walked, and every step seemed to get worse. The next morning, a supply chopper came with a brand-new set of jungle boots. I had never realized how important good footwear was until I had none.

Looking at my new boots, I wondered how the VC did it. They wore the "Ho Chi Minhs"—sandals made from used American tires.

The local people went to our dumps and retrieved the thrown-out tires and tubes. They would take them back to their huts and cut the tire treads into soles. The inner tubes would serve as straps for holding the treads to their feet. I guess it's all what you get used to. Still, what a difference my shoes made for me.

We walked until the end of the day. Some other units received sniper fire and we were mortared, but now our company was moving out into a clearing where choppers began to arrive, taking us back to the USS *Okinawa*.

We arrived back on the ship May 13. The attitude of the men was not as somber as I had expected it to be. Everyone arrived as if we never left. The resilience of our company was apparent. Captain Reczek had done a fantastic job, as had our forward observers and all the SLF Marines. We lost our executive officer when Lieutenant Sutton was wounded, but Reczek was already looking for his replacement. We had gotten our first taste of battle, and I wondered what we had won.

Did we take the ground we fought for? No, we didn't. Did we win the hearts and minds of the people? No, we didn't. What we did win was a numbers game. We killed, wounded, and captured more of them than they did us.

I listened to the stories from everyone about our first encounter with Charlie. We'd had our trial by fire, and as we spoke together, I noticed the old salts began to show a closeness we hadn't seen before. They were just like us.

One of the old salts talked about the day we thought the NVA were massing for an all-out assault and going to overrun us.

"Remember that night when Puff showed up?" he recounted. "Earlier that day, Lieutenant Francis was going to send us on a suicide mission. So, he goes up to Malloy and tells him this crazy plan where we attack the NVA down in the valley, right? But, thank God, Malloy shakes his head and says, 'No Way.' I mean, Malloy just totally and immediately rejects the idea."

Lieutenant Francis, outraged at Malloy's disobedience, went to Captain Reczek and suggested the plan to him, but Reczek rejected his appeal as being too foolhardy.

"Then Reczek says, 'But I appreciate your willingness to think outside the box,'" the old salt laughed.

I thought about the idea Francis had come up with. Now, knowing of all the traps that were set against other units, there was a good chance we would have been wiped out. Thank God for Sergeant Malloy and Captain Reczek. I could only imagine what Sergeant Malloy was thinking about Francis going over his head. Platoon sergeants usually lead by experience, and the boot lieutenants listen to the older, more experienced sergeants.

For the time being, however, Lieutenant Francis was gone. During the operation, he exposed himself to fire and was lightly wounded. I'm sure Malloy was relieved to know that Francis was gone and that he was now in total command. He didn't have to listen to Francis's crazy plans anymore. Still, Reczek put Francis in for a Silver Star. For his leadership and courage during the operation, Captain Reczek was awarded a Bronze Star.

CHAPTER

FOUR

DAYS PASSED, AND THERE was still no letter from Kathy. It was really starting to bother me. Her letter was the first letter I looked for, and she was the first person I wrote to after boarding the ship. I asked if she was okay and told her I loved and missed her. I began sending letters to everyone who knew her to find out why I didn't get any letters from her. One thing I did know: I was going to have to wait a while to get an answer. Our letters took a long time making it halfway around the world, and their replies took just as long to get back to us. A truly good thing about writing letters home is that we didn't have to pay for postage. We only had to write "Postage Free" in the top right corner of the envelope. It made it easier for us to write home.

We had four days to clean ourselves up and recoup before the next operation, Operation Beau Charger. On May 17, we were once again called to the hangar deck for a platoon meeting. Lieutenant Francis and Staff Sergeant Malloy were there.

Lieutenant Francis had recovered enough from his wound to return for duty.

Malloy said, "Marines, we are going in the DMZ tomorrow."

The DMZ was the dividing line between North and South Vietnam. It ran from the hills of Khe Sanh in the west to the South China Sea in the east. I knew from the stories I had heard that the fighting in the DMZ was going to be different than fighting in the jungles and rice paddies.

"The North Vietnamese Army has established positions south of the DMZ, and that puts them in South Vietnam," Malloy continued. "This is where we want them. We are not sure how many NVA we're up against because they have been secretly infiltrating the area for some time. There could be as many as what we were up against on Beaver Cage. It could be an entire division, perhaps ten thousand troops. Whatever their number is, we are going to destroy them. Before we do, we have to relocate about ten thousand civilians who live in this area. Unfortunately, this is exactly where the NVA have taken up their positions, using the civilians as bait. You are not allowed to fire at anyone until they fire at you first."

I looked over to Pilgreen, and I could read his lips as he soundlessly mouthed, "Yeah, right!"

Malloy continued, "These civilians will have to be relocated for their own safety, and we don't need any civilian casualties. Once all civilians have been cleared, this will be a free-fire zone and then you may kill anything that moves."

"All right!" someone said.

Malloy didn't smile. He just continued, "Men, this has all the makings of one epic battle. Many battalions will be sweeping from the south moving north toward the DMZ. We are expected to destroy the NVA in the area all the way to the DMZ. Our battalion will come in from the sea with a surprise flanking movement. The other battalions are on their respective operations. They are the Second Battalion/Twenty-Sixth Marines, First and Second battalions of the Ninth Marine Regiment, and the First and Third battalions of the Fourth Marine Regiment. They are on Operation Hickory sweeping north right now."

Wow, I thought to myself. *That's five thousand Marines.*

"All battalions will be sweeping north and northwest moving toward the DMZ. Second Battalion/Third Marines is on Operation Belt Tight and is also sweeping north at this moment."

I was amazed at the manpower we were committing. Malloy continued, "The Fifth ARVN Regiment is on Operation Lam Son 54, plus thousands of Vietnamese Police have been called in to help with the transition of the civilians, escorting them south."

I wondered how it was going to work, using the Vietnamese troops and police. We would have another five thousand, which equaled ten thousand troops on our side. Epic, indeed, but I wasn't sure how much faith we could put into our South Vietnamese counterparts. There were rumblings among the Marines that they couldn't be trusted. Some were known to run at the first sign of battle; others were thought to be traitors giving away our plans. Some were just scared to die and ineffective.

"We take off at 1400 hours and land southeast of Con Thien at Landing Zone Goose. Once we land, we will set up our perimeter and establish our LZ. We will immediately move west to find and relocate the noncombatants out of the area."

Someone yelled, "Dismissed!"

Pilgreen came up to me and said, "Ever notice how the North Vietnamese keep coming into the south, but we can't go over the borders to get them? How about they get to try and kill you first before you can shoot them? They also get to place their artillery on the north side of the DMZ, but we can't go over there to knock it out. Kinda makes it hard to fight a war. Whatcha think about that, Taylor? Kinda makes ya wonder, doesn't it?"

I looked at Pilgreen, thought about it, and frowned. Thoughts of Kathy and whether she was okay quickly pushed Pilgreen's question from my mind, though. I sure hoped she was okay!

Morning came. Some of the old salts wanted to get a little extra sleep but couldn't because of all the noise the guys were making. A few idle threats were tossed back and forth, but everyone settled in. Lunch was being served. Steiner, Mac, and I went early to get in line for what was to be our last meal on ship until we got back from Operation Beau Charger. We grabbed a silver tray in the mess hall and walked down the line. There were all types of lunch meats and breads, fried chicken, and slices of beef. Other foods displayed were an array of vegetables, mashed potatoes, and french fries. We found a place to sit.

Next to us were four Navy guys, and their conversation caught our attention. One of the four said, "A lot of wounded Marines and body bags came in on the flight deck a little while ago. I guess they got hit pretty bad, at LZ Goose. You know, they went out several hours ago. I was told that when they tried to land, they were hit by heavy machine-gun fire and one chopper even crashed—killed everyone aboard. Once the rest were on the ground, artillery and rockets rained down on them. I think up to seventy were either killed or wounded. Five choppers came back so badly damaged they were taken out of service."

"You know," Steiner said, "that could have been us."

There was a moment of quiet apprehension as I pictured the scene. I imagined readying myself near the doorway as the chopper before us spun out of control. We set down in a hot LZ with bullets punching through the fuselage. Marines sprint away from the open ground—some tumbling lifeless into the grass, others disappearing in the clouds of the explosions.

I looked at Steiner and Mac, who were also lost in thought, and said nervously, "Do you think I might be able to get a note from my mother not to attend this field trip?"

Steiner cracked a smile. "I already tried that, and Malloy flat-out turned me down," he said.

At one in the afternoon, we heard the PA system blast.

Now hear this:
BATTLE STATIONS! BATTLE STATIONS!

We headed up toward the hangar deck and prepared to go out to the choppers. That's where Staff Sergeant Malloy told us that our original landing site, Goose, was changed to LZ Owl, farther south. Steiner and I already knew why. What the Navy guy was saying in the chow hall was true.

Choppers waited on the deck, and we started our march out to them. Pilgreen sat on the floor by the door. We had now done this enough that it was becoming routine.

"Here we go again," I said.

"Four more months and a hook, I'm outta here," Pilgreen replied.

Pilgreen's thirteenth month was in the middle of September, when he would get to go home to Alabama. I had nine months left. It was pretty sketchy to think about how long I had to go. It felt like an eternity.

"I worry about that last month," Pilgreen said. "You know, the extra month we as Marines have to spend in country."

None of us knew why we had to serve the extra month, but we all felt that it was because we were Marines. All the other armed forces did twelve-month tours. A lot of Marines "got it" in that last month of their tour, and this was Pilgreen's greatest fear.

The choppers revved their engines, and we headed into the wind, gaining altitude increasingly fast. It didn't take long to see the *Okinawa* cruising off the coast of the DMZ. When we looked out the chopper door, we could see the bright, white sand along the approaching coastline in the distance. It looked so beautiful, but we all knew it was deadly. There was a river to the north, and I thought it might be the Ben Hai, which divided the north from the south. I remembered what Pilgreen said about not being able to go after them on the north side. The area north of the Ben Hai River didn't look any different from the area south, at least from the air.

The coast was now directly under our choppers, and we headed inland. We started our descent into what we all knew would be the abyss of the DMZ. There was a profound commonality in ideologies between the Marines and the North Vietnamese: it was to annihilate each other at all costs—to do whatever it takes to create havoc, chaos, and death against each other in this swath of land dividing the north from the south.

We entered an area that was dense with trees but with a space large enough to get four choppers in. We heard a bunch of sounds as if someone was throwing rocks at the chopper. It was the sound of bullets going right through the thin skin. The gunner manning the M60 machine gun sprayed an incessant fire into the tree lines below, focusing left, then right. There were a few NVA in the area, and they had opened up on us, hoping to kill a few Marines before we landed. I felt helpless listening to the sounds of bullets hitting the fuselage.

The choppers set down, and we all exited briskly while blasting the tree line in front of us. The firing stopped. Whoever was shooting at us had apparently decided to relocate to another area or to hide in spider holes. The ground was half sand and half dirt. There was a layer of grass on top of the soil with bare spots of bright, white sand. Mortars had hit there previously, creating blast marks everywhere. Three-foot weeds were clumped together all over the landing zone. Trees and brush surrounded us everywhere we looked.

I heard sniper fire in the distance. We moved into positions to protect the landing zone. Our men were heavily laden with packs on their backs, flak jackets, and M16 rifles. Machine-gun crews had just landed with the heavier M60 machine guns and boxes of ammo. We were ready for a fight.

Captain Reczek got the Marines moving in a northeasterly direction. Our platoon was given the job of covering the right flank of the company. Snipers picked at us along the way. Normally we would maneuver to annihilate the threat, but we had to remain focused on accomplishing our mission of relocating indigenous people out of the area. Besides, they could have been trying to draw us into an ambush, so going after them would not necessarily be a good idea. Meanwhile, the NVA were sending thousands of troops in several spearheads to overwhelm the Marines south of the DMZ.

As we continued to move north toward our original landing area, LZ Goose, I noticed our company had picked up about twenty-five old men, women, and small children. It pained me to see these old people bent over and sadly struggling along within our unit. They didn't carry much of anything.

I thought of the refugees fleeing from the German war machine in World War II. Those refugees had hauled all their belongings in large carts pulled by horses. These evacuees were carrying bags of rice and a few other household items they needed for survival, and little more on their backs. Old mama-sans and papa-sans wore black pajamas. There wasn't a single person between the ages of eight- and sixty-years-old. I wondered if the missing age group was a part of the South or North Vietnamese Army. Were the people with our platoon just old people wanting to survive or Communist sympathizers acting as lookouts for the elusive enemy?

As we moved through the hostile area, we went in a westerly direction, picking up an additional 15 people. By 6:30 p.m., our platoon had about 40 to 50 civilians. The company had an additional 225 indigents. Tanks and amtracs picked up the people and their belongings. Marines loaded them aboard anything that had tracks.

A couple of hours passed, and it was getting dark. Our movement slowed because we had to wait for the amtracs to return for more civilians. We definitely overstayed our visit, because as soon as the amtracs arrived we started getting hit with mortar fire. The rounds went over our heads, but everyone still dove for cover.

There was a tree line in the distance where we figured the gooks had set up their mortars. That's where the rounds were originating. Tanks and amtracs moved forward to take up positions to attack the tree line and secure the area. As the armored vehicles moved forward, an RPG rocket was launched and streaked toward one of the amtracs. We heard a *boom* and the amtrac exploded, killing everyone inside. I averted my eyes to avoid the carnage. The amtrac had been filled with civilians—women and children. You could tell from the blast that no one could have survived.

The tanks immediately pulled back, as fifteen more RPGs were fired. Smoke trails followed the rockets toward the tracked vehicles. Fortunately for us, the rockets missed their intended targets.

Jets came in overhead, and the mortars ceased firing from the tree line. As the jets banked toward the tree line, the last of the civilians were hurried into the last amtrac. The jets were F-4 Phantoms. They started diving in from west to east, and they had the tree line zeroed in.

The F-4s dropped their 500-pound bombs directly on the tree line. Huge explosions erupted and we could see trees, dirt, and debris flying everywhere. The sleek, silver-colored, fast moving aircraft followed each other up again for another run. They came in a second time, on the same forty-five-degree angle. They let their cargoes of explosives fall again on the tree line. The ground shook. I felt like I was at the scene of a train accident as I watched in horror and thankful exhilaration. It was like watching live TV but we couldn't turn the channel. I was grateful that we didn't have to experience that kind of firepower.

The incursion of the jets had stopped the firing from the tree line for now.

We dug in for the night. It was really hard to dig our fighting holes. The soil was mostly sand with just enough dirt to give it a little strength, barely holding it together. Our foxholes kept collapsing. I'm sure the NVA had the same problem. As dusk fell, a mortar barrage of about forty rounds crashed directly on our lines. All night long, we got hit and then there would be a lull in the action. We would then send our artillery on their positions. They, in turn, sent mortars and artillery back on our positions. Just trying to stay alive was a full-time job. Throughout the night desperate cries rang out: "Corpsman up!"

THE NEXT DAY, WE began sweeping the same area we swept previously. As we started to move, sniper fire erupted from our front. We held up, and then the mortars started again. They exploded randomly all around us. The NVA seemed to know exactly where we were. They were ready to deliver whatever they had on our positions at a moment's notice. F-4 Phantoms arrived again and blasted the suspected positions. When the jets arrived and dumped more 500-pound bombs, the mortars stopped firing at us and we were able to move out. The jet incursions kept the NVA off-balance and kept their heads down. After we moved out, mortar rounds hit exactly where we had previously sat.

We kept moving for several days, picking up more of the local population. They were evicted from their homes, which made the area a "free-fire zone." From then on, anybody remaining in the area, whether they were truly combatant or not, could be killed.

On the twentieth, we picked up another 135 rural farmers, and on the twenty-first, another 84. Then, on May 23, we observed a twenty-four-hour truce in honor of Buddha's Birthday, with no incidents reported by anyone.

By now I was extremely dirty. My utilities were loaded with a grease-like grime. Dirt and sand covered all the green from my waist down. Days of digging foxholes that kept collapsing, plus kneeling and crawling in filth, caused us to be filthy. There were no bathrooms in the DMZ. Trying to find a place to dispose of our digestive waste was nearly impossible. No one wanted to be around when we dug our hole and squatted. The fact was that once a day we each had to go and make that disgusting run. That alone would make us vulnerable to a sniper's bullet. Then on top of that, not taking a bath for days was as dirty as one could get. After the third day, it didn't make any difference. We were dirty, and we were going to stay that way for quite a while.

We kept moving, sweeping back and forth over the same area in the DMZ, and getting hit as we set in for the night. Mortar rounds blew up all around us constantly. After getting hit over and over, Captain Reczek realized that we were getting hit every time we set up for the night.

One evening, we set in and dug our foxholes exactly the way we had the previous night. Just before dusk, Reczek made the company saddle up and abandon the holes we'd dug. We moved about fifty yards south from the original site. You should have heard the grunts complaining! The Marines in the hole next to me bitched like crazy.

"What a bunch of crap!" someone said.

"Why can't they just make up their frickin' minds," the other whined.

As darkness set in, the rounds came in as expected, but they exploded in the area that we had just evacuated. Reczek had figured out how to trick the NVA into thinking we were somewhere we weren't. We recognized that Reczek was flexible, getting smarter every day, and that he truly cared about his men.

On the sixth day, we received intense machine-gun fire and mortars from another distant tree line to our north. Our forward observer began talking to the F-4 fighter pilots. He was able to zero in to the pilot the exact place where the firing was emanating. This time, the jets came in from the sea. They came in screaming low and fast behind us. They darted in a westerly direction, lowering their altitude as an ear-shattering roar rushed over us. A feeling of power went through me. The jets banked hard right and set up for their run on the tree line. The two F-4s headed directly for the tree line side by side. It was like watching a football game, where the home team player was running to the end zone for a touchdown. We were screaming for him to score.

"Kick their asses!"

"Blow the bastards to hell!"

The jets were lower than usual and about fifty yards above the trees. It didn't look like they were being fired on, but I'm sure they were. As they approached the tree line, we could see silver canisters being released, two from each wing. The canisters rolled end-over-end directly toward the tree line.

I thought to myself, *Oh my God, they're dropping napalm!* Eight explosions happened simultaneously. The jets had dumped their entire load. Bright red flames erupted along the entire length of the tree line. Then a huge, round ball of a ferocious, billowing, red-and-black volcanic-type eruption made its way above the trees. The flames settled down a little as the round, black clouds continued upward. Everyone's eyes were wide at the onslaught that happened in front of us. We were extremely happy because the jets sure calmed things down again; we didn't get any more fire from the NVA.

We swept for several days until the twenty-sixth. All that happened was harassing sniper fire. Our mission was now complete. All Marine units on the operation had lost a total of 142 men, with 896 more wounded. Out of that total, our battalion lost 23 Marines and had 99 wounded. On the twenty-sixth, all the First Battalion/Third Marines headed toward the ocean where landing craft were sent to pick us up and take us back to the USS *Okinawa* before our next mission. At least we would have mail call and I could see if there were any letters from Kathy.

By now, there had to be a letter waiting for me.

CHAPTER

FIVE

AFTER BEING ON THE ship for three days, there was talk of a new mission brewing, and sure enough, Jones came down into the squad bay.

"Listen up, everyone!" he said. "Tomorrow is June second; we are going on another mission, this time to Death Valley. The name of the operation is Bear Bite. There will be a platoon meeting at 1500 hours on the hangar deck tomorrow."

The next day on the hangar deck, Jones and Francis began to describe what we were to expect. Staff Sergeant Malloy came forward, interjecting our plan of attack, before Lieutenant Francis could say a word.

"Men, we are headed to the Thua Thien area, which is in the Quang Tri Province," he said. "This area is known as Death Valley. Death Valley is a fertile valley that is located between three mountain ranges. It's a hornet's nest of Viet Cong."

I instantly hated the name Death Valley.

"The VC will be setting up booby traps everywhere," Malloy continued, "especially in tree lines where they expect us to pass. You never know which tree line they will lace. We are expecting mainly butterfly mines and bouncing betties. If any of these devices go off, take cover immediately. Charlie is known for taking advantage of our delays. They also love to slow us up so they can prepare ambushes and preset mortar barrages."

We were taught in booby trap school that the most horrendous booby trap of all is the bouncing betty mine. The reason for this is because it is the hardest mine to detect. The mine is totally buried in the ground with the exception of three little prongs. Once one of the prongs is activated, it would release a mortar projectile three to eight feet into the air and explode, sending hot shards of steel in every direction. The individual who sets it off usually dies. Everyone within fifteen feet around him becomes wounded with shrapnel. If it explodes at three feet, it blows off your legs; a little higher, and it blows your stomach apart. Higher, and you can imagine what happens. I dreaded the thought of setting out in the morning.

Nighttime came fast on the ship, and it was time to go to sleep. All the lights went out except the dimly lit exit lights. A lot of Marines settled in the ship's cafeteria to write letters home to a wife, sweetheart, parents, or friends. I sat in the chow hall drinking hot coffee into the night. As I looked around the cafeteria, some of the guys talked while others played card games, especially poker. I didn't get involved with the poker games because the same guys kept winning. I thought they were very skilled, the luckiest people alive, or were just flat-out cheating. My lousy pay of one hundred dollars a month plus sixty-five dollars combat pay didn't go very far, and I wasn't going to take a chance at losing it.

In six hours, reveille would sound. The cooks made loaves of bread for the following day's meals. The smell alone made my mouth water. If we were up late enough, we could sneak into the galley where the racks of fresh, homemade bread were kept. This evening, as Steiner and I left the cafeteria, we quietly entered the confines of the kitchen and stole two loaves of that magnificent bread. We were like mice stealing the cheese and hiding away, eating it in a hidden cavity of the ship. I put my nose to the loaf, closed my eyes, and took in the smell.

"Mmm," I said. "Just like Grandma used to make."

By 4:59 a.m., the squad bay was silent. All the men were sleeping in their bunks stacked four high, one on top of another. The lights came on at 5:00; I heard someone snoring a few bunks away. At 5:45, most were in the squad bay finishing up last-minute details before moving out to our place of departure.

The word came down from Sergeant Jones that we were moving out of the squad bay in ten minutes. As we left the squad bay, Marines passed out ammo and grenades. A loud sound came out of the speaker system.

Now hear this:
BATTLE STATIONS! BATTLE STATIONS!

I was feeling pretty good until I heard the sound of the PA, but the announcement triggered a Pavlovian response and filled me immediately with fear. Looking around the hangar bay, I wondered what the Navy guys were thinking about us. I suspected they were probably glad they hadn't joined the Marines.

We headed for the stairs that took us to the flight deck and waited for our turn to advance to the choppers, getting ready to depart to the skies. The first set of choppers had already taken off. My platoon was going to be in the second wave, and we waited for the choppers' return. The choppers began landing on the *Okinawa*, and we anxiously prepared for our turn. Jones was there at the top of the stairs, along with some Navy flight deck personnel, as we started moving up. As soon as we were in position, we were sent out, five at a time. The first group of five would be designated to the closest chopper. The next five would move out to the next chopper, and so on. This continued until all choppers were full. The order was given to lift off.

As I sat there in the waiting chopper, my mind seemed to be on hold, with no thoughts at all. I found myself just staring blankly at Wakefield, one of the old salts from Khe Sanh, and waiting for the first choppers to accelerate their engines. The gunner with his special green flight suit and helmet looked over at me and smiled. I smiled back and gave him a thumbs-up. He gave me a thumbs-up in return. We still hadn't taken off, and I looked beyond the gunner and outside the chopper door.

The ship was about ten miles from the shoreline and running parallel to it. A brisk wind hit the flight deck, and I wondered if it would affect our takeoff. The engine roared, and then the chopper started moving awkwardly at first. The scent of exhaust fumes filled the cargo bay. A gust of wind caught the spinning rear blades, causing the tail to slide a little to the left. The pilot corrected the misalignment immediately. We moved upward and proceeded forward. All choppers were in the air, and the USS *Okinawa* started looking smaller as we pulled away. I saw the huge elevator platform that moved the choppers from the hangar deck to the flight deck. The elevator platform was located in the middle of the ship and on the port side. The elevator had a large, cavernous opening where the crews maneuver the choppers in and out of the hangar deck. Men were moving all over the flight deck. They began to look like ants on a plastic model I might have put together as a young boy. Little by little, the ship disappeared. In the distance on the horizon was a speck of white. This was our shadow, the hospital ship, USS *Repose*.

Our chopper kept climbing. Soon we were high over the coast of Vietnam. The gooks must have been able to see us and know that we were coming. Below, I saw hooches and little, square, green-and-brown patches of farmland. We started our descent, and the loud roar of the engines began to fade. The sudden descent plugged my ears, so I yawned and felt a rush of noise fill my head. Steiner pointed his finger down, but when I leaned over and looked out the door, I couldn't see what he was pointing at. I saw the hooches and fields much more clearly the closer we got. Still there were no signs of life. The Vietnamese I was looking for would look small from this altitude, but I should be able to see the local farmers. My curiosity overwhelmed me. I needed to see more from the window behind me, so I got up from my sitting position to a crouch and looked out. The ground was closing in, and the engines kicked in to slow the chopper's descent. Marines maneuvered to get on their feet just before we touched the ground. The choppers made a swift landing, and we all departed out the door, one at a time.

We ended up in a field of scattered bushes next to a series of rice paddies. This landing was different from our other landings. The chopper pilots didn't take off immediately. They waited until all the choppers landed. Once they had, the lead chopper took off. One by one they peeled away. The first wave of Marines had already spread out and secured the landing zone. As the choppers vanished into the distance, we waited for orders. Obviously, we didn't have long to wait. We were going to be a sweeping force.

Some abandoned railroad tracks ran parallel to our march, their bridges long since blown away by VC sappers. The tracks were purposely raised to about eight feet to clear the monsoon rains and rice paddy waters. We followed the tracks southward for a while and then crossed over to the other side. I was always alert for danger and expected to get hit at any time. The Viet Cong were excellent at using various positions and obstacles to camouflage themselves so they could snipe at us. I was worried they might use the tracks to hit us in some way. My vigilance was becoming an instinct.

Our company of three platoons, with an accompaniment of weapons, began receiving a lot of menacing fire. Several times a day, a medevac chopper was needed to evacuate a wounded Marine. We swept through several villes without incident, and then would sometimes receive sniper fire from the ville that we'd just left behind us. Whenever this happened, the entire company would stop. During one of these "breaks," I retrieved a can of Del Monte mixed fruit cocktail that my sister sent me. I specifically looked for the cherries inside. Funny how something as small and simple as a cherry could bring back a sense of home.

Somewhere in the early afternoon, the company was moving through some trees and a dense growth of underbrush when it happened. *Boom!* One of the Marines had stepped on a bouncing betty. We all hit the deck because we didn't know what happened at first. A black cloud rose up from where the explosion had been. Men lay everywhere, and some were moaning.

"Corpsman up!" someone yelled.

A medevac chopper arrived within twenty minutes, and corpsmen evacuated one dead Marine and four others who were wounded, two of them critically.

It would soon be my turn to pass through the booby-trapped tree line, and the thought was horrifying. I yelled to the Marines next to me and said, "Instead of all of us going through in different spots, let's group together and all go through the same spot."

"Great," said Walstad. "Who goes through first?"

"We could draw straws, and the one with the shortest straw will go first," I said.

Damn if I didn't draw the short one.

"Here it goes," I said, taking in a deep breath.

I knew not to go through the path of least resistance. That was where they placed their mines. I spotted a place that would be harder to get through than anywhere else. There were no telltale signs of butterfly mines, and the ground was too rooted to bury a bouncing betty. The entire platoon was careful about traversing the obstacle and, as luck would have it, no one set off another trap.

It was the fourth day out and late in the afternoon. Our platoon hadn't had any sniper fire all day, and we set in by a village that was definitely VC-controlled because we had received fire from it before. The village was known as "hard core," and the VC were definitely somewhere around.

I heard a chopper coming in, and I suspected we were finally getting our resupply of food, water, ammo, and mail. I was hoping it would bring mail. Sure enough, two of the guys from our squad brought four cases of C-rations and a bunch of mail. The food was passed out first, and then came the letters. I had two. One came from my Dad, and another came from Patricia Kelly. I remembered the Pat Kelly who graduated with my girlfriend, Kathy, from St.

Aquinas High School in Chicago. I sat on the edge of my foxhole and opened the letter.

Dear Bill,

Everyone knows that you have been trying to contact Kathy, and I happen to know she has not been writing you. I hate to be the bearer of bad news, but I think it is too cruel not to tell you. Kathy got married to the guy that lived next door to her.

The letter went on, but I just dropped it. I threw my hands over my eyes and cried like a baby. My heart was shattered, and my stomach ached. I fell into the bottom of my fighting hole, crying my eyes out. I was halfway around the world in this godforsaken place where it seemed like everyone was trying to kill me. I really didn't know how to take life at that moment. My head spun with sadness, anger, and then hatred. How was I going to continue on? The VC hadn't gotten me, but the love of my life did: she shot me in the heart. Many horrible things passed through my mind, but I decided that all I could do was continue to survive and make it home alive.

OUR PLATOON LINES WERE set up in such a way that we could keep an eye on the people as we entered the village. We knew the village was hostile. Our lines stretched into the ville about fifty yards. My squad was directly in the village with five, two-man fighting holes. We had nine men plus Sergeant Jones. Jones and Muller, my team leader, had been called to the CP in the center of our lines. They were gone for some time. I watched the people in the village, and they kept their distance from us. They went about their daily chores and didn't do anything out of the ordinary.

My foxhole was dug along a six-foot-deep runoff trench that had a trickle of water in the center. I thought it must be a drainage ditch for directing the torrent of water away from the village during the monsoon season. My field of fire was to include the hooches in front of me and the trench.

I ate dinner and watched little kids playing around the hooches. They were so cute. One of the little kids who was about eighteen months old came over to see what we were doing. I smiled at the little guy. He smiled back, and it wasn't long before his mom yelled something in Vietnamese. He went running immediately to her. To be honest, I really wasn't in the mood to play or interact with him anyway.

Jones came over to my squad area. He was going to each foxhole laying out a plan that was devised by Captain Reczek and Lieutenant Francis when they were aboard the *Okinawa*. They had agreed that once we came upon a hostile ville, we would lay a trap for the VC. Jones came up to my foxhole, where Pilgreen and I set in.

"We're going to lay a trap for the local VC," he said in a low voice. "This village is VC-friendly, so there's a good probability we'll get sniper fire at some point when we're leaving the area. What we're going to do is this. Your squad will get camouflaged before dawn and hide in the brush along the drainage trench. The platoon will get up at the regular time. As the platoon gets ready to move out, I'm sure the gooks will eventually expose themselves. This time you guys will be waiting for the bastards. Get those sons of bitches once and for all!"

I could feel the adrenaline flowing throughout my body. We were down to a nine-man squad instead of the regular fifteen. Even with nine of us, we could still put a hurt on Charlie in the morning. I felt angry and was ready for a fight after getting that letter.

We woke up a half hour before daylight. Quietly, we got our stuff together and cut small branches and stuck them in our helmets, flak jackets, and packs. I found a perfect bush growing alongside the trench about eight feet tall. I sat in the middle, underneath the branches for cover. Inside the bush, I was totally camouflaged. All kinds of branches and growths coming out of the ground gave me perfect cover. The other Marines hid in equally good covering positions along the trench. Slowly, the early morning light approached our hidden positions and then the village on the other side of the trench.

As dawn bloomed, it became just another sunny day in Vietnam. We watched as the Marines slowly transitioned from night watches to being awake and starting their day. Some Marines went to relieve themselves, while others started making their favorite food of the morning. I sat there and waited. It felt like it took forever. I wished I had eaten something earlier. I became hungry, and my stomach began to growl. All I needed was to give away my position with my morning stomach noises. As it was, we had to remain still and as quiet as possible. The people who lived in the hooches started their morning routines. The little kids came out and started playing. The mama-sans were getting water out of the water urns in front of their hooches and started fires to cook their first meal of the day.

The Marines who were not part of our ambush were not moving out. *What's holding them up?* Damn, I wanted them to move out! Finally, I saw them getting their possessions together. They put their cartridge belts around their waists, threw their packs on their backs, and picked up their rifles.

The little kids had moved away from their hooches and started coming closer to us. I was quiet because I didn't want them to see me and give away my position. The little kids had crossed the trench and were moving a lot faster than the Marines moving out. *I'm sunk*, I thought. The kids were looking on the ground to see if the Marines had left anything of value. One walked right past me and was looking at the platoon of Marines in wonder as they moved out. He started rooting around in my fighting hole. He walked toward me, searching for something on the ground, and then stood right in front of me. He looked up and saw me hiding in the bushes! The kid had a look of wonder on his face.

Damn! The kid sees me.

"Di di mau," I whispered, which means "get lost" in Vietnamese. I waved my hand as if to shoo him away—fingers down and flicking out as if to scatter a fly.

"Di di!" I said again.

He smiled at me and then cocked his head with a questioning look on his face. I realized the kid thought this was a game. I smiled, and he giggled at me. He then saw the other guys hiding as well. He couldn't figure out what we were doing, but I think my smile had put his suspicions to rest. This was just a game for him. Muller looked at me and put his head down, shaking it from left to right.

Then Muller heard something, looked right, and gave out an alert sound.

"Pssst!"

We all looked at Muller, who was now pointing across the trench, into the village. Sure enough, three VC were diddy-bopping into the ville, totally unaware that they were being observed by a squad of nine Marines. Two of the VC had AK-47s over their shoulders and held them casually by the barrels. The other VC had a machine gun, which he was carrying by a handle in the middle of the weapon.

Hell, the company of Marines was just leaving and only about forty yards away from where they had been set in! *The nerve of these guys*, I thought. The three VC went to the backyard of a hooch about seventy-five yards to our right as we looked into the village. There was a thick hedgerow about eight feet tall on both sides of the hooch that completely concealed the backyard where the VC slipped out of view. The trench went jagged into the direction of the hooch. The kid watched with a weird look on his face as we crawled on our stomachs into the trench.

"Get down and stay down," said Muller.

When we all made it to the base of the trench, we started moving toward the hooch and the hedgerow. Our shoulders were tight up against the left side of the embankment so as to not reveal our movement.

Muller was totally pumped. He said in a whisper, "Everyone lock and load."

I had already done that. A round was in the chamber, the safety was off, and I was ready to go with a twenty-round magazine. Slowly, we moved down the trench to an area that was closest to the hooch. All nine of us crawled out and went into crouched positions in the center of the hedgerow. They couldn't see us, nor could we see them through the thickness of the evergreens. Muller put his finger to his lips and pointed to his ears. We listened and could hear them talking, but we didn't understand a single word they were saying.

Slowly, Muller got up and walked up the thick hedge toward the front yard and saw a slight opening between the branches. It was barely wide enough to fit one person. We were going to have to go through this opening one at a time. There would be a struggle getting through the entanglement of branches. Muller moved his finger to his lips again to give the quiet sign, and then signaled for us to approach him so we could crash through the bushes to either apprehend or kill the VC on the other side of the hedge.

"On the count of three, we'll all rush in," Muller whispered.

He held his index finger up to announce one, then the middle finger to announce two, then he put up the ring finger and made a mad dash through the bushes. Muller pointed his M16 at the shocked VC, and they got up and ran. He pulled the trigger to fire and all he heard was a click. His M16 didn't fire!

Muller started fumbling with his rifle to find out what was wrong. Steiner was second through the hedge and saw three of the VC running. To our surprise, the entire back end of the property was wide open, and they scattered in different directions. Steiner fired his M16 the second he made it through the hedge. I was the next to come through and immediately fired my M16 full automatic in the direction of the running VC. I reloaded another magazine and followed Steiner into the rear of the yard.

As I ran through the yard, I noticed a woman sitting on the ground with all the weapons the VC had been carrying. They were so surprised that they had left their weapons behind. Pilgreen covered the woman with his M16 as Steiner and I commenced to try to locate the three VC who escaped. They had only a few seconds of a head start, but they were totally out of sight. I thought the only way the three of them could have vanished so quickly was because they must have been hiding very close—probably in a concealed spider hole. I looked for footprints and they were everywhere, leading in all directions. I looked around and saw a small graveyard of their ancient ancestors. *Another great place to hide*, I thought, but I found nothing. There was a lot of sand, small trees, and brush everywhere. The direction they headed had small rolling hills, and they could be anywhere. After about twenty minutes, Steiner and I gave up the search and went back to the yard where the woman was.

"Why didn't you shoot?" I asked Muller.

He shook his head. "I told you to lock and load, but I didn't follow my own advice. I took the safety off before we went through the hedge, but I didn't have a round in the chamber. I can't believe I messed up like that."

"At least we captured one of them and all their weapons," I said.

The VC woman we captured was a mature woman, about twenty-eight years old, and taller than most of the women we had encountered. She had black pajamas draping from her body. We made her squat down and tied her hands behind her back. Muller and Jones tried to get her to talk. She just gave all of us dirty looks. The rage she felt for us was undeniable. Her attitude wasn't like most of the enemy combatants we had caught. The enemy we captured were usually terrified and didn't look at us at all. Not this one. She fit the definition of a hard-core zealot.

I don't know what came over me, but I had my own internal rage. *I'll show her*, I thought. *The way I feel, she better not fuck with me.* I was determined to scare the hell out of her and get her to open up. My adrenaline was at a peak. Knowing there had been a lot of Marines wounded and killed leaving this village upset me even more. How many Marines did they actually kill before we got here? How many had she killed? I had a sense of being as aggressive and determined as she was, and I was going to teach her a lesson. I watched as Jones kept asking her questions over and over. She had the angriest look and meanest disposition of anyone I had ever seen.

Jones had the .45-caliber out of his holster and was giving up trying to get her to talk.

"Fuck this," he said, stepping away from her.

I didn't understand why. I thought he was being way too easy on the bitch.

"Let me give her a try!" I said, grabbing the .45 from his hand.

He was taken aback, but he didn't stop me. I walked over to her, pulled the slide back, which cocked the .45 and sent a bullet into the chamber. She stood up, hands still behind her back, and turned her face away from me. I put the .45 to her left temple and stepped into her line of sight.

With the meanest face I could muster, I said, "Thang Viet Cong dau?" (Where is the VC?)

She was angry and defiant but did not appear to be scared.

I screamed it again. "Thang Viet Cong dau?"

Without a single hesitation, she spit directly into my face. I looked at her in shock and anger. I felt the tension of the trigger under my finger, the hammer only milliseconds away from dispatching the bullet into her brain.

NO! No, this isn't right! This isn't me!

I stepped backward, startled by the demon that had occupied my psyche. I wiped her spit off my face and handed the pistol back to Jones.

He looked at me in shock. I think he was glad I didn't pull the trigger.

I went back into the backyard and surveyed the guns and ammunition we had just captured. I felt like a fool. I felt like I had been in a poker game, with all the chips on the table, and she had called my bluff. I didn't even have a pair of deuces.

A chopper came in, and we watched as two Marines loaded the female VC and the cache of weapons and ammunition. I felt glad that I didn't shoot her. I wondered how it would have affected the others to see her brains blown out of her head. I wondered how it would have affected me. I had become confused about the war and what we were doing there. The fate of that woman was now in someone else's hands. It might have been a fate worse than the bullet.

A COUPLE OF DAYS later, I was walking along a trail, next to a field, when I noticed a path-side pagoda. I surmised it was a place where the locals prayed. It seemed odd to me. The pagoda was against a rock wall and sitting on a crude cabinet. The cabinet was elevated about chest high, and I began to inspect it. This was a kind of altar, and it had a panel that was cracked in the rear. I reached around, feeling inside the crack, and noticed there was something inside. I retrieved it through the small opening. It was a quart glass jar filled with crushed peppers—some farmer's offering to a long-lost ancestor.

I had found a gold mine. Our C-rations were very bland, and now I had some seasoning. I saw Rangel from Third Platoon. He was on the far left, and I was on the far right. He had seen me checking out the altar.

"What did you find?" he asked.

I showed him my prize. His eyes opened up like he had just seen Madonna, the mother of Christ.

"Hey man, I'm Mexican. You're holding the Holy Grail," he said. "Can I have some of that?"

I had a lot of respect for him. He had been wounded two times and was considered an old salt.

"Sure," I said, and we became best friends at that moment. I managed to move to the center of the platoon, and Rangel moved next to me. As we walked along the trail, he told me that he would soon be turning twenty.

He looked me dead in the eyes and said, "I don't think I'm going to make it out alive. I'm in my thirteenth month, and I keep thinking I'm going to die! I only have three more weeks before I rotate. I don't think I'm going to make it home. Man, I seriously think they have me zeroed in. I've been hit two times already."

"Hey, man, just keep the faith and be careful," I said. "I know you are going to make it."

He shook his head and said, "I hope so, man." Just then, there was a call from his squad leader to get back in formation.

After sweeping for an entire day, we arrived at a small village along the ocean. The VC or NVA had somehow evaded us all day, or else there had been some bad intel. The order was given that we were to dig in and spend the night just outside a seaside village. Our command knew that Charlie was here somewhere and expected us to get hit. There was a good probability that we would experience something soon, but we were prepared. If the enemy hit us, they were going to pay one hell of a price.

It was a fishing village full of South Vietnamese people, with small sand dunes everywhere. The people pretended to ignore our efforts to set in for the evening, but we knew they were watching our every move. I caught them looking at us as we dug our foxholes.

Of course, we had to take off our cartridge belts and packs to dig the fighting holes for night watch. Each hole connected to the right and left. We continued the same pattern in a very large circle until all three platoons were connected. The CP was in the middle as usual. Mortars and Rockets stayed in the CP area.

Pilgreen and I were told to dig our position facing north of the lines. There was just one minor problem. The holes we were about to dig were composed of the driest sand I had ever encountered. There didn't seem to be a bottom to the dry sand, either. We were about to find out how problematic this was going to be.

Pilgreen and I were partnered and took turns digging. He started first. With his deep Southern accent he said, "Taylor, what the fuck is up with this dang sand?" His emphasis was on the word *fuck*. "Check this out, Taylor." He started to dig, and for every four shovels of sand thrown out, three collapsed back in.

"Hell," he said. "I could do this all dang night and never get this hole dug. It gets wider before it gets deeper. It's a joke."

We both started cracking up and then stood there for a minute just calming down from the laughter. When I looked at the Marines around us, they were all swearing as if they were crazy men.

"Hey, look at Drust cussing up a storm over there," I said.

Pilgreen looked to his left and then right and saw Steiner using algebraic formulas to stop his hole from collapsing. Steiner had got his hole started, and then before his very eyes all his sand went crashing back in. We couldn't get enough of the show that was before us.

Everywhere we looked, Marines were swearing and throwing their shovels. We laughed for at least half an hour. The Marines became even more agitated when they saw us laughing at them.

Pilgreen and I had to get serious with our own hole. It took a little while, but we used various types of thick brush and debris to firm up the sides. Once it was dug, we were able to start eating. I pulled out my peppers.

Pilgreen commented, "Where'd you get those, Taylor?"

I told him the story and shared the peppers with him. Now all I needed was a nice cup of hot coffee. I made a stove from an empty food can to heat the coffee and used my metal canteen holder as a cup. The instant coffee really hit the spot.

The area seemed to be secure enough. Little children were playing and running around. The villagers apparently made their livelihood on fishing and some farming. Certain plants seemed to be able to thrive. The food quality was poor, to say the least. Farmers grew corn, peppers, and banana trees. The peppers seemed to thrive more than any other crop.

I opened a can of C-rations and seasoned it with the hot peppers. As I was finishing my meal, the local kids wandered by and began talking to me. They seemed friendly enough and I got caught up with them, feeling like I was home again. Children always touched my heart. There had to be seven of them, cute as you can imagine. It made the war seem far away.

All of them had crazy little hats. A couple had the pointed Vietnamese bamboo hats. Another had a hat right out of a fifties movie, similar to what Humphrey Bogart would wear. Three of the kids had button-down shirts, and the littlest one had on a dirty T-shirt. He was the one who touched my heart the most. His innocence allowed me a momentary exit from the war. The oldest one didn't smile much. He seemed distant for some reason.

One of the kids had a big smile and asked me for cigarettes. He motioned with his hands like he was smoking and actually said, "You give me." I thought that he liked to smoke or otherwise use them to barter with. Of course, I didn't give him any, but I did give him some of my unwanted food. My gift consisted of creamer and sugar packets left over from other C-rations.

I grabbed one of the little kids who got really close, and I started tickling him. The two smallest were laughing very loud and hard. Pilgreen ignored me, as he was more interested in just taking it easy and resting from the long march earlier in the day. After tickling the children, I looked around and noticed something strange.

Two of the older kids had gotten close to my rifle and cartridge belt. Too close, I realized. They looked as if they'd been caught with their fingers in the cookie jar.

I yelled at them, "Di di!" and they took off running. The little children I had been playing with didn't understand and were shocked at my new attitude. I yelled to the little children, "Di di," and then, in English, "Get out of here!"

I checked my gear, and one of my grenades was missing. I deduced that it might have fallen off sometime before we entered the ville, but maybe one of the older kids had taken it. I grabbed my rifle and the cartridge belt and looked over my shoulder. I noticed one of the older kids looked over his shoulder as he ran away. It looked like he might have had something in his hand. I looked at Pilgreen for only a second, and the kid was gone. I felt a rush of guilt come over me. How could I have been so stupid? I rushed over to Pilgreen and told him what happened.

"Whatever you do, don't let anyone know," he said. "Especially don't tell Sergeant Malloy or Jones. They could court martial your ass."

I didn't know what to do. Why should I report it? If I lost it, I could get in trouble by being negligent. If I allowed myself to be suckered in by the kids, I was still negligent. Trouble, no matter what I do. *Leave it alone*, I thought.

I didn't see any more children that evening. Pilgreen and I spent the usual fifty percent watch, all night long. During my watch, I kept thinking that maybe someone might throw that grenade at me.

At the crack of dawn, I could see everyone stirring from their watches. There were no smiles as most of us didn't get a good night's sleep, especially me. I felt somewhat relieved to know that my grenade hadn't killed or hurt anyone. Some guys were looking for a place to relieve themselves. Little walks in different directions would mean most had a destination for their most discreet moment. The word came around that we were to move out in twenty minutes and continue the sweep. This time we heard that we were going to move inland, in a more south and westerly direction.

I figured I had time for a quick breakfast. It would be my cold, ten-year-old scrambled eggs in a can. To go along with my eggs was a nice cup of instant coffee. I heated it up on the homemade stove I'd constructed the day before. Breakfast over, I heard someone say, "Saddle up!" Everyone put on their cartridge belts, flak jackets, and packs.

"Get ready to move out," yelled Muller.

Third Platoon was going to take point, and we were to follow them. Our platoon was going to be on their right, in a staggered line. We just started to move out when there was a big explosion. Crap, what the hell was that? We all got down and took cover. After about twenty minutes, the word came down that Rangel was hit by a booby-trapped grenade. His wounds were light, but they were calling in a medevac chopper to evacuate him from the field. I deduced they must have strung a fishing line across the path that Rangel was walking. When his foot pulled the line attached to the pin, it set off the grenade.

I suspected that it was my grenade that did it. Pilgreen looked at me, raised his eyebrows, and gave me an index finger over the lips.

I learned a huge lesson that day to be more careful with the people, no matter how innocent they might appear to be. I managed to work my way over to where Rangel was being patched up. He was sprayed with shrapnel on the back side of his body. All his wounds were superficial. He had managed to get far enough away from the grenade before it exploded to not do any real damage. I felt so guilty.

"Aww man, I'm so sorry you were hit," I said.

Before I could say another word, he looked at me with the biggest smile on his face and said, "Are you kidding me? This is the greatest day of my life. It's my third Purple Heart and my ticket out of this place!" Rangel looked directly in my eyes and said, "Get it? I'm going home alive, Taylor! I'm outta here at last."

I found out that day that if you were hospitalized two times, each time for at least forty-eight hours, or if you were wounded in three different engagements, you were sent home and wouldn't be sent back into a combat area for two years. Rangel's Vietnam tour was up, and he was going home. His thoughts about not making it out alive in his last month were unfounded, and he had only two more weeks before his scheduled rotation date out of Nam.

Just maybe I'll be able to go home one of these days too. Then I remembered that I had eight more months left in country. I was in perilous times and wondered about making it home alive or in a body bag, like so many others had.

OUR COMPANY WALKED ALL day. The temperature was well over one hundred degrees. It rained very little. The amount of rain that did come was just enough to make the heat worse by adding humidity. The farmers worked in their rice fields from dawn to late morning. They would then rest for the hottest part of the day and be back at it again until dusk. While they worked in the fields, they never talked to each other. They wanted to get their crops to flourish and focused on their tasks of farming. We walked through their paddies regardless of what they were doing.

Our direction was toward the mountains in the west. We entered a jungle area near the mountains, away from the roads. This place was abandoned land and contained ten-foot-high stalks of elephant grass. The narrow leaves reach three feet in length and are an inch wide. They have pointed tips and razor-sharp edges. This dark green plant flourishes and creates walls of grass that seem endless. Every platoon had two Marines who would carry machetes to hack through it. The lead man would always be bleeding from paper-like cuts from the sharp edges of the grass. As we followed, any part of our exposed flesh would also get sliced. The grass was also loaded with dusty seeds, and it was at least ten degrees hotter and more humid wading through the growth. Platoons got tangled and bogged down. Carnivorous leeches would attach themselves to any exposed flesh as we passed through. I heard many stories of platoons getting ambushed in the quagmire of grass, but ours never did. Captain Reczek always seemed to have a good read on our direction and destination.

It was difficult walking through the jungle in horrible, one hundred-plus-degree heat every day. I had drunk all my water as usual, and the pain of my thirst had become unbearable. I could no longer coax my mouth to produce the saliva I needed to wet my throat. In Okinawa's jungle training, the instructor said that if you were thirsty and in the situation I was in, to find a thick bamboo stalk. The stalk has sections and stores water in the sections for the dry season. Cut a bamboo stalk and lay it across your lap. Then, put a hole in one of the sections and suck out the water inside.

So I searched for a stalk of bamboo and found a nice, thick piece. I hacked away at it like a Wisconsin lumberjack and dragged it around until we took a break. The bamboo had a hard outer skin, and it seemed impossible to make a hole in it. I tried using the point of my KA-BAR, and then tried the bayonet. Neither knife worked. My thirst was getting to the point that I couldn't stand it any longer. In desperation, I sawed at one of the sections using the serrated side of my KA-BAR knife. I worked my ass off until a hole appeared. I sucked at it and nothing came out. There wasn't a single drop in any section. Even the bamboo was thirsty and had drunk its own supply.

I looked around. There was a very shallow, stagnant pond of water twenty feet away. I walked over to it and wondered whether or not to fill my canteen with the nasty water. I needed to do something because I was dying of thirst. I retrieved my halazone tablets, got on my knees, and put my canteen in the water very gently to keep the bottom debris from flowing in. In the depths of the muck, I noticed movement in several places. Like bolts of lightning, large leeches raced out of the muck and aimed directly toward my hand and the canteen, swimming like snakes. I yanked my canteen out of the water, and they vanished back into the muck. I couldn't believe my eyes or the fact they were keeping me from the water I needed so badly. I tried again, and this time they reached me faster because they were closer. I was fighting the leeches. I wanted their water, and they wanted my blood. I played this game until my canteen had enough water to quench my thirst. Of course, I put twice the number of halazone tablets inside and a full package of presweetened Kool-Aid to kill the taste. I then had to wait another miserable hour for the halazone to work. At least I had figured out how to get water to drink.

THE NEXT DAY, WE were back on our sweep. There was a large stream flowing in the same direction we were walking. It was beautiful—I was mesmerized and thinking about home and about fishing at Kelly Lake in Wisconsin. As I moved my left foot forward along this worn path, Pilgreen grabbed me from behind. He jerked me backward, and I fell on my ass. I was shocked at the sudden action he had taken and stared at him with a confused look from the ground. He pointed at the area in front of me. There was a patch of leaves on the trail. Pilgreen thought they looked awfully suspicious. I thought they were only leaves and I wasn't paying attention, but he was. He grabbed me just in time.

I got up and we both apprehensively approached the leaves. Pilgreen took his hand and slowly moved them aside. Sure enough, there were small sticks holding the leaves in place. The sticks and leaves concealed a hole that was about two feet deep. It was a pit with punji sticks facing upward and sideways. If I had taken that step, my body weight would have certainly carried me toward the sharp bamboo spikes. The Vietnamese spread feces on the spikes to cause infection in the wound, creating even more problems. Pilgreen had saved me from a horrible and painful situation. Pulling one's foot out of a punji pit is next to impossible. Marines have to dig the hole wider and lower to get at the punji sticks. Then you are medevaced with the sticks impaled in your foot. You need surgery to free your foot, and then you must get ready to take care of the impending infection from the feces.

Several days later, we set in for the night. Drust and I were going to be foxhole mates for this evening. Drust was an old salt from the Khe Sanh gang. He felt more comfortable with his old Khe Sanh friends and didn't take a liking to the new guys. Drust always had an attitude and complained about everything. We dug our foxhole about forty yards away from a hooch that was next to a village. There were two small kids about six and eight years old watching us in awe.

Banana trees laced in and around the entire village. The trees lined the perimeter of the rice paddies, and the whole scene looked like something out of National Geographic. Every hooch had dirt mounds that were bunkers sitting outside the dwellings. We allowed the villagers to have these fortifications for protection from the ravages of war. To the west we could see the mountains, which looked similar to those in Colorado, but without snow.

Up to this point, I had been without a way to tell time and I had been using everyone else's time pieces to stand watch, so I bought my own from the ship's store. Being in the bush at night without a wristwatch was almost as bad as having no rifle. It was a necessity. And since I couldn't be lighting a match every time I needed to check the hour, I got a Timex with hands and numbers that glowed in the dark. To keep the glow from giving away my position, I kept it in my vest pocket. The afternoon sun was beginning to set when I saw something moving in our hole. It looked like a piece of wood crawling and trying to climb up the side wall to get out. We inspected the large moving object closely. It was the biggest, fattest centipede I had ever seen in my life. It was nine inches long and was at least one inch wide. A massive number of legs were moving desperately in unison. If I had seen it in a zoo, I would've still been aghast. I imagined myself sitting on the edge of the foxhole and that damned thing sneaking up my pant leg and biting my privates.

Drust grabbed his KA-BAR knife and started stabbing it. The skin was like leather, and he found it extremely difficult to puncture. We took turns stabbing it until we cut it into pieces, and even being cut up, the legs continued to move. The strange, mangled creature, with all its hundred legs still trying to run away, grossed me out worse than a dead corpse. What else was waiting for us out there that we didn't know anything about?

The chopper had delivered the mail earlier, and Jones walked the lines passing it out. I got a couple of letters, and Drust got just one that looked official. When he opened the letter, he started going nuts.

"Those motherfuckers!" he yelled, looking at the letter. "Those cocksuckers!"

I stood up and asked what was wrong.

He picked up his M16 and immediately fired full automatic into the village. Incoherent screams came from his mouth. I had gotten down because I thought I could be his next victim. He started to reload his rifle with another magazine. I was able to jump up from the crouched position and tackle him to the ground before he could fire another round.

Jones came running over to us, as did other Marines, and yelled, "What just happened?"

I said, "Drust was reading that letter over there and just cracked up."

Three of us held Drust down. He was still screaming, kicking, and clawing like a madman the whole time. I was in total shock. Jones picked up the letter.

"Sorry to inform you," he read. "Your brother was killed in Vietnam around the City of Saigon."

Jones dropped the letter to his side and tried to rationalize with Drust, but soon realized, as I did, that Drust needed to get out of the field as soon as possible. A corpsman came over and sedated him with a shot in the leg. Soon, he was on a chopper headed back to the USS *Okinawa*. Jones sent men to see if anyone was hurt in the village, but they didn't want anything to do with us. I thought about how crazy the war continued to get. I never saw Drust again.

ON JUNE 15, WE reached our next objective. We congregated in a field where we waited for the choppers to lift us out and on to our next operation.

This operation was called Choctaw. Staff Sergeant Malloy was in front of the platoon waiting when Lieutenant Francis showed up. Francis was less than enthusiastic and obviously had something on his mind. The platoon gathered around the lieutenant's perimeter in a semicircle.

"Our battalion is being called upon to search and sweep toward the First Battalion, Fifth Marines," he said. "It's their turn to set up a blocking force. Our battalion will sweep a large swath of rice paddies and villages. We know the Fifth NVA Regiment has been sent to the area to destabilize it again. It is suspected that NVA units are also supporting the local VC. We are going back to the Que Son Valley, so expect a lot of VC units mingling in and around the villages. Our landing zone will take us to our next objective, which is forty miles south of Da Nang. We will be up at daybreak and in the choppers by 6:45 a.m. Our landing should take place no later than 7:30 a.m. Once we settle in, get your platoons to spread out and then we'll start our sweep. We have to cover a lot of territory in a short amount of time, so let's start looking like Marines and kick some ass out there."

Already the month of June had been difficult. We'd searched for large units of VC and NVA, but only found small bands of harassing VC everywhere. The NVA had retreated somewhere, but where? There had been no signs of them at all.

We woke at 5:00 a.m. The time came faster than anyone liked. I could hear the choppers in the distance and watched the horizon for our squadron of UH-34s. To our surprise, it wasn't our squadron at all, but rather, it was the CH-46 Sea Knights. The chopper was long like a hotdog and had two rotors of spinning blades. There was one large blade assembly forward and another at the rear. It could carry fifteen to twenty Marines into combat in a single load. This equates to an entire squad with packs and weapons. When it was our turn, we ran single file to the rear of the chopper. Marines ran the length of the chopper and sat down on long canvas seats. Sergeant Jones yelled to move forward. Marines didn't want to be on top of each other, but we were forced to push closer together. Each Marine moved in a little and gave enough room for all to fit. We sat in two rows and faced inward toward each other. The six-foot back door was attached to the floor with hinges. It was in the down position and used as a ramp for loading. Slowly the back door started to rise and then closed. I could hear hydraulics locking the door shut.

The jet engines began spinning both sets of blades. The sound was nearly deafening. I could hear the stresses in the chopper. The rear lifted first. I had never flown in a chopper so large before, and I wondered how it could lift such a heavy cargo. The first group of choppers started moving forward and drifted like a plane taking off down a runway. Our chopper moved forward and then up, following the lead choppers. No one was talking, and I could see the two pilots totally engaged in the takeoff process. They wore green helmets and talked to each other and to their squadron.

Right behind the pilots were two door gunners covering both sides of the helicopter. There were large, gaping windows just behind the pilots so the gunners could maneuver their machine guns and belts of ammo. There were four round portholes on each side of the fuselage. They served as observation windows to look outbound. No one cared to look at anything. I just knew that, in about twenty-five minutes, I would be back on the ground searching for Charlie.

The descent was fast. The helicopter blades started spinning hard to slow down the flying behemoth. The ass-end was coming down first. The rear two wheels touched down. The order was given to stand up and get ready to run out the rear opening. The chopper's hydraulic door came down as soon as the back end came into contact with the ground.

"Get the hell going!" someone in the front of the chopper yelled. We weren't even on the ground.

By the time the front wheel hit the ground, everybody was out the door and spreading in various directions. Our choppers landed near where the previous wave of choppers and men had landed. Members of our group were sent out to make contact with First Platoon. When the choppers lifted off, the loud roar of their engines was nothing compared to the influx of debris they had created. The operation was completed in record time and, before we knew it, they had vanished out of sight.

The next wave of choppers was coming in on the other side of our position, putting us in the middle of the sweep. Several Marines were sent to make contact with Third Platoon as they began their landing. *So far, so good*, I thought. No sniper fire on the landing. We were told that a recon unit had made sure there was no enemy around as we landed. Assuming everything was perfect, we were to begin the sweep precisely at 8:00 a.m.

But it was already after 8:00 a.m., and we hadn't yet communicated with the other platoons. I could see the officers were getting frustrated. Lieutenant Francis was pointing in all directions and waving his arms above and below his head. I pointed at the lieutenant.

"Hey Steiner, I think we have an orchestra conductor in our platoon."

He looked and started laughing, and yelled back, "Yes, and we got front row seats."

It was hot, so I took off my helmet and began to wipe the sweat off my brow with a green towel that I often kept around my neck. We stood there waiting for what seemed to be forever for the order to move out. It was almost 9:00 a.m.

The officers and platoon sergeants started yelling at us to get moving, as if we were to blame for the tardiness. Getting a late start means that somewhere down the line we would be having a very short lunch break.

We moved swiftly to get to our first objective. It was above my pay grade to know what the actual objective was. I just followed orders and kept a low profile, like Pilgreen always said. One thing I was sure about was that we were going to sweep straight across miles of countryside to find Charlie. It was going to be a big cluster fuck because the operation had been disorganized from the start. To make matters worse, I felt like we were being herded like cattle through the rural areas. As I understood, our job was to look for anything unusual as we passed through the small villages.

It appeared we were going north, because the mountains were to our left. I could see the clouds above the distant mountains. Clouds always seemed to be hanging over the mountains, but rarely above us.

One specific village seemed pretty large, as it had more than twenty huts. Every home had a round stone container outside at the front entranceway. The container was filled with rain water that had been collected for the family. All the containers had a wooden, hand-carved, circular top that fit perfectly. The top kept the contents from evaporating and, at the same time, kept the bugs out. The stone kept the water cool. When we ran short of water, we would lift the lid and fill our canteens. It was certainly better than a stagnant pond somewhere.

Old men and women crouched next to their hooch entrances. All the women had tar-black teeth. When we tried to communicate with them, all we saw was that nasty black tar. Anything they said sounded like a bunch of mumbo jumbo. I was told that the women chewed betel nuts. In training, we were told it gives them a rush, something like having six cups of strong coffee. It was also used as an ancient cure for indigestion. The tar-like substance provides a coating to keep cavities at bay.

Some of the inhabitants looked at us as if we were no more than a small dog passing through their village. Most of the people ignored us as if we weren't even there. The only people living in the village were old-looking, in their seventies and worn from a hard life in the fields. Or there were little children running and play-ing. No young adults were seen at all. We were told that younger women were not there because the Marines might rape them, but we knew better. Our thoughts were that younger men and women from the ville were VC, and everyone knew we were looking for them. After all, they wanted to kill as many Americans as they could without getting caught or killed themselves.

After passing through the village, there was another rice paddy and another ville. We kept pushing always toward the next village and then the next. The rice paddies we passed through were in squares with dikes to walk on. At times there were rows of trees dividing the paddies where we might get ambushed. Other obsta-cles were rivers and creek beds that made long ditches. A few hours into the sweep, we ran across a dried-up creek bed or monsoon washout. It was so camouflaged that I almost fell into it. The creek bed was obscured from flat land and, I would imagine, from the air as well. It ran in front of us, but on an angle. To my left, it was behind me, and on the right, it drifted to the front of us. It looked like the perfect hiding place for Charlie, and we had to cross it.

About six feet deep and eight feet wide, the creek bed was filled with tall, wild grass that grew as high as the ground we were standing on. This made it almost impossible to see. Marines to my left were already down in the tall grass of the ditch crossing to the other side. I held my M16 rifle on full automatic as they crossed and stood guard as Marines to my right started entering the ditch. My adrenaline was on full throttle. After all, we were supposed to be looking for the enemy.

Among the Marines who were around me, I was the last to enter. As I got into the ditch, I imagined what the VC might do if they were there. I noticed that the dirt walls of the creek bed were eroded, making a concave umbrella effect and providing even more potential cover. We were moving like a mindless herd of cattle, and nobody else seemed to be concerned, but everything inside me was screaming out, *We should not be taking this natural obstacle for granted.*

I felt the need to investigate everything a little further, thinking that it should only take a few seconds. We were already being driven hard, and it was getting hotter as the day moved forward, so I knew the agitation level was up.

"Hurry up, ladies!" the sergeant yelled. "Get your asses moving, or I will do some ass kicking myself!"

I decided to check out the ditch anyway. I didn't want us to get ambushed from behind. I started looking around the dense grass. Mosquitoes buzzed around in the cool recesses of the ditch. In one of the recesses, I thought I heard a sound. I wondered if it was an animal. Could it be the enemy? Was my imagination playing tricks on me? I pointed my M16 in the direction of the sound. Then I heard it again. It sounded like a human scream!

"My God!" I said. "What was that?"

John Steiner, who was already out of the ditch and on the other side, said, "Taylor, come on. Get your ass moving. The sergeant is going to get pissed off!"

"There's something down here!" I said. "I think it's a gook!"

"No shit?"

Steiner knew I wouldn't kid about such a thing. He yelled to everyone within earshot, "Hey you guys, Taylor's got a gook down here! I'll cover you." He was pointing his M16 in my direction.

About ten Marines approached and crowded around the top of the ditch, looking for potential trouble. Hell, some of the guys were dying for some action. Charlie sure can be elusive most of the time. I crept close to where I heard the sound. Then I heard it again. *Crap, what do I do?*

"I heard it too!" someone on top said.

"Check it out, Taylor," said Ski. "We have you covered."

An incredible amount of firepower was now pointing in my direction. I looked at Ski's M16 and said, "Yeah, like you shoot the gook and me too. Is that what you had in mind, Ski?"

"Then just throw a grenade into the spot where you heard the noise!" Ski said.

"I'll take care of it myself," I said. "I'm going in a little closer. Just keep me covered."

I edged into the side wall and noticed a small cave.

"There's a small cave down here!" I reported.

"Just throw in a grenade and get it over with, Taylor!" Walstad commented.

I didn't think the enemy would keep making noises and giving away their position.

"Come on, Taylor," yelled someone.

"Shit! I'm going in, guys!"

The bright sun had dilated my eyes to the point that I was practically blind as I entered into the small cave. I started to feel around and felt something soft, like a towel, blanket, or cloth of some sort. There was something in it.

"I think I found something," I said.

Someone said, "It's a booby trap. Put it back and throw in a grenade!"

I thought, *Why would anyone booby trap something they would never expect me to find?* I backed out of the cave and pulled the object into the light of day. It appeared to be a blanket filled with something moving.

"Shit," I said. "It's a baby!"

The baby was about nine months old. Immediately, it began to cry.

"Nice going, Taylor!" Ski blurted out. "You captured the smallest gook in the history of the Vietnam War."

"Shit," another Marine said. "Here comes, Sergeant Jones."

"What the hell is the holdup?" Jones yelled, his aggravation level through the roof. "The lieutenant, the captain, and the colonel are screaming. Let's get moving now."

"Hey Sarge," someone said. "Taylor's captured the smallest VC in history."

Jones just stared at me as everyone filled him in on the situation. Then everyone broke up in laughter as the story was highly embellished with Marine humor. That's when Lieutenant Francis came over.

"What the fuck is the big holdup here?" he screamed. "The whole battalion is being held up because of you assholes."

"Taylor has found a baby hidden in a cave, sir," someone said.

"What?" Francis exclaimed. With a look of puzzlement and disbelief, Francis squinted at the baby. His radio operator handed him a handset.

"Sir," the radio operator said. "It's Captain Reczek."

"Aw, crap," said Francis. He closed his eyes, shook his head, and grabbed the handset.

"I have a slight problem here, sir."

All we could hear was yelling coming from the handset right into Francis's ear. Francis was trying to get a word in edgewise and said, "Yes, sir. I know, sir. I understand, sir. Of course, sir. Just one thing, sir. One of the Marines found a baby in a cave in the ravine we just crossed. What should we do with the baby, sir? Okay, got it! I understand. Francis out!"

Francis handed the handset back to the radioman.

"Okay," he told everyone. "The captain says get moving, *now*!"

"What are we to do with the baby?" Jones asked the lieutenant.

"The captain said to bring it along."

"*What*? We can't do that!" I said. I looked up at Jones and pleaded with my eyes. "Let's just leave the baby where I found it. The parents have to be around here somewhere. They'll come back and find the baby gone!"

"The captain said bring the baby along," Jones replied.

"Sarge, we have to leave the baby here," I said again, but Jones turned away.

"Taylor," he said. "You're such a pain in my ass."

Just then the blanket opened up and we discovered he was a boy.

"Sarge, we are going to make this kid an orphan if we bring him along. Let's just leave him here. The captain won't miss the baby, and anyway, what if we get hit? The baby would be in the middle of a firefight."

The little guy was clinging to me like I was his father. It was as if he sensed that I was protecting him.

Jones said to one of the Marines standing on top of the hole, "Give Taylor a hand out of the ditch."

I climbed out of the ditch while holding the baby. The baby was hanging on to me for dear life. Sergeant Jones knew what I was talking about. I gave Jones one more plea.

"It doesn't make any sense to take the baby with us," I said. "I'm sure the captain didn't mean for us to take the baby. Can you get confirmation?"

Sergeant Jones looked at me, cocked his head as if to say, *Really?* He said, "Taylor, the captain gave an order. I don't think you want an insubordination charge when we get back!" He looked at me matter-of-factly and continued. "You're in charge of the baby until we can get it choppered out of here. Make sure nothing happens to him."

Jones left and ran to the center of the line. I knew it wasn't right to take the baby. I thought about disobeying the captain's order, but the other Marines were back on line sweeping, and beginning to separate away from me. I started walking fast to catch up, the baby still in my arms.

He was a healthy little tyke and looked well taken care of. I looked around in the distance to see if anyone might be looking for him. I couldn't help but think that the child's mother was watching in horror as we walked away with her baby. Even if they didn't see me take the baby, they would soon realize he was gone. The only future I could see for the child was that it was going to end up in one of those horrible orphanages. It tore me up inside knowing I was doing something wrong.

I CARRIED THE BABY for hours, always protecting him from the rays of the sun. We stopped for lunch. The baby didn't seem to be hungry at all. I tried to feed him cookies from one of my C-ration dinners. He pushed them away. I tried to set the baby down, but he wouldn't have anything to do with that either. I was able to set my rifle, pack, and cartridge belt to the side. I sat him on my lap, and he finally took a rest from holding on to me. I decided to call him Charlie. I tried to think of how one might feed a baby in the middle of the wilderness. I knew he had to be hungry. Then I remembered a *Three Stooges* episode where the bald-headed stooge, Curly, fed a baby by using a rubber glove as a baby bottle.

But where would I get some milk? *Wait a second*, I thought. *We have instant powdered milk in our C-rations for coffee.* I asked for donations of milk packets from everyone and received quite a few. Everyone was willing to donate to Charlie. Then I went over to the corpsman, Doc Eastman.

"Hey Doc, do you have any rubber gloves?" I asked.

Sure enough, he did. I washed the powder out of the glove with a little water. Then I heated some water in my metal canteen holder and added the milk packets to the concoction. I tasted the mixture and it had a little sweetness to it. I asked Steiner to hold open the glove as I poured the heated ingredients inside. I twisted the glove at the wrist and then I bit a little hole into one of the fingers as Curly had. I cuddled the baby close to my body and fed it to him.

"Look at Taylor; he's breastfeeding," one of the Marines commented.

A roar of laughter came from the group. I just shook my head. The baby seemed to like my concoction at first, but shook his head and then rejected the finger of the glove altogether. I couldn't figure out why.

"Maybe the hole isn't big enough," Steiner said.

"You know, you may have something there," I said.

So, I bit a little larger hole, which was difficult at first because of the thickness of the glove. Once the milk came out faster, the baby drank it like crazy. He fell asleep in my arms. I knew he was exhausted. It wasn't too long before I heard the call to saddle up. I tried to move, but the baby clung to my every motion. I finally got all my gear on. We moved out, and the baby took a long nap in my arms as we proceeded on the sweep.

We finally reached our first destination point for the evening. The lines were set and fields of fire were established for the evening watches. Two ambush patrols were sent out. Of course, there were listening posts just outside the lines to alert us in case of an attack. After checking our fields of fire, we had to dig our fighting holes.

The baby was clinging to me. I tried to hand him to Steiner. Little Charlie would have nothing to do with that. Steiner shrugged his shoulders and dug the entire hole because he understood the situation we were in. Steiner was falling in love with the little guy, as were some of the others.

The sun was setting over the mountains. Before I made my own dinner, I started my little ritual of feeding Charlie. Steiner had Charlie laughing with some playful antics. One by one, the guys came over to our foxhole to check in on the little guy. The baby was beginning to get more comfortable with the entire platoon.

Little Charlie was becoming our little mascot. Everyone started worrying about him, because he gave us a sense of home and normality. I held the exhausted little baby in my arms and rocked him to sleep as he drank the instant milk. About dusk, the baby woke and I gave him some more homemade food. I noticed that he needed a diaper. I went into my pack and got one of my T-shirts, tore off the bottom, and made a diaper. The top part of my shirt was used to cover him during the night. I held him all night long. A couple of times I tried to put him down, but he would wake and begin to cry and I didn't want him to give away our position.

The next morning, we got up and continued the sweep.

I managed to get enough creamers to keep him fed. I dipped cookies into milk to make them soft and easier for him to eat. Another Marine came over with a puppet he had made from an extra pair of white socks he had. The Marine drew eyes, a nose, and a mouth on the sock with a pen. Then he put on a little puppet show for the baby. Charlie actually started laughing. This raised our spirits a lot.

"I see you still have that baby," the sarge said as he entered our area. "Looks like you're doing a good job."

"What are we going to do with him?" I asked.

"I'll talk to the lieutenant," he said.

It wasn't long before the lieutenant appeared and acted surprised to see I still had the baby.

"Oh, yeah, the baby," he said. "We are getting resupplied tomorrow, and I made arrangements for the baby to be lifted out of here."

"Where do you think the baby will end up?" I inquired.

"That's not our problem, Marine."

I couldn't help but think of the coldness with which Francis said that. I held on to the baby all night long.

Morning came, and I was exhausted. I made myself coffee and broke out cold scrambled eggs from my C-rations can. I made the baby his milk and fed him a little warmed egg which, to my surprise, he ate willingly. We started our sweep again. Charlie and I had moved several hours before we stopped for lunch. I could hear, in the distance, a chopper approaching. It was getting closer. I wondered if this was it. Were they coming for the baby? I looked at the baby, and my eyes started to fill with tears. I could see the baby turn to me with concern, knowing something was wrong by the expression on my face.

One of the Marines from the command post ran over and said, "Bring the baby to the LZ. He's being lifted out right now."

Shit, I knew it. My stomach felt ill. I stared at the baby. All I could think was that this baby was going to an orphanage. I felt as though someone had ripped my heart right out of my chest. What was I going to do? I tore into my pack, looking for my writing gear. It was at the very bottom of the pack, so I flipped it upside down and emptied the entire contents on the ground. I could hear the chopper coming closer. Frantically, I started to write my name and address, but the pen didn't work so I shook it wildly. The guys were yelling for me to bring the baby to the landing zone.

"I need a pen!" I yelled. "Someone help me!"

Some of the guys looked for a pen while others just sat back, watching the show.

"Taylor, I got one," Steiner said, and he threw it to me.

I got a small piece of paper and wrote. "To whom it may concern, I found this baby in a cave. I want to adopt it. Please contact the Taylors at ..."

I wrote my name, address, unit, and service number. I then ran to Doc Higgenbottom for a safety pin, which I used to fix the note on the baby's homemade gown. The chopper had almost arrived. The CP didn't like choppers waiting on the ground.

"Hey, Taylor!" someone yelled from the CP. "Get the baby moving, now!"

I ran toward the chopper. It was a UH-34, with slanted eyes painted on the front as if it were a large predator looking around as it landed. The baby was terrified as the chopper came in. Dust, sand, dirt, and small rocks flew everywhere. I turned around and tucked his little body close to mine and shielded him from all the flying debris. The rotor was loudest as the chopper landed.

Four Marines disembarked very quickly. The door gunner threw some boxes on the ground and motioned for me to come forward with the baby. Little Charlie was now crying with terror and holding onto me for dear life. I didn't want him to go, either. The door gunner was yelling incoherently and waving his hand to me. I ran over to him and the gunner grabbed the baby. He couldn't seem to pry the child away because the baby was still holding on for dear life. Or was it me holding onto him? The gunner gave one big pull, and the baby was ripped from my arms. Little Charlie was crying, screaming, and kicking with his hands held out as if to say, "Come and get me and don't let them take me away."

I grabbed the gunner by his shirt neck and pulled him close to me. With all the passion I could muster up I said, "Take care of him. I love him!"

"I will," said the gunner, as he looked directly into my eyes.

"Whoever gets this baby, make sure they get this note," I demanded.

"OK! Now move off!" he instructed.

The engine of the chopper started to roar. I was still by the door and the door gunner. I had to back away from the chopper. The dirt and debris were flying, and it felt like the blades of the chopper were dangerously close. I ran away to escape the hell and ferocity of the spinning blades. As I turned to look at the chopper, dust and dirt were flung into my eyes, blinding me for a couple of seconds. It was hard to locate the baby by the door of the chopper. I tried to see him one last time. The tail of the chopper lifted and it started to rise and move forward, up and away. I watched the chopper become smaller. At the door, the gunner was holding onto the chopper with one hand and the baby in the other as they disappeared from my view. Tears were running down my cheeks, and I waved until the craft was out of sight. I turned and slowly walked away, heartbroken. I wondered if I would ever see the baby again.

I yelled out, "God, I hate this war!"

CHAPTER

SIX

ON JUNE 25, WE were called to assist Fourth Marines in the Thua Thien Province on Operation Maryland. The battalion commander ordered choppers to take us in to assist local efforts in finding and destroying enemy units around the area. When we arrived in the choppers, our landing was unopposed. All three platoons, including Weapons, started a sweep right away through an area that had green, rolling hills and hooches peppered throughout. Between the hills, each hooch had a little garden and a small rice paddy. Our platoon swept the area and set in for a few hours.

Lieutenant Francis sent out three different patrols using three fire teams from Second Squad. All four-man fire teams had been whittled down to just three men each. Muller took Steiner and me down a winding road, with me as point man, looking for any signs of the Viet Cong. As we rounded one of the hilly turns on the road, I noticed a yard coming into view on my left. As I got farther into the turn, a hut came into view. I had my M16 firmly at my right side and at the ready with my finger on the trigger. I had walked fully into the turn when I noticed two men and two women standing very close to the hut and talking to each other. They all had AK-47s leaning next to them on the side of the hut, just out of their reach. Instantly, I raised my M16 at them and they froze. I had them dead to rights. If they moved, they would have surely died.

Muller and Steiner ran up to where I was standing and pointed their M16s in the direction of the VC. We all had them in our sights. We pointed to the ground and instructed them to lie down. The two men got down immediately. The two women needed a little coaxing but finally went down. They all laid there for a few minutes while we secured the area and searched the hut. Nothing was found other than the four VC, their AK-47s, and several magazines each. They wore the telltale black, loose-fitting pajamas.

One of the ladies was very young and very beautiful. I had seen a lot of captured women, but I had never seen one as beautiful as her. I knew we were fighting both sexes, but it seemed strange to actually have caught such a pretty woman. I was in awe at her beauty. Usually the female combatants were unattractive, dirty, and skinny.

We found some rope, tied their hands, and then walked them back to where the platoon was set in. I couldn't wait to show our trophies and was looking for a long awaited "atta boy."

Right away, Jones and Lieutenant Francis came over. They immediately took the prisoners to the CP.

Jones asked me, "Where did you find them?"

I told him the story, and that was that.

"Return to the lines and eat some C-rats. We'll be moving out soon," he said.

I found a nice place to sit down, broke out a can of Beef Spiced with Sauce from my pack, and started cooking it. I sat there watching everyone around the VC, talking. The VC were squatting next to each other, looking around at their surroundings and each other. The pretty woman gave the young Marine who was guarding them a shy look. I watched all the VC, but my eyes kept zeroing in on the pretty one. I was curious to see what was happening and what we were going to do with them.

The pretty woman smiled at the Marine guard. I didn't recognize him; he was probably new to the unit. She pointed to her crotch, indicating she had to urinate. She then motioned her head toward the bushes which were between me and the squatting VC.

With a mouth full of spicy beef, I cocked my head and peered at her through the bushes, still enamored by her beauty. I hadn't seen a pretty woman in months. Yet, I wondered what was going on. Vietnamese women in the countryside would relieve themselves just about anywhere. They would squat and roll up a pant leg, spread the bottom of their silk pants wide, and just go. I didn't realize it at the time, but this woman wanted her privacy, and it appeared that the new Marine was going to let her walk into the bushes.

She walked up to the Marine. He untied her and let her go into the bushes. In one swift motion, she squatted while pulling her black silk pants down over her knees. The Marine guard was watching her, and she looked at him like she wanted privacy. When he turned his head to grant her that, she bolted, bottomless, and sprinted out of the bushes and away from the guard.

Instinctively, I grabbed my M16 and took a quick bead on her. All I could see were her firm butt cheeks bobbing up and down as she sped off like a jackrabbit. I considered pulling the trigger, but all I could do was watch those cute little butt cheeks running away. The next thing I knew, she was gone. She had gotten away.

Of course, everyone was yelling at the poor young Marine who was totally naive about how things operate in the field.

I would later give myself the excuse that if I had fired, I might have hit someone in our lines. That definitely would have been worse, but the fact is, I had let an enemy combatant run away and had done nothing to stop her. The other three VC were watched closely by two experienced Marines and were sent to the rear for the next chopper out.

On June 30, we were choppered back to the USS *Okinawa*. All June consisted of was looking for a fight, but we had found only small skirmishes. We gained a lot of field experience, but the month had exhausted us. We finally got back to the sanity and the friendly confines of the ship for what we hoped would be at least a few days of rest.

WHEN WE BOARDED THE *Okinawa* on the thirtieth, we had been in the field for an entire month. As we got off the choppers, we handed over all our ammo and grenades. It was time to get some real sleep, grub, and clean clothes. As we entered the squad bay, almost right away, we had mail call for letters and packages. I got a package with a salami, pepperoni, and crackers. There were more cans of Del Monte fruit cocktail and a package of Planters nuts from my dad. Unfortunately, the salami and crackers were spoiled rotten. Taking a gander at the wrapping, I noticed from the postal markings that the package had been mailed over three weeks ago and probably exposed to all kinds of heat. It was no wonder my goodies had spoiled.

I needed some uninterrupted sleep and fell asleep the second my head hit the pillow. It had been a long and exhausting month.

The next day, I went to Mass and Communion on the flight deck. I was asked to be an altar boy for the service, and it gave me comfort knowing I was still in touch with my faith in God. I was surprised there weren't more Marines there with me.

The next day, Staff Sergeant Malloy very abruptly called the entire platoon to the hangar deck and said, "The ship is headed for the DMZ. Bravo Company from First Battalion, Ninth Marines was ambushed out on Operation Buffalo. Word has it, they've got barely enough men left to make a platoon."

This meant that as many as two hundred Marines were either killed or wounded. Perhaps only forty had survived. After only one night of rest, we were going to have to go to the DMZ to assist the surviving Marines and get our fallen brothers out.

Malloy continued, "We never leave our dead behind, and First Battalion, Ninth Marines need help evacuating their dead. The entire battalion is going in. Bravo Company will be in the first wave. Line up over there because we're passing out food, ammo, and grenades now. Get your gear together because we're going out tomorrow."

I wondered if our platoon was going to be hit when we landed. I remembered the last time we went to the DMZ on Operation Beau Charger how aggressive the NVA had been there. They just kept coming at us, whittling us down with mortars, artillery, and snipers. I knew what to expect, and I wasn't looking forward to doing it again. I had thoughts about Alpha Company being hit at LZ Goose. At least we would have Reczek and Malloy leading us into the battle.

A series of emotions had come over me. There was sadness we wouldn't have the break I'd been looking forward to. I was pissed off because there wasn't time for the ship's laundry to wash our filthy uniforms. I was terrified about going back into the dreaded DMZ, but also furious that the NVA had killed so many Marines. Unrested, filthy, and up in arms, I was looking forward to exacting some payback.

We all filed in line to get our ammo for the field. I took nine boxes of food to break down and put into my pack and then got into the ammo line. That was where the bad news hit me. They handed out the ammo everyone had brought aboard from our previous operation. Many of the rounds were covered with corrosion, and a green mold-like substance was eating away at the copper.

"I can't believe this shit," I said aloud. "What the hell are they trying to do, kill us before the gooks do? Are we expected to go in the DMZ with this shit?"

"Shut up, Taylor, and just take the rounds and clean them," Jones said. "Now, move on."

They handed out only a few hand grenades. I rolled my eyes. I felt so insecure and denied. I noticed boxes of supplies that had just arrived on the other side of the hangar deck that no one had opened.

I said to Jones, "What about that stuff over there?"

"That's not our concern right now; move on, you're slowing up the line," he said.

One of the waiting old salts said, "Come on, Taylor, move it along. We don't have all day."

I shook my head and grabbed a few handfuls of the most sickening garbage I had ever seen and a few grenades. The ammo I had returned when I boarded was perfect, but now I was forced to take someone else's neglected ammo. I walked to the squad bay below, hating the situation I found myself in.

I went immediately to the chow hall and started writing letters home. I explained to my dad that I wasn't sure I would be coming out of this one alive. We were going into the DMZ again tomorrow to get our fallen Marines. I had the worst feeling I ever had in my whole life. I wrote fifteen letters and then noticed I was the last one in the chow hall still writing. I took my shower, and it was so late that there wasn't anyone walking around. All the Marines had gone to sleep. I was getting ready to retire when I came up with what seemed to be a good idea.

I grabbed my bayonet and slowly walked into the gangway that led to the hangar deck. No one was awake because everyone was sleeping for the next day's mission. I moved up the ladder that leads to the hangar deck. The deck was dark, but strategically placed night lights gave just enough light to get around. I sneakily entered onto the darkened deck and crouched down. My senses were keyed as if I were in Vietnam and sneaking up on the Viet Cong. There wasn't a soul or a sound. *This is going to be easier than I thought*, I said to myself.

Slowly, I worked my way along the bulkhead in the darkened shadows, which would make me almost invisible to the naked eye. Working my way farther along the bulkhead wall, I still didn't hear anyone, so I tiptoed to where all the boxes sat that had come in earlier.

Bingo, a bonanza.

Treasures surrounded me. I couldn't believe my eyes. There were cases of grenades, M16 ammunition, C-4 explosives, and all kinds of food. I went straight to the cases of the M16 rounds. I busted open the top and grabbed fifteen cardboard boxes of twenty perfect rounds in each box and put them in my leg pockets. Then there were the cases of grenades. I took as many as I could put in my jungle shirt side pockets. Everything had to be put back together and given the appearance that it had never been touched.

I should have left right then and there, but I saw the C-4 explosives case. I wanted one large stick to take with me in the field. The engineers were the only ones with this awesome explosive. They molded the explosive and used it to blow bunkers or explode booby traps and unexploded ordnance. I was going to use it for heating my food. If you tear off just a small piece, you can light it. Once lit, it gives off a blowtorch flame. I could heat my food in seconds, which would be much faster than with the usual heat tabs.

The box I needed was much harder to get into than the others and, of course, on the bottom of the pile. Moving as quietly and rapidly as possible, I took the boxes that were on top and moved them to the side. When I finally got the box I wanted, I used my knife and pried the plastic band and wooden top from the box. It was difficult trying to remove the layers of wrapper that covered the explosives. If the wrapping looked like it had been tampered with, it could bring someone's attention to the stolen items. This was taking more time than I thought, but I really wanted the C-4.

I finally got the wrapper off and opened the lid to the box. It was unbelievable. There were many large sticks inside. They were long and square-shaped, like quarter sticks of butter, but ten times larger, and they felt like stiff silly putty. I grabbed one stick of the C-4, replaced the lid, and slid the box back into its original position. That's when I heard the sound of footsteps coming my way.

Holy crap, if I get caught I could go to the brig (jail) for sure, I thought. *Why didn't I just leave when I had the chance?*

My heart started pounding. I hid behind one of the stacks of boxes and didn't move at all. The sound of the footsteps got louder. I then noticed the C-4 box was slightly out of place and the wrapper had flipped up. I closed my eyes hard and said, *Damn!"* to myself. I had only seconds to move one of the boxes that I had moved aside. That would at least cover the wrapper. With all the stealth I could muster, I grabbed the box and lightly placed it over the C-4 box. I slipped back into my hiding place just as a Marine guard walked directly to where I had just set the box.

He stopped, looked around, and listened for any kind of sound. I was surprised he couldn't hear my heart; it was pounding out of my chest. I took short, silent breaths. He stood there a while, and I didn't move one single bit. He started to walk away. I peeked around one of the boxes and saw him put his .45-caliber pistol in his holster. I hadn't realized he had drawn his weapon. Heading to the back of the ship, he reached into his pocket and pulled out a pack of smokes. He pounded the top of the pack on his hand as he walked to the fantail (the open back of the ship). I checked the rest of the hangar deck, and there didn't seem to be anyone else around, so I slowly retreated into the shadows and retraced my footsteps back the way I came. The need for a cigarette may have saved me from a horrible fate. I would have lost a stripe for sure. It was not that I cared so much about a patch on my shoulder, but it would've meant a reduction in pay.

THE NEXT MORNING, WE all readied ourselves to take off, and then the sound system blasted.

Now hear this:,
BATTLE STATIONS! BATTLE STATIONS!

Bravo Company was the first unit to land in the DMZ, so we expected them to spread out and set up the LZ for us. It was almost our turn to leave when Malloy walked up to us on the hangar deck.

"Bravo Company was hit when they landed, so our LZ will now be a mile farther south," he said. "We'll be the first platoon to land and set up the new LZ there. Once we move out, Alpha Company will land and follow us. Our mission will be to sweep toward Bravo Company and help them out. Alpha Company will meet up with us. Then, as a battalion, we'll move west toward Con Thien. The word is that Third Battalion, Ninth Marines is also getting hit, and the gooks are in the process of surrounding Con Thien. We have to sweep the area and secure First Battalion, Ninth Marines' easterly flank. The NVA have the 304-B NVA Division and Ninetieth NVA Regiment in the vicinity, and they are massing them in order to overrun Con Thien. The NVA may be using nerve gas, so we're passing out gas masks to take with you into the field. Along with that, you'll be issued a shot of atropine to take if they deploy the gas. The instructions are: You have to slam the needle into your thigh and squeeze the atropine into your body. The antidote will then be released into your system. There are lots of other Marine units moving into the area. We're bringing in more support from everywhere we can. Get ready, because we are moving out in a few."

"Everyone saddle up," Jones said.

I was ready with extra M16 ammo in my utility pockets. My shirt pockets were stuffed with grenades. I hadn't seen Lieutenant Francis, nor did I look for him. Someone said he was with the CP and Captain Reczek. They would be in direct radio contact with our platoon and Staff Sergeant Malloy.

The choppers were waiting on the flight deck and warming up as usual. We entered the walkway to the deck and then ran to the awaiting choppers. I was the second Marine to exit through the heavy metal door on deck. I ran out following Pilgreen. We climbed in, and I moved against the wall on the far side of the opening.

The choppers took off almost in unison this time. The pilots were getting good at the maneuver. We climbed as usual, and no one spoke. I reminisced for a second about what it would be like to be home in that moment instead of looking at the gunner, sitting by the chopper door. He was young-looking, but he had that "thousand-yard stare." It appeared as though he had seen more than his share for his age. There was no laughter, no smiling this time out. Everyone realized this was for keeps.

We crossed from the sea to land. The white sand was visible below as we headed inland. Once inland, we veered in a southwesterly direction. The area had a lot of trees for cover and protection. I saw a big opening between the trees where the choppers were headed.

When our choppers landed, we immediately jumped off and set up the perimeter. Thank God we had another easy landing; recon had been right about the safety of our new LZ. Hundreds of Marines were landing right behind us, brought in by the huge CH-46 Sea Knight choppers. Their huge twin blades spun hard as they landed and a dozen Marines exited through the rear.

With all the Marines landed, we headed in a northwesterly direction, going on an angle toward the area where B Company had been hit. It was extremely hot and everyone was sweating, but no one removed his flak jacket, knowing that mortars could soon be raining down upon us. Malloy kept everyone moving toward Bravo Company.

"Now don't be stupid and drink all your water," he said. "We have to conserve as much as we can. There is a long march ahead of us."

Apparently, the thoughts of Beaver Cage and all the heat casualties gave us caution, because we stopped more often to rest. Every time we stopped, we always stayed in the tree lines for cover.

After a minibreak, our platoon would proceed again toward our destination. As we walked, a tall cement structure came into view. It appeared to be a Catholic Church. The building was three stories high, with a four-story steeple. There was a statue of Christ with outstretched arms in the very front of the church. It seemed so surreal that I broke out my Brownie camera and took an incredible photo of the church in that valley of death. We continued a little farther, and that is when I started seeing dead NVA bodies everywhere. They had been there a while, because we could see the discoloration in their faces. Flies swarmed around their swollen bodies. The smell was putrid. I squinted at the smell and reeled away.

I noticed an NVA canteen lying beside one of the dead corpses and grabbed it as a souvenir. Then I stepped back and took a long look at the dead soldier. Hell, he was six feet tall. I always thought the gooks were short. I suspected this guy might have been Chinese. Were we fighting the Chinese too?

As we moved north, we saw unexploded ordnance everywhere. All kinds of craters riddled the landscape around us. A lot of action had happened here before we arrived. We made another stop because it was incredibly hot.

I looked at Pilgreen and said, "What the hell happened to you?" His pant leg was ripped from above his knee all the way down to his foot.

"This shit is worse than the hills of Alabama, that's fer sure," he said.

PFC Bob Collins was next to him. He was so hot that he took off his flak jacket and utility shirt and went bare-chested. As he sat there sweating in the sweltering heat, he drew in the flavor of a Camel cigarette.

"I don't like this shit at all," Pilgreen said.

"Saddle up!" Malloy yelled.

Collins took his last puff and flicked it like a bullet.

We put ourselves together and headed on our way. As we moved closer to the DMZ, we saw jets pounding the NVA in the distance. Clouds of smoke followed each run. This meant we were getting closer to the fight. We were moving in the direction of where the jets were bombing. I could hear the explosions in the distance. The closer we got to the action, the more destruction we saw around us. The tops of all the trees around us and every piece of greenery had been blown to bits. It looked like an F5 tornado had passed through the area. Small trees were devoid of leaves, stripped of all bark, and now only three feet high. The ground was littered with craters from 500-pound bombs.

I took off my pack and dug a foxhole for protection like everyone else. Once my hole was dug, I stood up and looked directly south toward the CP where our mortarmen had set up. I saw a guy running with his pants around his ankles. He was running like hell and jumped into a foxhole headfirst. No sooner did I see him than mortar rounds started zipping in at us like crazy. I dove for my hole.

The only way a mortar could get me was to drop directly in on top of me. I lay as low as I could in a three-foot-by-two-foot fighting hole that was waist deep. The mortar rounds exploded around me. One was so close that it felt like it could have killed me if I had been outside the hole. About eighty rounds hit us before the barrage stopped.

Someone yelled, "Corpsman up!"

I knew someone had got hit and needed help. I looked around and saw the crater from the mortar round that landed close to my hole. Liquid oozed out of my pack. I picked up the pack as the substance dripped to the ground. Shrapnel had torn through my pack, which had been lying on the ground next to my hole. It was the fruit cocktail my dad sent me. Both cans were leaking and dripping from the shrapnel. "Those motherfuckers got my fruit cocktail!"

"You're lucky as hell they didn't get your nuts and sausage!" Pilgreen said, laughing his ass off.

Everyone busted out laughing. But it didn't last long because Sergeant Jones came over and told us we might have to attack the tree line in front of our position. It was 7:30 p.m., and the tree line was several football fields away.

"Are you fucking kidding me?" I said. We would have to attack across open ground all the way.

Hell, are we fighting like in the days of the Civil War? This is how people get killed!

I wondered if it was Lieutenant Francis making the call.

Mortars started in on us again, and we all dove for cover. They exploded on the ground above me as I lay in a ball with my knees up to my chest, my head down, and my hands over my head. All in all, two hundred fifty explosions blasted around us. Artillery, plus heavy and light mortars and rockets, rained down on the entire battalion. No one mentioned anything about the tree line anymore. I hoped they had scrapped that idea for good.

As the evening progressed, I knew it was going to be a bad night with only five hours of broken sleep. Thank God I had Pilgreen as my foxhole partner. Pilgreen was a survivor. He managed to avoid being wounded but also stayed engaged. I took his advice to always keep a low profile and continue to survive.

"Play it smart," he would say. "Keep thinking. Always be looking for a place to go in case we get hit, and keep your damn head down. When you hear firing, get down as close to the ground as fast as you can, and don't play the hero unless you can't help it."

Jones came over to our hole and said, "Malloy thinks the NVA might attack us this evening, so be prepared."

I didn't sleep much because of all the rounds continuing to explode around us. The sound of flares going up like fireworks would light up the night. Someone would hear something and fire at the direction of the sound. Everyone stayed awake. When daylight came, there had been no attack. In the early morning, I ate my canned eggs and sipped on some hot coffee, courtesy of my plastic explosive I stole from the ship. I shared the C-4 with Pilgreen, and he made additional hot coffee for the both of us, which was a real premium, given the circumstances.

Word came down to saddle up. The entire battalion was going to sweep the Trace, in no man's land. The Trace was a six-hundred-meter-wide bulldozed strip of land up against the DMZ.

Charlie Company was in the middle of the battalion marching west toward Con Thien. Alpha Company was to our left flank, and Bravo was on our right—1,500 men marching to only God knows where. I thought of the poem, "The Charge of the Light Brigade."

Theirs not to make reply,
Theirs not to reason why,
Theirs but to do and die,
Into the valley of Death
Rode the six hundred.

Bravo Company was getting hit with small arms and mortars. Alpha and Charlie companies continued to move slowly forward. Delta Company was at our far-left flank. Mortars again rained on us, and everyone went for cover. The entire battalion was getting hit from all directions. Alpha moved forward but was soon under artillery fire. We settled in and dug fox holes for another night of terror. The word came down that a small tree line to the north of us had to be taken. This was where an NVA Regiment with more than a thousand men had taken positions and was directing attacks along the entire line in front of us. Our artillery blasted the area. Jets hit the tree line incessantly. Command figured this should whittle the NVA down to just a few men.

The next day was July 6. We had to attack the tree line and eliminate the North Vietnamese threat. Our artillery continued its barrage on the tree line. Then the jets came in, dropping 500-pound bombs again, while more jets followed with napalm. This certainly had to weaken their forces. It had been effective the last time when we were in the same area on operation Beau Charger.

The jets moved away, and the artillery stopped. Then the order was given to stand up and move forward, firing our M16s at the tree line in the distance. We had to follow orders. I was just one man in the outfit, but I was terrified that we were going to move forward. How many movies had depicted this very scene with the good guys massacred as they charged across open ground under the order of a bugle?

Following his own orders, Staff Sergeant Malloy stood up and yelled, "Let's go, men!"

At least we had three heavy-duty tanks leading the charge. The tanks fired and blasted away at the tree line. In unison, our platoon opened up, full automatic. Slowly and aggressively, everyone moved forward. As soon as we entered the open field and the cover melted away, all hell broke loose on us.

Malloy and Sergeant Pike were given orders by Lieutenant Francis to attack a bunker that was in front of their position. Both men were hit almost immediately with large-caliber machine-gun bullets. Sergeant Eddie Martin, one of the squad leaders, watched in horror as they both dropped as quickly as they had charged forward—the .50-caliber tracer rounds still spraying the ground around them. The rounds were so massive and powerful that they seemed to explode like miniature grenades when they struck the dirt. Malloy's shoulder had a huge hole in it, and he was bleeding profusely. Next to him, Pike was lying facedown with a large hole in his back. Sergeant Eddie Martin found cover, but it took time, he told us later, for the reality of what he'd just witnessed to sink in—for him to accept that Malloy and Pike were gone forever. If anybody could survive a bad order, it should've been those two seasoned veterans.

Twenty RPG rockets came at us from the tree line. Most of the rockets were aimed at the tanks, simultaneously disabling all three of them. An ample supply of .50-caliber machine-gun emplacements sprayed the ground around us.

Marines were dropping everywhere. Bullets buzzed and whisked all around me as I ran back from where we had just come. It seemed like it took forever to find cover, yet it was only seconds. I couldn't believe I wasn't hit like so many others around me. Pilgreen and I returned fire at the tree line. There were only about six men left in our squad.

All the firepower we had used on the North Vietnamese before the attack hadn't done jack shit. The NVA had managed to live through it all. I couldn't figure it out. It was like a magic act. What the hell happened? Why did so many of our guys get wounded and killed? Our morale was broken, and my confidence had taken a hit at the loss of Malloy and Pike. Thank God we still had Sergeant Jones, who immediately took charge as temporary platoon sergeant.

Jones yelled, "We have to pull back south of our position because a squadron of B-52 bombers will be coming in to blow the shit out of the damn tree line and the Trace."

In the meantime, more jets were called in, and Jones came over to our position. "You know," he said, "Captain Reczek said that since Operation Beau Charger, the NVA's been building reinforced underground bunkers north of Con Thien and, I bet, right here too. We could bomb them until we ran out of bombs and still wouldn't kill them. I bet that's why we got hit so bad. They just hunkered down until the jets were gone. We probably didn't kill a single one of them. Bunkers or not, those B-52s are going to blow the shit out of them."

Unlike the jets that had been screaming over us earlier, B-52s were high-flying bombers. We might see only their vapor trails far up in the clouds. But each is capable of carrying thirty-two 1,000-pound bunker-buster bombs which, on impact, would literally shake the earth a mile away.

"Where's Malloy?" I asked Jones.

"We'll have to come back and get him," he said. "Sergeant Pike too. Okay, everyone on your feet. We're pulling back."

We pulled back quite a bit as our artillery zeroed in on the tree line. We found a spot and settled in again. Hours passed. We could hear a faint sound of planes from high above but couldn't see them. I looked up, and there was nothing visible. I saw a glimmer of the faint, white vapor trails. We heard a distant whistling sound that kept getting louder. Everyone got down as the sound increased and became so unbearable that it felt like the bombs were coming right at our positions. The whistling got even louder; then huge explosions shook the ground like an earthquake. The bombs exploded as if they were firecrackers, but with the force of an avalanche, one after another. Billowing gray and black smoke-filled clouds rose in the air. It drifted in a northeasterly direction, ultimately toward the DMZ. There wasn't a sound coming from the north. If there were NVA in those bunkers, I guess we could call them massive grave sites now.

We settled in for the evening. Aside from the hiss and the eerie glow of an occasional flare drifting to the ground under a small parachute, the night was dark and uncomfortably quiet. There was no small arms fire, no sniper rounds, no mortars, artillery, or even the subtle chatter of wildlife. If I slept at all, the sleep would have been uneasy in the ghostly silence. Each time I came near to sleep, I would think about the NVA sneaking up on us, or charging in a sudden, violent break to the stillness. Adrenaline would surge through my veins, my heart would race, and again, I would be wide awake.

THE NEXT DAY, WE could see support tanks arriving from Dong Ha. They were assisting the Third Battalion, Ninth Marines. Their mission was to get the dead Marines from all the battles that had taken place. Our Bravo Company, First Battalion, Third Marines were now out there to recover our own battalion's dead.

The gooks knew we always came back for our dead, and there was a good chance that the bodies of our boys could be booby trapped like they had done to the First Battalion, Ninth Marines a few days before. They were also known to hit us when we were in the open, trying to retrieve our dead, but there was no more contact that I could see. It appeared the B-52 strike had broken the backs of the NVA and they pulled back across the DMZ.

In the distance, we could see Marines in the open putting as many Marine bodies on the tanks as they could. Bravo Company got Malloy and Pike, plus a few others, and brought them back to the rear. There were hundreds of North Vietnamese bodies everywhere. They would come for their dead later in the night. There was a stink in the air. Whenever we got a north wind, the putrid smell of rotting flesh filled our noses.

The next day, we regrouped and started moving toward an extraction point so we could get back to the ship. We headed away from Con Thien and were sweeping in an easterly direction toward the ocean. I saw Bumgarner carrying a mortar tube.

"Hey, Bum," I said. "I saw one of your mortarmen running for cover with his pants around his ankles. He ran past your mortar position at the CP."

"Yeah, that was Henderson," Bum laughed. "He was so scared he wanted to take a crap in the foxhole that he and Rodriguez had just dug. Rodriguez told him to get the hell out of the foxhole and do his business elsewhere. So Henderson got out of the hole, walked a safe distance from their foxhole, pulled his pants down, and was in the middle of a dump. That's when he heard the mortar rounds coming in. He didn't have time to finish. He just ran with his pants around his ankles and dove in the foxhole headfirst. I don't know what was worse—the yelling from the foxhole, or the mortars that were landing all around us."

Everyone thought that was hysterically funny.

Operation Buffalo was over; 159 Marines had been killed and 845 wounded. We had lost quite a few from our platoon, including

Malloy and Pike. Our side claimed that we had killed 1,290 soldiers of the People's Army of Vietnam. There were another 530 probable deaths and no one knows how many we wounded. I'm not sure the NVA did either.

Before we returned to the ship, the battalion commander wanted us to clear an area south of the DMZ around Dong Ha. It was obvious that we were tired, but we had to go on one more operation called Kingfisher. Once Kingfisher was completed, we would go back to the ship and lick our wounds, resupply, and get down for a well-deserved rest. The entire battalion went on line and started sweeping around Dong Ha to make sure the enemy was gone.

We made two forced marches, checking for signs of the NVA. Our officers had to send in their assessment of the operation and articulate their after-action reports and recommendations. The reports would be a good measurement to see how successful we had been on Operation Buffalo. As far as I was concerned, my attitude toward the war was changing fast. I now understood what Pilgreen was trying to get me to understand in Okinawa. Everything was FUBAR (fucked up beyond all recognition).

For two days, 1,300 Marines were spread on a line the equivalent of fifteen football fields, clearing the area around the city. I wondered if we were going to run into another NVA trap. Of course, Charlie was hiding in small units everywhere, and skirmishes occurred throughout the battalion. Operation Kingfisher continued with other battalions, but the SLF had to get back to the ship. We continued our sweep to our landing zone, where the choppers came in to pick us up and take us to the big lady we all loved and appreciated, the *Okinawa*. It was July 18, but July wasn't done with us yet.

EVERYTHING WAS IN A rush on the ship. We were steaming to an area near the coast, between the DMZ and Da Nang, near the city of Hue. After a couple of days, we were on outbound choppers once again.

Our choppers landed in the hills just off the coast. The three platoons of Charlie Company were being split up, and our platoon split up even further into squads. My squad was sent up a mountain road on Highway One. We walked for hours up the steep, paved road. To our left, if we looked down, we could see the shoreline in the distance. There weren't any guardrails to keep vehicles from falling from the mountain. To our right was a steep cliff. The road wound around the hill to our right.

Wakefield led the patrol. He was one of the original old salts from Khe Sanh and had transferred in from recon. Sands and Don Smith were exhausted from the forced march, as were the rest of us. I never heard so much bitching in my life.

We rounded a bend on the road and came across a cool stream that flowed briskly off the steep hillside—the sweetest little waterfall you've ever seen. We all took a break and refilled our canteens. I threw in my halazone purification tablets and knew not to touch the water for an hour. Some of the older guys, who were short and at the end of their tour, were fed up with the war and didn't use their tablets or take the malaria pills the corpsmen had given out. They hoped they would get so sick they would be taken out of the war altogether, or at least visit sickbay for diarrhea and fever, getting them out of the field for almost a week. Many of the old salts had only a couple of months left in country. For some this would be August, and for others it would be September. No one looked forward to their dreaded thirteenth month. They feared what we all felt. Are we going to make it out alive?

Second Platoon had seen a lot of action, and it was showing in the men. We had not received the R&Rs that were promised for months. The excuse officers gave was they didn't have enough men to run the platoon. Even when we would get replacements, we never had enough to get us close to full strength.

Late in the afternoon, we reached the highest point on the road. We climbed the rest of the way to the crest of the hill.

Steiner said, "Hey guys, look!"

He was looking at the valley below. We all stood there admiring the beauty of it. Down in the valley, we could see a swath of dark green vegetation. The ocean had carved a small bay in the shoreline. The cliffs gathered all around a small village, and it seemed secluded from every other place in the world. It looked like an exotic Shangri-La, like in James Hilton's novel *Lost Horizon*. Then again, was it a quiet little fishing village? Maybe it's a perfect place for the VC to hide. It would not be our mission, but we would continue to watch it from our position.

To the south was the continuation of the road we had come up on. It wound downward and continued through a wide valley that stretched for miles.

Our job was to set in and sit and watch the area for any movement from our high vantage point. We dug our fighting holes and put ponchos over our heads as roofs. Sticks were used as poles to hold up the ponchos, keeping the morning dew off our bodies.

We had a Vietnamese scout with us to use as an interpreter. He was a little worn, compared to us. No utility jacket—just a green T-shirt and utility pants ripped at the knees. He loved to smoke American cigarettes and was in heaven to be with a squad of Marines. In addition to bumming cigarettes from everyone, he loved eating our C-rations, as if he were dining at the Waldorf. He became a part of the squad while he was with us.

Nighttime came, and I sat with Steiner in our hole. It had gotten really dark and our conversation waned. Steiner had first watch, and I was drifting off to sleep when a strange sound awakened me. Steiner grabbed his M16, jumped up, and looked directly in front of our fighting hole. I jumped too and listened.

"There it was again," Steiner whispered. "Was that the sound of a tiger directly in front of us? Fuck, I didn't know they had tigers in Vietnam! Are you telling me we have to fight tigers too?"

We heard the roar only a few times that evening, and then the sound dissipated into the night. I figured it had probably got our scent or heard us and was checking us out. The creature went farther inland as the night progressed. We woke up the next day, and I could hear everyone clamoring about the tiger.

Harvey, a tall, thin, black guy from Chicago with a good sense of humor and soft-spoken manner, overheard us talking and ran over to our hole.

"Damn, I thought I was imagining that shit," he said. "I heard it too, and it scared the shit out of me!"

Pilgreen said, "Hell, it made me feel like I was right back home in Alabama, although it did keep me alert for the rest of the night."

"I didn't know they have tigers in Alabama," I said.

"Nope, they shur don't have tigers, but they do have cougars," Pilgreen said.

Several days later, when we rejoined the platoon at the bottom of the hill, Walstad asked Pilgreen, "So how was it up on the mountain?"

"Y'all ain't gonna believe this shit," Pilgreen said. "We had a tiger come up to our lines the other night!"

"Are you shitting me?" queried Walstad.

"No shit, man—honest! Just ask Taylor."

"Is that true, Taylor?" Walstad asked.

"Naw, he's shitting you," I lied.

"Taylor, really," Pilgreen erupted. "Tell him about it!"

I looked over at Steiner, who was listening to our conversation.

"Hey, Steiner, did you hear anything about a tiger on the hill we were on?" I remarked.

"Nope, I don't know anything about a tiger," Steiner said. We both walked away.

"Really, one did!" Pilgreen insisted.

Walstad just shook his head and walked away.

There was no more action for Charlie Company, and we were grateful for that. The battalion had done a little damage to the VC on the operation. Bravo Company had found ten thousand pounds of rice. A couple of Marines had been wounded by booby traps, but the battalion had killed three VC and captured twenty-two more. July and Operation Buffalo had proven to be disastrous to my platoon. Half the men were either killed or wounded, and we had lost the best platoon sergeant and squad leader in the company. Broken, we headed back to the ship by chopper on July 29.

CHAPTER

SEVEN

I HAD SURVIVED ANOTHER month and now had only seven more to go. I hoped August was going to be easy like June had been. I knew, however, that no matter where we were sent, it was going to be hot; after all, August is the hottest month of the year. I think even the commanders needed a break from the constant action.

On August 6, Jones called us to the hangar deck to inform us of our next operation. Jones was now leading the way as Malloy once did. He was no longer our squad leader and had been promoted to platoon sergeant.

He said, "Okay, guys, tomorrow we're attacking from Mike Boats, and we'll do a beach landing. Elements of the V-25, VC Local Force Battalion, and other smaller VC units have infiltrated the Hoi An area south of Da Nang. They are threatening stability in that area, so we're going to do something about that. Early tomorrow morning, Charlie Company will transfer to the USS *Duluth* and then board the Mike Boats from there. We expect to surprise the VC when we move inland from the shore. Reczek thinks it's going to be a soft landing, but we can't know for sure. Other battalions will be landing inland and sweeping toward us. We will land at Blue Beach. Our operation's name is Beacon Gate."

Jones was made for command. Malloy was the best, but unfortunately, Malloy was becoming a distant memory. I had a great deal of respect for Jones because, before he took Malloy's position, he was my squad leader and I witnessed his leadership skill in that role. To me, he was like a younger version of Malloy. He was about six years older than me, so maybe about twenty-five. Jones was excellent at reading maps and setting up ambushes with precise fields of fire. Whenever Jones would lead our patrols, if we had nine Marines it felt like twenty. The man always had his shit together.

While he often consulted with the old salts for their experience, it never felt like Jones ever settled into any particular clique. That's one of the things I always liked about him. He conferred with everyone and carefully considered what others had to say. He was approachable, in other words. We could reason with him, and he never took advantage of his rank in a way that would belittle anyone.

He was all business too—a professional Marine who took his job seriously. I never caught him shooting the shit about girlfriends back home or whatnot. When he huddled with the fire team leaders in our squad, the discussion was always about strategy and tactics. He didn't kid around much, but he could muster a bit of humor from time to time.

With Jones now leading the platoon and Corporal Muller, my former fire team leader, in Jones's old position, I felt like the platoon was as good as it could possibly be. If Jones was a young version of Malloy, Muller was a young version of Jones, not another grab-ass shit-bird like some of the others. Though I didn't know it at the time, the platoon was indeed as good as it was ever going to be.

The next day, we transferred to the USS *Duluth* just as Jones had said we would. The ship's speaker blared out.

Now hear this:
BATTLE STATIONS! BATTLE STATIONS!

The platoon climbed down the net ladders to the awaiting Mike Boats. One by one, the boats moved away from the ship and formed a circle pattern until all were ready. We must have circled for half an hour, and several of the Marines became seasick. The circling caused a violent up-and-down movement from multiple waves caused by the other boats. All it took was one guy running to the side of the boat and losing his breakfast to send many others following immediately behind. I was one of the lucky ones who were able to control the queasiness, but if we had circled any longer I would have been one of them. When the entire company was finally assembled in all the boats, we headed toward the shore in file, and the ride became smoother. The sick Marines had to tough it up and settle in for the ride.

Then I realized that it must have felt the same for those Marines who hit the shores of Iwo Jima in the Pacific during World War II. Visions of John Wayne as Sergeant Stryker in the movie *Sands of Iwo Jima* flashed through my head.

As we came closer to the shore, one of the crew members told us to get ready to disembark.

Jones yelled, "Lock and load!"

The engines of the boat moved full speed until the front end caught the sand and began to slow the forward movement. The front ramp lowered halfway. The boat motors revved one last time, and the front ramp slammed to the ground. We all ran ashore, spread out in a line and hit the sand.

I looked ahead and all I could see was a beautiful, sandy beach with a tree line in front of us. No one fired his weapon. There was no one around. We moved forward to the edge of the tree line. The entire company arrived and also moved into the trees. We didn't see anything out of the ordinary.

For four days, we walked in a wedge or straight across in a line. The operation concluded with just minor contact, and on August 9, we headed back aboard ship. It had been a trial run for things to come. No sooner were we back aboard ship than we had to go on another operation.

Sergeant Jones called the platoon together on the hangar deck of the *Okinawa* late on the afternoon of August 11.

"Men, we have to go out again," he said. "This operation is called Cochise. It's back in the Que Son Valley."

I heard Ski sigh, "Not there again."

The Que Son Valley was where we had our first operation, Beaver Cage. We lost fifty-five Marines on that one. One hundred fifty-one were wounded. I glanced over at Ski, but he was gazing down at the deck with his arms crossed and his top lip between his teeth.

"Intelligence reports that the Third NVA Regiment and the First VC Regiment have reentered the valley," Jones continued. "They have every weapon Charlie Company has and maybe a few more. We can't let them take over that valley. Tomorrow at 0800 hours, we are assaulting back into the area. We'll hit the ground running."

All the Marines retreated to the squad bay in the depths of the ship. The old salts began bitching the moment we arrived.

"I'm too short for this shit," Ski said. "I only have a couple of weeks left before I rotate home."

"I only have three weeks," Pilgreen said. "Then I'm back home in Alabama."

There was a whole group of old salts who were close to rotating, like Cooper, Harvey, Sands, Muller, and Shoeships, our only Native American. I could feel their despair, but the truth being told, I would rather have been in their shoes, leaving in a couple of weeks, than staying for another seven months.

The next day, we heard the sound blaring from the ship's PA.

Now hear this:
BATTLE STATIONS! BATTLE STATIONS!

At 7:00 a.m., a hot August morning, we all waited in line to go out to the flight deck. When we were all loaded, the choppers lifted off the ship, with Second Platoon in the lead to LZ Grouse.

As we began to land, we received sporadic sniper fire from tree lines near the LZ. We could hear the rounds hitting the metal skin of the chopper. Everyone squinted at the sounds because there was always the possibility that one unforgivable round had your name on it. The VC hid and used the surrounding cover to shoot at us.

Once on the ground, as so many times before, we found it difficult to locate the snipers. The Viet Cong could easily blend with the population who sympathized with them. We knew from the beginning that the missing men and women from the villages were the ones firing at us upon landing. If we found any villagers between the ages of sixteen to fifty-five, they would be interrogated.

On this landing, we ran across a thirty-year-old man who looked suspicious. He had on a red shirt, not black PJs. He was wearing a watch, which was a complete giveaway. Farmers were usually too poor to own a timepiece. Our interrogator was a South Vietnamese soldier, who was assisted by an American intelligence officer. The interrogation wasn't a pretty sight to watch. The best thing I could do was to walk away. I tried to wrap myself around the idea of questioning these people in a more humanitarian way, but it appeared the only way we could get information was to slap the shit out of them, along with screaming and yelling threats. The man was choppered out to the rear, and I wondered about his fate.

I looked around at the people in the area. They were farmers out of the Stone Age, barely eking out a living. We were modern day invaders intruding on their land. I don't think many of them had any formal education at all. They probably didn't even know the meaning of the words "communism" or "capitalism." They just wanted us gone. We certainly weren't making friends and laying groundwork for peaceful unity.

As I tried to understand the reason for being in Vietnam, an awareness came to me. Who were we actually fighting? My answer was simple. We were fighting the North Vietnamese and the Viet Cong. But who were the VC? They were the South Vietnamese people. They lived and struggled in the farm areas, and there were thousands of them. They were the innocent-looking people we saw during the day as we walked. In the next minute, they were the snipers who shot at us. The only thing I could count on for sure were the Marines around me.

I remembered a conversation among some of the old salts back in the squad bay aboard the ship. They'd been talking about getting short and staying alive long enough to make it back home.

I realized things could get really scary when you had to depend on people who were short and now more concerned about their own survival than that of the team. The VC was here for the duration. But I also knew that Jones had power over everyone, and that he was going to lead us with confidence and control.

It became crystal clear what Pilgreen was alluding to in our previous conversations. Steiner, on the other hand, had already figured out the craziness we were in. He knew as I did, that in order to survive, we had to keep alert, stick to our Marine training, and work together. Pilgreen had survived the tour so far, and he was determined to get back home to Alabama alive.

We moved to and set up our blocking force destination, creating concealed positions and digging our fighting holes. Our battalion would be the anvil in the hammer-anvil maneuver, and the Fifth Marines would be the hammer, sweeping the enemy toward our positions. Alpha, Bravo, Charlie, and Delta companies were set in place, waiting for the gooks.

One evening, the enemy attacked or stumbled into our lines. Bravo Company took the hit this time. We heard firing but didn't know yet it was Bravo that was in trouble. A couple of Marines were killed and a few wounded, but their two M60 machine gunners tore into the enemy unit as it attacked. Many of the enemy were killed that night. The reason they had attacked with such unrealistic courage was discovered in the morning. Little plastic bags of white powder were found with the bodies. "Little bags of courage," I called them. We all speculated about the bags' contents.

Had it not been for their M60s, the boys of Bravo Company could've been wiped out. Many of them complained about the fact that their M16 rifles kept jamming. There is nothing worse than fighting the enemy and not being able to fire back.

Lieutenant Francis would always say, "You men have to keep your weapons clean, and we keep telling you this all the time. If you clean your rifles, they won't jam."

We did clean them. They jammed anyway.

AFTER OUR BLOCKING FORCE assignment, we were sweeping again, looking for the elusive units we were told were "everywhere." The operation started uneventfully for Second Platoon. No contact whatsoever. I felt no indication that we were in danger. Alpha and Bravo companies were far to our left flank and spread out. Charlie Company was also spread wide. We encountered villages near which were a complex set of tunnels throughout rolling hills. We went through villages and came into the area with the rolling hills. As we swept through the small hills, we stumbled upon one of the tunnel systems. Orders came down to try to check them out as fast as we could.

My squad gathered around one particular tunnel entrance that went into the side of a small hill. The opening was about three feet high. It went parallel into the hill, and when we looked into the tunnel with a flashlight, it seemed to have no end.

"I need a volunteer to go in," Sergeant Jones said.

Everyone just looked at each other.

"You're not getting me in there. No way!" Cooper said.

Muller, who was my squad leader, just smiled, shuffled his feet, and looked away.

"I'm too big," Sands said. "There's no way I'm going to fit in that hole."

Everyone looked at me. I always wanted to prove I was brave, so I said, "Okay, I'll go."

I threw down my pack, cartridge belt, two bandoleers, and my flak jacket. It felt good to strip down because of the excruciating heat of the day. Sergeant Jones handed me his .45-caliber pistol and flashlight. I felt the adrenaline flowing through my veins as I got ready to enter the darkened hole. I got on my hands and knees.

The light of the day made it difficult to see in the dark as I entered the tunnel. My eyes would need a minute to adjust to the darkness. I put the flashlight beam down the hole. I could see the tunnel went pretty far. I said to myself, *Shit, this is crazy.* Why did I volunteer? *It's too late to back out now,* I told myself. I started to move farther into the tunnel. My mind started playing tricks with me. I envisioned someone at the other end shooting down the hole directly at me from the darkened recesses beyond. The shooter would be certain to hit me because my body covered almost the entire width of the hole.

I kept crawling, keeping my attention down the tunnel with the .45 pistol pointing forward the whole time, just in case. The pistol was cocked and set to fire a round. I got about fifteen feet into the tunnel and could then see what appeared to be the end, where it veered right or left. There was another thirty feet to the turn. I knew I could die if I didn't focus down the tunnel where someone could be with a gun.

Jones started yelling to me, "Hurry up. We don't have all day, and we have to move out soon!"

I wished he wouldn't have yelled at me because if there were gooks in the tunnel, they would now know I was coming. Jones would have to wait. I was going to make it at my own speed. Suddenly something brushed against my face, like a thick spider web. It was heavier than a spider web. It was like a ribbon hanging from the ceiling. I jumped back because it felt horrifying. It seemed to be invisible, and yet it touched me. What the hell was it? *Shit*, I thought. My focus had been down the tunnel and not close up, making near things invisible. I scanned for the foreign object with my flashlight.

When I caught the object in the beam of light, it glistened, translucent. *My God*! I shivered, *What the hell is hanging there?* I carefully approached. It wasn't moving at all. When I got closer, I recognized that it was a snakeskin. All I could think was to abandon ship and get the hell out of there. Whatever had worn that skin could still be in the tunnel.

"Taylor, what the hell is wrong with you?" Jones was saying. "Get going and find out what's inside."

I backed out so fast that I hit Jones in the face with my ass.

"What the fuck, Taylor," he said. "What the fuck are you doing?"

Then he saw my face was white as a ghost.

"What?" he asked.

All I could say was, "Snakes! They have snakes hanging from the ceiling. Forget this, I'm done."

Jones knew it was going to be a lost cause. Steiner giggled.

"You should have seen your face," he said. "What happened?"

I told him they booby-trapped the hole and hung a snake from the ceiling. "Lucky for me it shed its skin, or I would have been dead," I said.

He shook with empathy.

"God, this place sucks," he said.

Lesson learned: no more tunnels or volunteering! I put on my gear and caught up to everyone who had started to move out without me.

"Shit. Hurry up, Taylor," someone said.

You bet, I thought. *I don't ever want to be left in this shit-hole place by myself.*

Second Platoon was still lucky enough to avoid action so far on the operation, but Lieutenant Francis was itching to get into a fight.

We set in for the night. The next day, we were expected to go on a long sweep in the morning, searching for Charlie.

BY EARLY MORNING, ALL the other companies were already in skirmishes. Communications indicated to Captain Reczek that VC units were peppered throughout the area, setting up ambushes. It seemed that they would hit one of our units and then evaporate into the countryside just to set up for yet another attack. Captain Reczek got hold of Lieutenant Francis on the radio.

"Hold right there and don't move out," he ordered.

It was eight in the morning, and Francis wasn't content with the slow movement the company was making. There was a tree line in our path that our platoon would eventually have to pass through. So, Francis took it upon himself to have my squad check it out and clear the path where we were headed.

Sergeant Jones told Lieutenant Francis that it didn't feel right to send the squad across open ground. As Francis insisted, Jones shook his head in deference to the lieutenant. It reminded me of how Malloy used to argue with Francis. Since our squad had to go out, Sergeant Jones decided to join us, leading us personally to the tree line. He used Ski as his radioman in a wedge maneuver to approach the trees.

I was on the far-right side. Walstad was next to me on my left with Muller next to him. Pilgreen was to his left but farther away, and then Harvey. We didn't usually take a corpsman out, but Jones decided to take Doc Hawthorne just in case. The rest of the squad veered off to the left with Jones in the middle and in the lead.

Jones led us to the top of a hill; it was eight-thirty in the morning. We all stood there for a few seconds and viewed the valley before us. The tree line in the distance was shaped like a long and narrow island, with plenty of heavy brush and downed trees lying all around. Fresh, green trees jutted high into the sky. The tree line extended to the right and then made a fish hook hard to my right flank.

A small haystack, five feet tall, was to my right. In front of us, the landscape made a long and gradual slope down to a ravine that dropped about four feet. In the ravine, a small creek ran from my left to right. On the other side of the ravine were four dry rice paddies that we would have to cross before reaching our objective, the tree line. I could see what looked to be short, dry plant stems jutting upward from the paddy. The rice must have been harvested some time ago. It was the dry season, which meant we wouldn't have to wade through ankle-deep water. To my right-front I saw a little boy on top of a water buffalo ambling along with no urgency toward a distant village. The valley looked poetic—like the impressionistic masterpiece of some nineteenth-century painter.

The farmers appeared to be slowly moving away from us. We walked down the hill to the ravine and lumbered in the creek bed. The ravine was fifteen feet across and cool water slowly passed in the middle.

I said, "Hey, Muller, let's get some cool water first."

"Get in tune, Taylor!" Muller barked at me. "Our objective is the tree line."

I was a little embarrassed to have Muller scold me. Our canteens were nearly dry, and I saw it as an opportunity to top them off. I didn't really sense any danger because our platoon had had no action at all in the area. After all, there were still farmers and children milling around.

"Everyone, move out," said Jones.

I jumped up and over the ravine wall and started walking into the first rice paddy. We were spread out pretty far apart—at least fifteen feet between us, side by side, as we walked.

It was already getting hot, and I thought how nice it would have been to get some cool, fresh water. Nevertheless, I had my flak jacket on and zipped it all the way up. I held my M16 in both hands as I moved forward. I felt a little tightness in the two bandoleer straps, so I adjusted them. When I looked up and around again, I noticed that the people who were in the field to my right had moved away and were almost gone. I figured they must have seen the Marines coming and were leaving the area for fear we might hurt them.

We entered the second stubby rice paddy, now pretty much halfway to the tree line and committed to go all the way.

I thought to sneak a quick picture of the farmers, children, and buffaloes before they disappeared. I grabbed my Brownie camera, which was in my pocket, and snapped a shot. I didn't think anyone saw me, but I was wrong.

Muller yelled again, "Taylor, what the hell are you doing?"

I had already put the camera away in my side utility pant pocket.

We entered the third paddy, and now we're seventy yards from the tree line. I focused and didn't see any movement or anything out of the ordinary. Then again, there was a lot of cover in the trees, so I kept my concentration there.

We got within forty yards and to the beginning of the last rice paddy dike. I looked quickly to my right and didn't see the people or buffalo that were there just moments before when I'd snuck the photo.

What the hell? Where did they all go?

My heart skipped a beat and I turned my attention quickly back to the tree line. Just then, it erupted with all that hell could muster. The entire tree line simultaneously opened fire at us with a deafening sound like forty jackhammers pounding away. Dozens of enemy AK-47 and machine guns sent their hell toward us. Grenades exploded all around us.

The millisecond I heard the first sounds of fire, I hit the ground and lay horizontal against the rice paddy dike. I'm sure that's what saved my life. I probably had the luckiest position in our group. I was in the corner of the paddy when I hit the ground. I was protected in front by the foot-high dike. It was just high enough to cover my stomach. A two-foot rise to my right protected me from flanking fire. Even though I had this great position, the machine gun bullets were skimming and hitting the dike in front of me. Luckily, the dike was thick enough to absorb every bullet.

In the short brush before the tree line in front of me, Walstad lay flat on his back. He lacked the cover of the paddy dikes that I had. He lifted his head and looked down the tree line and at the hook to my right. I will never forget the look of terror that struck his face just before twenty or thirty bullets pounded into the ground around him, literally drawing an outline just inches around his entire body. As each bullet missed him by mere inches, he unloaded a complete magazine of twenty rounds at whatever he was staring at. After emptying his M16, he scurried into a secluded depression and disappeared from view.

Other guys were screaming, "Help, I'm hit! Help me!"

I tried to move, but machine-gun bullets dug into the dike in front of me along the length of my body. I emptied a magazine blindly over the dike toward the tree line every time this happened. After doing this a few times, the thought occurred to me that I might need to conserve ammo. I was trapped behind the dike and could not see any way out of it.

Hawthorne rushed over to Muller, Ski, and Jones. They were lying up against a dike in the paddy next to me, even closer to the tree line than I was.

"Who's hit?" yelled Doc Hawthorne.

"I'm hit in the shoulder and the foot," Ski said. "Jones is dead. Muller's hit in the elbow and can't move his arm."

I watched as Hawthorne poked his head up quickly over the dike. He assessed the situation and then quickly ducked down again. Watching him do that, and knowing how accurate and close those gooks were, scared the living hell out of me. Then, without any warning, he stuck his head up again and *Bam!* The back of his head exploded, sending blood and brain matter into the air.

I froze in horror. That's all I had to see! I was trapped and sure I was also going to die. I just kept firing a small burst every now and then to let them know someone was still alive to fight back. I thought if they rushed us, we wouldn't have a chance.

It seemed everyone in the squad was hit but me. I called for Walstad, but he never answered. Ski yelled out to me, "Where did Hawthorne go?"

"Hawthorn's dead," I said.

"Shit!" Ski exclaimed.

About forty-five minutes passed. I knew I needed to be free of most of my gear so I could move around more easily. The sun pounded down on us as we lay there baking. I lay on my back and slid the bandoliers of M16 magazines off my shoulder and then took off my pack and flak jacket, keeping them close to me.

"Where the hell is the rest of the platoon?" Ski yelled.

"I don't know, Ski," I said.

"Go get help. I'm bleeding!" he pleaded.

"I'm pinned down," I yelled back. "I can't move! Why don't you radio for help?"

"The radio is dead!" Ski said. "The bullet that hit my shoulder went into the radio and knocked it out."

LIEUTENANT FRANCIS MUST HAVE realized we needed help and he had to try to get us out of the mess he created. He had two squads left to get the job done. The lieutenant's radioman tried to communicate with our ill-fated squad by radio, but no one answered. Francis called Eddie Martin over. Martin commanded First Squad, which was formerly Pike's squad before he was killed in July with Staff Sergeant Malloy.

"I want you to gather your squad and get the trapped men out of there," Francis said. "I suggest you move your three fire teams forward in alternating movements on the left side. One team moves while the other two cover them."

Martin shook his head the whole time Francis talked. Martin's bottom lip protruded forward while the sides of his mouth sagged down at the corners. He kept shaking his head while looking down saying, "No" over and over again.

"What do you mean, 'No'?" Francis said to him.

"That's what I fuckin' said. I'm not going to do it," Martin said. "It's suicide to go out there. It's crazy, and I'm too short. There's no way I'm going out there."

Francis argued with Martin for quite a while, but Martin was adamant and therefore immediately relieved of his command. Meanwhile, valuable time had been lost. Martin was going to be sent to the rear to be put up on charges, but obviously, he couldn't have cared less. No matter what they did to him, it would be better than dying. Martin had told us how hard it was for him to believe that Malloy and Pike had been killed. I think that watching them get hit right next to him instilled a fear he couldn't shake. I think he decided he wasn't going to die for that shit-eating country like they did. His only thought was to go home and be done with it all. Francis made Sergeant Kochmaruk the squad leader, replacing Martin.

There were about ten men in First Squad. Among them was Harvey, the tall, thin, black guy from Chicago. He was another short-timer who had never batted an eye when it came to getting his fellow Marines out of a jam. He jumped right up and grabbed his M16. Two machine-gun teams finally made their way up to Francis's location. Francis assigned one of the teams to go with First Squad and give them covering fire from a hidden position. The other team was Roger Bacon's. Swiftly, he moved his machine-gun team toward the right on top of the hill to cover First Squad's assault. Sergeant Kochmaruk was given the same orders and moved around to the left, flanking the tree line.

Francis walked over to Wakefield, who led Third Squad, and put him on standby. If First Squad ran into trouble, Third Squad would be next to go out.

First Squad proceeded down the hill, and Francis followed them to the ravine. Kochmaruk and his squad then moved out of the ravine toward some abandoned hooches for cover. Their cover extended toward the tree line for one hundred yards, but then they would have to cross another hundred yards of open ground to get to the wounded men. It was past noon, and Kochmaruk would have to pull a John Wayne. In World War II movies, John Wayne was the one who always led the charge of courage to get a tough job done, even under seemingly impossible odds.

AT NOON, WE HAD been out in the sun baking for almost four hours. There were no clouds above us for relief. The firefight had subsided, but the gooks kept us pinned by shooting whenever we tried to move. I had a lot of time to think out there and eventually came to realize that the only reason I was still alive is that they were using me for bait. If they had wanted to, they could have rushed and killed us all within the first twenty minutes.

The enemy knew our guys were going to come, and they waited in the tree line for them. We were trapped too close to the tree line for jets or artillery support. I needed to get back to the rear to reveal where the machine-gun emplacements were and who was wounded and dead. Oh, and to survive, of course. How was I going to do this? When I moved at all they fired at me, forcing me to keep down. Their rocket-powered grenades were launched at us and exploded in front of the paddy dikes often enough that I knew I couldn't move.

About one in the afternoon, I heard firing taking place on the other side of the paddy. I thought help was on its way, but whoever it was, they didn't realize how intense the fire could be, and, like us, found themselves in a world of shit. This ambush was set to perfection, and no one could get close to the tree line without getting hit. Still, it sounded like someone was at least trying to help us.

The fire I had heard was from Kochmaruk's First Squad and their attempt to cross the paddy while the two machine guns of Bacon's team opened up on the tree line from the hill. All of

Kochmaruk's men were hit, including Kochmaruk. Out of fifteen men, Harvey was the only Marine who made it to the trapped men at the ambush site. Kochmaruk's squad managed to crawl back to the ravine for cover—every one of them wounded.

The brave Marine from the South Side of Chicago had made it to within thirty yards without getting hit. Now with Pilgreen, Harvey kept looking over the dike to see how he might maneuver his way to help Muller and Ski.

"Keep your head down, dammit!" Pilgreen yelled at Harvey. "These guys mean business!"

"*Okay*, man," Harvey said, readying himself to jump over the dike. As he rose to make a dash for the trapped men, he was shot and fell over backwards. Blood gushed from his head and his legs twitched in a spasmodic response to the last jumbled signals from his brain. Pilgreen turned his head away.

Ski was still trapped and wounded in the paddy in front of Pilgreen.

Pilgreen yelled out to Ski, "Come on, Ski, you need to move along the dike toward me!"

"I can't do it," Ski said. "They'll hit me again!"

"Just stay against the side of the dike for cover!"

Ski had been bleeding for hours and had to be weakened—not just physically from the loss of so much blood, but also psychologically, from the very sight of it.

"I can't make it!" he cried to Pilgreen. "I can't!"

WITH FIRST AND SECOND squads down, Third Squad was all Francis had left to work with. He made his way out of the ravine and back behind the hill. Francis went over to Wakefield and instructed him to assault straight over the hill into the middle of the tree line. It was going on 2:00 p.m.

I was now in my fifth hour of being trapped. I decided I needed to make a break for it. Before going, I had to devise a plan. Pilgreen and the others were twenty-five yards away from me. If I were to move along the dike to their position, I would be in range of the enemy machine guns to my right where Walstad was targeted. I scrapped that idea.

The firing toned down because we had all stopped moving. I hadn't heard a single shot in the last half hour. I pictured, in my head, that if I were the enemy sitting in the tree line for five and half hours, I might lower my guard, not expecting someone who was trapped to just get up and start running. I thought they had to be running short of ammo by now, having fired at us all day. Their guns were still as they waited quietly, looking for new quarry.

I went to my cartridge belt. I filled the long utility pockets on my pants with M16 magazines. I grabbed two hand grenades and put them in my side utility jacket pockets, then took a drink, and emptied my canteen. I made my Act of Contrition because I didn't expect to survive what I was about to do.

I said to myself, *Now get up and run!*

I did exactly that. I made it all the way back to the next paddy dike without one shot being fired at me. I couldn't believe my luck. I'd been right about my strategy of catching the gooks off guard. I was now a lot farther than I was just a few seconds ago. There was quite a distance to go, and I could still be hit if they started firing at me. I waited for a while and decided not to run this time but to crawl, keeping my head down the entire way to the next paddy dike.

As I crawled frantically, rocks and short, dry rice stalks stabbed into my arms and legs. I got halfway through the paddy when they started shooting at me. The rounds were wild and off target. I'm not sure how many gooks were firing at me, giving away their positions. A rocket grenade was fired at me and came close when it exploded. My entire left side was sprayed with debris and shrapnel. I decided it was best to run the rest of the way.

I got up and dove over the next paddy dike. I had only two more rice paddies to go and decided to run the entire way out of the dikes. As I ran, I could see the hill in front of me taking the rounds that were meant for me. Dirt puffed up all along the hillside. I dove into the ravine and finally felt safe. There was cool water, but I didn't have my canteen any longer or the purification tablets that were in my pack. Feeling safe, I leaned against the ravine wall facing our lines. Then I heard something in the ravine.

Holy crap! Those gooks could use this ravine for cover to flank us.

I didn't feel safe any longer. I jumped up to the other side of the ravine where there was a drinking well, just like you would see on a small farm in the States. I went behind the well for cover. A tunnel entrance went directly into the side of the hill where we had been standing five and half hours earlier. I started to enter the tunnel that veered to the left toward a haystack, but it was dark and I couldn't see anything inside. I didn't have a flashlight. I thought I heard something or someone inside, not far away, so I slowly backed out of the entrance and stood there, hesitant, trying to figure out what to do. As I stood there, snipers tried to pick me off from the tree line. I could see the rounds hitting the hill around me, but they were missing me by six to eight feet. I still didn't want to be hit by a lucky shot, so I got down behind the well again. I needed to get to our lines and pass on all the information I had about the tree line, so I jumped on the hill and started running up.

I saw Mac, Shoeships, Steiner, Sands, Cooper, and Wakefield along with the rest of Third Squad coming over the crest of the hill to my right. As soon as Mac came over the crest of the hill, he was hit. He grabbed his hand and fell to the ground, rolling down the hill. Sands rolled down the hill, wounded also. Men were falling the second they crested the hill.

I knew the fire couldn't be coming from the tree line because their fire hadn't been accurate when they tried to shoot me by the well. I looked to my left front and realized that the tunnel by the well led directly to the haystack. Now it made sense to me. The sound I had heard in the tunnel was the gooks getting into position to fire at the Marines coming to help us. They must have had a machine gun hidden in the haystack and were slaughtering Wakefield's Third Squad. I reared up and opened fire on the haystack, full automatic from my position. I emptied a magazine and grabbed another from my pocket, firing another twenty rounds.

One of the Marines that had crested the hill saw me and pushed me to the ground.

"They're in the haystack!" I screamed.

The Marine looked over at the haystack and said, "If they were there, there's no fire coming from it now. Get back over the hill."

With that, he was gone, running down the hill toward the ravine to help the wounded back to safety.

All the wounded Marines had moved back to the rear. Francis was in the ravine with a handful of Marines that weren't wounded. I went over to the other side of the hill where the platoon had gathered that morning. Marines were walking and running around. I tried to catch the attention of one of them. Finally, I got the attention of one of the Marines.

I said, "I know the positions of the machine guns, and I know where a tunnel is and who is wounded."

"Yeah, we know all about it," he said.

No one was interested in a single thing I had to say, nor did anyone seem to give a shit. I sat on the ground with my knees to my face, wrapped my arms around my legs, and cried. My platoon was gone, for all practical purposes. Most of the short-timers or old salts that had been my companions had been killed or wounded in their thirteenth month. As of that moment, Second Platoon didn't exist. Sutton was lost, Malloy was dead, and now Jones was dead.

Doc Johnson was the only corpsman left out of three in our unit. He came over and squatted next to me.

"Are you okay?" he asked.

"I really don't know, Doc," I said.

He looked me over and noticed blood streaming down my left arm from my shoulder. With adrenaline running through me, I hadn't even noticed that I'd been hit.

Doc squeezed my arm and a piece of shrapnel came out. He patched me up with a field dressing and off he went, saying something about putting me in for a Purple Heart. It was 3:00 p.m., and that's when the Huey gunships arrived. Finally!

PILGREEN WAS STILL TRAPPED by the tree line but wasn't hit. As the gunships blasted the tree line, he finally got Ski to move.

"They're shooting at me!" Ski complained.

"Just keep moving," Pilgreen yelled at him. "Push, Ski!"

Ski worked his way from his safe position in the front corner of the paddy toward the dike behind him where he was more exposed. Listening to Pilgreen's urging, he managed to make his way along the dike wall. Now he was going to have to make it over the dike, totally exposing him and Pilgreen to the gooks in the tree line. Pilgreen kept urging Ski to move closer so he could help pull Ski over the dike to safety. Ski said he couldn't do it because he was hit in the leg.

"What about the other leg?" Pilgreen said. "Push with the other leg."

As the Hueys circled for another pass, snipers resumed their attempts to kill Ski.

"Dig your good leg into the ground and push," Pilgreen said. "I'll grab you and pull you over the dike."

As the gunners in the gunships opened up again on the tree line, Ski made his decision to move. He pushed with his good leg and managed to get enough of his body on top of the dike where Pilgreen then yanked him hard enough to get him over. Ski was exhausted and also weak from the loss of blood.

"Come on, Ski. Let's get the hell out of here," Pilgreen said.

Taking advantage of the Hueys that continued to blast at the gooks, Pilgreen urged Ski, pained and sluggish, to push harder down the dike toward the left flank and then to safety.

As the low-flying Hueys passed slowly over us ripping into the tree line, hundreds of shell casings fell around us, each ringing with a metallic tink as it hit the ground or another casing.

As ordered, Kochmaruk made a heroic charge to the tree line and received the fate that would have been Sergeant Eddie Martin's. He was killed, leaving only seven of us left in the entire platoon. I'm not sure why Francis never came to me or where he was. He had to be humiliated at the fact that his entire platoon was, for all practical purposes, wiped out. The only Marines who were left at the tree line were dead. All the wounded were in the process of being medevaced out. Among them was Walstad.

He had not been hit but was shell-shocked and shaking. He still had that same look of fear on his face—his eyes wide open, his arms held close to his chest, and his whole body trembling. He cowered away from those who approached.

Choppers were being shot at as they landed and took off. I was instructed to go to the CP. When I got there, I was told that I didn't have to stand lines that evening. It was to be the first time I didn't have to spend a fifty percent watch since joining my platoon in February. I was relieved to hear it.

LATER THAT DAY, AN officer appeared and called the seven survivors of my platoon together.

He said, "Listen men, you have to go back out to the tree line under the cover of darkness and retrieve our dead. You are the only ones who have been out there and know the lay of the land. Remember, we never leave our brothers behind."

I knew what he said was true, but I didn't want to go back. The fear of being trapped and running into the gooks again overwhelmed me. It was 8:00 p.m. and getting dark. I hadn't eaten since 8:00 a.m. My pack with my C-rats and cartridge belt were at the tree line. I wondered where I was going to get something to eat. I asked an officer about getting some chow because my pack was at the tree line.

"You'll have to wait 'til morning," he said. "Choppers have been bringing in ammo and taking out the wounded. There was no resupply of food for anyone today."

Resupply was usually every three days, and today was day four. No one had much left to eat. I went around asking if anyone had something to spare. Steiner was the only one to offer me something. He threw me a small tin of peanut butter. I took it with gratitude and opened it with my P-38 can opener. I spooned out all that I could and carefully licked the last bit of peanut-tasting ooze from within the tin. I licked it clean, being careful not to cut my tongue, and then settled in for a quick snooze.

Four hours later, I woke up screaming. I had dreamed that I fell into a well and was trapped at the bottom. When I looked up, I could see only a little bit of light at the top. It was a small well, and my arms were stuck tight against my sides. I screamed for help, and it was my own screaming that woke me from the dream. Apparently, it had woken up some of the men around me as well. They glared at me, agitated.

"What the fuck, dude," one of the Marines said, shaking his head.

I felt embarrassed but then quickly fell back asleep. It seemed that no sooner than I'd closed my eyes, I was shaken awake again by the officer.

"It's time to go to the tree line," he whispered.

I grabbed my M16 and a couple of grenades and stood up to talk about our mission. Pilgreen was going to be the point man going out. He knew the lay of the land and the best way to the tree line. Steiner, like me, did not want to return to that god-awful place. Any sane man would have been like Eddie Martin when he said, "No way in hell am I going out there."

Steiner and I took it in stride. Like it or not, we were going to follow Pilgreen.

The Alabama boy looked us over and noticed Don Smith had his dog tags dangling. He handed him a roll of black electrical tape.

"You gotta tape those up," he said. "We don't want those making noise."

He noticed the heavy load around Wilson's waist—his canteens, medical kit, and magazine holders.

"You should take that belt off, Wilson," he said. "Remember, we gotta carry back our guys."

We all stood in line. There was Wilson, Doc Higginbotham from Third Platoon, Don Smith, Steiner, and me, with Pilgreen leading the way. Pilgreen's sudden command presence reminded me of Jones and Malloy.

"Let's get this thing done," he said. "The sooner we get out there, the sooner we get back."

I felt confident following him to the tree line. When we left the safety of our lines, we went down the left side of the hill into the ravine. I wasn't familiar with that side of the hill at all.

Pilgreen whispered, "Y'all keep quiet now, ya hear? I don't want to get killed because some stupid motherfucker was making noise."

Pilgreen crawled down and we all followed his lead, moving slowly and stealthily. My heart was pounding, knowing where I was. A thick fog had permeated the air. We slowly walked along the creek bed with Pilgreen leading the way in the darkness. He would stop every once in a while, turn his head to listen for danger ahead, and at the same time keep an eye on the column.

Wilson tripped in the darkened ravine and the shushes that followed were louder than Wilson's trip. Pilgreen just shook his head and put his index finger to his lips. The sound of an artillery shell went over our heads. It was a smoke projectile perfectly placed by our FO. Several more went over our heads and into the tree line area ahead of us. This projectile, once it hits, explodes and releases smoke canisters that emit large amounts of thick smoke for up to a minute and a half. It was our signal to move out and get the bodies. We slowly crawled out of the ravine onto the foggy, smoke-filled rice paddies, keeping our profiles as low as we could. The smoke and fog had reduced our vision to only a few feet.

Slowly, we crawled closer to the tree line. Finally, we were just a few yards away. There wasn't any wind, so the smoke from the canisters hung over our heads, which allowed us to get closer to our downed men. Pilgreen was using all the instincts he'd learned from hunting in the hills of Alabama—instincts that were heightened for the slightest indication of movement. We laid there for what seemed to be a long time and then Pilgreen slowly moved forward toward our dead comrades.

Harvey was the first Marine he came across. Pilgreen pointed to me and then Harvey and continued forward. Doc Hawthorne was just a few feet away. Moving along, he climbed over the dike and came to White's body and then Jones's. All the bodies had their pants lowered to their knees. I ignored this act of insult and kept doing what I knew I needed to.

I hovered over Harvey's body. I knew I had to move him, but how was I going to do that and crawl back at the same time? I grabbed his cold stiff hands and attempted to pull his body toward me. I heard a sloshing sound inside his head and chest. I immediately let go of his hands, sickened by the sounds. *What the hell is that?*

As his body baked in the sun for hours, his insides must have liquefied. Everyone was now making a lot of noise, including the dead Marines. The struggle was taking us too long. I looked down the paddy and noticed that my pack, cartridge belt, and extra ammo were gone. All the bodies had been stripped of anything of value. I thought, *We have to get the hell out of here.* Wilson tried helping me, but it was too difficult to move the bodies. A loud, horrible eruption of gas came from Harvey's corpse. The smell was sickening. I just wanted it done.

Pilgreen grabbed Jones's body and did an over-the-shoulder carry and ran past me. Wilson helped me load Harvey's bloating corpse over my shoulder. He felt like two-hundred pounds of pure dead weight. I could hardly stand with him on my shoulder. I struggled as I walked swiftly back toward the ravine. The other men picked up the remaining bodies and followed Pilgreen and me.

I felt a sense of relief as I approached the ravine, but Pilgreen didn't stop. He was moving alongside the ravine and toward the hill. I then realized that he wasn't stopping. He was going all the way back. I didn't think I could make it because my back was struggling with the dead weight, and now I had to make it up the hill. One of the other guys saw that I was struggling and came up next to me and tried carrying Harvey's legs, but all that did was throw me off balance.

Pilgreen made it back up the hill, but I stumbled and went down. Harvey's head hit the ground and turned toward my face. A gurgle sound came out of his mouth and I almost puked. I pushed myself up and tried to pick him up, but I was drained of all energy. Wilson grabbed Harvey and was able to throw him over his shoulder. As I followed Wilson, I watched Harvey's head swing like a ball on a string from left to right. His arms, hanging down, swung as well.

We all made it back. The enemy hadn't been there like I thought they might be. After stripping the bodies, the gooks had scattered to the wind like they always did, knowing hell would be upon them in the morning.

Francis came up to Pilgreen and said, "You've been promoted to lance corporal because you were due for promotion. On top of that, I'm putting you up for a meritorious combat promotion to corporal for what you did out there."

Francis smiled at Pilgreen, expecting appreciation. Pilgreen, remembering what had just taken place, cocked his head at Francis.

"As far as I'm concerned," he said, "you can take this promotion and shove it up your ass for killin' all those guys with your heroics and your fucked-up mission."

Pilgreen didn't want anything from Francis or anyone else. His tour was up in a couple of weeks, and he had almost gotten killed at the very end. Francis never did give Pilgreen his meritorious promotion. I thought he deserved a Silver Star.

CHAPTER

EIGHT

WE MADE IT BACK to the ship to lick our wounds and regroup. For the rest of the battalion, it was just another mission. For me and my platoon, it had been a total disaster.

Operation Cochise ended on August 29. Our battalion had nine Marines killed while inflicting fifty-five confirmed enemy kills. We had lost Sergeant Jones, and he was going to be hard to replace. Francis was still our platoon commander. There was no one left in the platoon to stop his reckless aggression.

Waiting for us on the ship were a bunch of FNGs. I wasn't going to treat them like I was treated when I first arrived in Okinawa. I introduced myself to them right away. I walked up to a tall, good-looking, nineteen-year-old Marine with a full mustache.

"Hi," I said. "I'm Bill Taylor."

The Marine smiled back and said, "My name is Bill too, Bill Burgoon. These are my friends who I went through infantry training with, Ed Niederberger, Ivan Hiestand, and Bruce Hodgman."

We liked each other right away.

I ended up being promoted to squad leader and lance corporal. Ed, Ivan, and Bill went to my squad, and Bruce was sent to Third Platoon. Some of Second Platoon's wounded had been patched up and were waiting for us on the ship. We still didn't have a full platoon by any means, but we had a lot more than the seven remaining from the last operation.

I was heartbroken when I found out Pilgreen had received his orders, and his tour was over. No one had to tell him what to do. He got his gear, jumped on the next chopper heading for Phu Bai, and then departed for the place we all knew as "the world"—home. I would have loved to say goodbye to him.

On September 1, our battalion took off from the USS *Okinawa* at 8:30 a.m. We were going to land in the Thua Thien province for Operation Beacon Point—heading again into the area known as the "Street Without Joy." I knew what to expect from previous landings, but the new guys were in for a rude awakening.

We were on our way to LZ Sparrow. I looked at Niederberger sitting in the chopper along with Burgoon and Hiestand. They looked like kids having their first ride on a Ferris wheel. They were full of anticipation, as I must have been many months before. I guessed I was the old salt now. If these guys were going to survive, they were going to need my help.

I yelled to the three new Marines and said, "You know, in this area where we're going, the North Vietnamese will use a lot of snipers and there will be a lot of booby traps around. You have to be alert at all times."

They nodded in agreement. Suddenly, I knew what Pilgreen must have felt like, looking at me when I was as green as these new boys.

I put this question to the three Marines. "What are we doing in Vietnam? Does anyone know the answer?"

Hiestand immediately said, "We're fighting for freedom."

"I know that's what they told you. I was just wondering what you thought," I said.

Hiestand had the same look of confusion as I once did when Pilgreen had said the same to me, and I could tell he started to wonder, as I once did.

Looking down out of the chopper's door opening, I could see the beach below. White waves hit the peaceful shore, as I had seen so many times before. The shoreline was huge and looked to be at least one hundred yards of pure white sand before the greenery appeared. The choppers continued their run over a marsh and then on to a grassy plain farther inland. As the chopper got close to landing, I saw a small herd of water buffalo and several farmers attending to the herd. One of them sheltered his eyes with his hand as he looked up at us.

It seemed we were centered between a razorback mountain range to the west and the ocean to the east. We exited the choppers and received sniper fire from our west. As we continued to land, patrols were sent out in pursuit of the elusive snipers, but they vanished quickly into the countryside. No one was hit, but it still gave us the fear of God as the rounds came our way. After walking for hours of sweeping toward our objective, we stopped for an uneventful night.

The next morning, the company continued in a V-shaped sweep. I knew danger was upon us, because we returned to the infamous hedgerow country. First Platoon took the lead as spearhead in the middle of a rice paddy. My platoon was back and to the left covering our flank. The first hedgerow came into view.

The hedgerows were natural hindrances that impeded our ability to move toward our planned destination. The hedgerow was the perfect place for the VC to plant their bouncing betty mines, both around and along the perimeter of the thicket. The VC would also hang butterfly mines in the limbs of trees and bushes. If a mine went off, they sometimes leveraged the resulting confusion to execute an ambush.

I told the new guys that we needed to make our own path through the hedgerows, and I carefully inspected the ground for anything that looked like little prongs sticking out. One could never be too careful.

It was about midmorning and First Platoon was slightly ahead of us and about to traverse a hedgerow when automatic fire erupted from our front. My platoon immediately hit the ground.

First Platoon's lieutenant yelled, "Rockets up!"

I looked to my right and saw Tom Harrison of Rockets running just behind the corporal of the team toward the lieutenant when the radioman, George Norbit, set off a bouncing betty mine. He was killed outright, and Tom was blown unconscious. Tom told me years later that when he came to, there was a hissing sound in his head and he felt as though he were in a vacuum. He dizzily sat up, and all he could see was the corporal lying down with his flak jacket wide open and his chest and abdomen covered in blood. The corporal struggled to get up, as a corpsman and two Marines tried their best to dress his wounds. Tom could see that the corporal was screaming, but he couldn't hear the screams because he was still deaf from the explosion.

Tom looked down at his legs because they were burning in pain. His right leg felt like someone had hit it with a baseball bat. All the men around him were attending to the most severely wounded, so Tom, using his bayonet, cut his pant legs open from the crotch down. His legs had numerous shrapnel wounds, some of which went all the way through. He took off his cartridge belt to retrieve his first aid kit. He removed his dressing to bandage his own leg, when Sergeant Avalos came over to help patch him up.

A medevac chopper came in, and all the wounded were taken out. We ended up overwhelming the area where we were receiving the fire and found only shell casings where the VC had been. Their plan had apparently been to ambush the Marines and have them run into the mined hedgerow for cover. The VC had quickly left the area because they had scored a victory and knew all hell would be on them if they stayed.

WE CONTINUED OUR SWEEP toward Camp Evans. Two tanks joined us in our forced march. We encountered a lot of water buffalo and rugged dirt roads. Hooches and a few old villagers were everywhere.

I ran across an old farmer who came up to me with his skinny cow. The cow's nose had a gaping hole that went all the way through from side to side—it had almost been blown off. The farmer kept pointing to my M16 and then the cow. I didn't speak Vietnamese, so I pointed to myself, and then pointed to the gun, and then back to the cow, hoping I understood him correctly. I thought I was being asked to put the poor cow out of his misery. The farmer kept nodding his head, pointing to the cow and nodding his head and pointing to my M16.

I asked the Marines around me, "Is this guy asking me to shoot his cow?"

"Yes, it looks like it," they all said.

Orders came to move along because we were in a sweep. The farmer walked with me and kept on with the pointing.

Steiner said, "Taylor, I think he wants you to shoot the cow."

I pointed my M16 directly at the cow's brain and looked at the farmer. He kept bobbing his head yes. I thought he wanted me to put the poor beast out of its misery, so I pulled the trigger. The cow's knees buckled immediately, it crumpled to the ground, and then rolled on its side. Niederberger, who was standing next to me, jumped out of the way of the falling beast.

"Looks like we're having steaks tonight," he said.

The farmer went nuts on me, screaming and yelling. I felt guilty, but I had to keep walking with my unit. The farmer followed at my side, yelling, and he handed me a leaflet with a picture of a cow and a soldier on it. There was Vietnamese writing next to the pictures and an amount of money on the leaflet. I finally got it. He wanted compensation for the cow. I just kept walking and shaking my head no. The farmer left me to try to convince someone else to pay for his cow.

As we were about to set in for the night, my entire squad was chosen to go on an ambush about a hundred yards in front of the lines. This made me very happy because it meant ten of us would share a ten-hour watch. Two of us would stand watch for two hours, and once we completed our watch, we got to sleep the rest of the night. Our normal watch was broken sleep all night long.

After dark, we left the safety of the lines and walked to a place that had great cover. We sat there camouflaged until midnight. The Marines who were on watch heard something and woke everyone up. I could hear a large group sloshing through a rice paddy just a few yards in front of us. The order was given to open fire. I shot nine magazines of twenty rounds in a matter of a minute when my M16 jammed. Luckily, the infiltrators never fired a shot.

After firing, we all pulled back, running through a rice paddy to the safety of our lines. The next day, we checked the area and found blood trails. I cleaned my M16, but it never seemed to work properly again.

One of the platoons found 7,100 pounds of rice later that day. Our choppers came, took 4,100 pounds of it, and destroyed the rest.

We finally reached Camp Evans. On this small operation, two Marines from our battalion had been killed and thirty-four had been wounded.

The next day, September 6, we ended up boarding trucks and were taken to a place known as the "Street Without Joy" for Operation Fremont. We were going to be a blocking force for the Fourth Marine Regiment. The Fourth Marines had been on Operation Fremont since July 7. It would be our job to stop any retreating enemy units.

The only action we saw was when a group of thirty-five VC walked toward our lines. We sent one hundred rounds of artillery on the VC unit. Nothing moved after the firing ended.

The operation concluded on the ninth. We were trucked to a landing area where the landing craft picked us up and took us home to the *Okinawa*. Of course, all our ammo was taken from us as we boarded the ship.

We ended up staying aboard the *Okinawa* for six long and beautiful days. I got to know the new men of Second Platoon well. Burgoon, Hiestand, Niederberger, Hodgman and I all did a lot of laughing and joking together, but the fun came to an end on September 16.

OPERATION BALLISTIC CHARGE IN the Quang Tin and Quang Nam provinces started on Saturday, September 16. Charlie Company was singled out to do an assault just south of Da Nang. The goal of Ballistic Charge was to maintain pressure on the VC and eliminate local bands of resistance who were regaining an upper hand.

Charlie Company boarded helicopters and was sent several miles inland. Alpha, Bravo, and Delta companies were to make a beach assault and move west toward us, pushing the enemy into a fight.

Our chopper was the first to land, and we received heavy sniper fire from every direction. We responded by firing full automatic at whatever looked suspicious. One of the choppers behind us took casualties from the snipers. I wasn't paying any attention to the sounds of enemy fire because our platoon was blasting away as we spread out. Once we established our landing area, the firing from the snipers stopped.

We were told that our corpsman was hit on the landing and he was being medevaced back to the ship. We had overwhelmed the VC so fast they quickly scurried off into their hidden camouflaged sanctuaries or went into their underground tunnels.

We moved swiftly north toward a village that was south of Hoi An. Hoi An was a very sizable city because it was along a large river that swept from the distant mountains to the ocean. There was a lot of river traffic, and the locals caught fish and sold them in the markets. There was no one around the village we entered except old, decrepit men and old women with teeth tarred black from betel nuts. They walked around randomly and didn't seem to belong to any hooch. They kept their heads down as they passed us. We spread out throughout the village, searching every hooch.

"Holy shit," a Marine yelled. "Look what I found! There are hundreds of punji sticks over here."

Another Marine yelled, "Sarge, look at all the rice I found!"

It was a half-ton of newly harvested rice. We knew it could be used to feed the local militia, so engineers were called up and instructed to destroy it all. I had conflicted feelings about it. Sure, it could supply the VC, but it could have just as well simply been the normal life and livelihood of the local farmers—an entire season's worth of toil and trouble blown away in a flash. These were, after all, the South Vietnamese, who we were supposed to be fighting for. How could we help the South Vietnamese when they often were also the ones who were trying to kill us?

We finished our job in the village and moved on. We proceeded to walk through a few rice paddies before entering another ville not too far away. Sergeant Martinez, the new platoon sergeant, told us to search all the hooches for weapons and contraband. These dwellings were all the poorest of the poor, basic one-room bamboo huts. The hooches appeared to be a place where the people could get out of the elements or just sleep at night to keep the mist off their bodies. It was easy to walk into a hooch because they had no true front door—just an opening with a makeshift covering. The floors were made up of compressed ground, covered by bamboo mats to keep the dust and dirt down to a minimum. A crude bed made from whatever wood or bamboo was available to them sat off the ground and in a corner or against the wall. Sometimes there would be more than one bed. Also scattered around inside were rickety homemade end tables to keep their utensils, pots, and pans on. It was like being transported three hundred years back in time.

Bill Burgoon and I checked a hooch together, looking under and around everything for weapons or anything that could be used against us. Ivan checked out the hooch next to ours at the same time. The hooch Bill and I were checking was a little bigger than Ivan's. The occupants were missing from our hooch, and I assumed they didn't want to be found. There were three beds in the hooch.

Bill was always smiling and joking, and today was no different. He pointed to the first bed. "I got this figured out," he said. "I know who lives here."

"Okay, who lives here?" I was very interested in his opinion.

"It's Papa Bear's bed here," he said. "And that one over there is Mama Bear's and, of course, that one ..."

"Don't tell me. It's Baby Bear's!" I interrupted.

"How did you know that?" Bill said, with a smile.

"So where did these bears go, may I ask?"

He shrugged his shoulders. "They went to find the Three Little Pigs," he said.

We walked out of the hooch as Ivan came out of the hooch he'd been searching.

Bill pointed at Ivan and said, "Look, Papa Bear!"

I laughed and grabbed my camera. "How about a picture for the fans back home?" I asked.

Ivan smiled and said, "Sure."

I took a picture of him exactly as he was coming out of the hooch holding his M16 in his right hand. He put a big smile on his face, a white towel around his neck.

"Okay, let's move out," Sergeant Martinez said.

I thought this was just an innocent village with old farmers and nothing more.

I took the lead out of the village with Bill behind me. Ivan was somewhere about five guys behind, for some reason. I noticed a grassy knoll to my right, which was lined with hedges and brush-like cover, about forty-five yards away. I realized that the top of the hill could be a potential danger and viewed it with a sense of caution, when a loud gunshot came from my right rear and the knoll. Everyone hit the deck.

Our sergeant told me to take Bill, Ed Niederberger, and another Marine to flank the sniper on the knoll. The four of us jumped up and ran to the left. We used what little cover there was to move around to the top of the hill. One by one, we advanced to the place we thought the shot had come from. After careful scrutiny of the area, we realized that the bastard was gone. He just wanted to kill a single Marine and scram. We checked everywhere, especially for any evidence of where he might have been in the brush line. The whole time, we pointed our M16s, looking to blow the sniper away. There was nothing—no evidence at all—no footprints on the ground and no rounds lying around. We kicked everything that might have been a spider hole. It appeared as if no one had been there, and we were at a loss.

We scurried back to the lines, looking behind us at all times. There were a lot of Marines standing around, but one was on the ground. I approached the wounded Marine. Two corpsmen were bent over, feverishly working on him. The corpsmen had the Marine's pants unbuttoned, his utility jacket up, and they had him lying on his side. I recognized Ivan lying there with his body exposed. The corpsmen found the entry wound in his chest area and the exit wound at his hip. Both corpsmen's hands were covered with Ivan's blood. Ivan was pale and moaning in pain. The corpsmen stopped his bleeding and laid him on his back, but it was obvious there was something else more serious going on with him.

"Mom! Mother, help me!"

Over and over, he pleaded out loud for his mother.

I felt awful watching him in horrific pain. I began to think about how he talked about his mom and family in Hobart, Indiana. His life was changed forever by a hidden sniper. Ed and Bill took it the worst. They had joined the platoon together after we had been wiped out on Operation Cochise, only a month before. Ivan had lasted only a month.

I then saw the white towel that he'd worn around his neck on the ground next to him. We always dyed our towels green, yet his was white. He had used it to wipe sweat from his face. I wondered whether the white towel had made him a target or if it was just pure bad luck.

I felt like we were in the arcade at a carnival of horrors. We were the little ducks and birds pulled on a conveyor in front of the VC who shot at us for a Kewpie doll. The dying and wounded Marines were stacking up. It felt like we were drawing straws as to who was going to get it next, and the random sniper shootings were getting out of control. I still had another four and a half months to go.

We could hear the faint sound of the medevac chopper in the distance. When the chopper arrived, two Marines jumped out. They helped move Ivan into the waiting chopper.

The new Marines who joined our unit told us stories about college students who were rioting and who marched against the war. They were somehow blaming us for the war. I just couldn't believe this was the truth. To make things worse, there was a race war that had started in the States, and I noticed that some of that bad blood was trickling into our unit with the newly drafted Marines.

I wished I was home and away from all the craziness. Was this what Pilgreen was talking about back in Okinawa during the training, or was it getting worse?

It all seemed so long ago.

CHAPTER

NINE

WE WALKED FOR A couple of days, and late one afternoon we stopped and set in. I was sent out on a listening post with Burgoon about a hundred yards outside our lines to cover our flank. There was no sun, and it felt like it could rain at any second. A weather front had come through, and a cloudy mist hung in the treetops not far above our heads. It felt eerie, the low cloud cover stationary and at treetop level. I had a perfectly clear view of everything under the cloud cover. To my front-left was a trail of tall, thin palm trees that ran into the distance from the front of our position.

I squinted my eyes toward the most distant trees, and that is when I first saw the people coming our way. I grabbed the radio headset, called the CP, and asked if there were any friendlies around us. As the people got closer, they appeared to be soldiers who were using the palm trees for cover and the cloudy mist for concealment from above. The men continued toward us; I could see no end to their line. The radio operator confirmed there were no known friendlies in the area.

"You'd better get an FO out here to my position as fast as possible," I said. "I can see over a hundred people walking along a tree line and more behind them."

Two Marines ran out to our position. The FO looked through his binoculars.

"Holy shit," he said quietly. "There are more gooks than I can count, and they are coming this way."

He got on the radio and got ahold of two jets that were a short distance away. Captain Reczek had called for air support before the FO had even gotten out to our listening post. The FO began talking to the jets above and gave coordinates from his map. I tried to figure out how they were going to do the maneuver, because of the low cloud cover. I knew the jets couldn't see the enemy, and yet the FO was talking them in. The first jet came in, broke through the clouds, and sent dozens of rockets precisely on top of the gooks. Explosions began to erupt the entire length of the tree line. The other jet came in right behind and honeycombed the tree line the same way. They came around for a second pass and completely devastated the area where the gooks had been. The area was in total darkness from all the smoke and debris.

When the dust cleared, we couldn't see anything moving at all. They must have died on the spot. I couldn't imagine how anyone could have survived such an onslaught. I didn't have any feeling for or against what had just happened. It was simply a matter of fact, warranting no compassion at all. What was happening to me? When I first arrived, I would have had some kind of feeling.

The FO reported there were one hundred fifty killed.

A CORPORAL NAMED MYERS came into the field because we needed a new squad leader. We asked him where he had been assigned before joining us. He told us he was assigned to Marine Headquarters back in the States. I asked him when he joined the Marines. He went through boot camp when I was in Okinawa training for SLF. He was meritoriously promoted to corporal doing office work, and he was now in charge of a combat Marine squad with no combat experience at all. I was pissed, as was everyone else. Screw this; we were about to riot right then and there.

Our platoon lieutenant came over and found out what we were all upset about. He wholeheartedly agreed with our concerns but explained that we weren't in a democracy and it wasn't Myers's fault.

He told Myers, "Listen to your fire team leaders and follow what they tell you."

Then the lieutenant said to us, "You men have to give him a fighting chance to get accustomed to the program here. This is the only way this is going to work."

Myers tried for a couple of weeks but didn't have the experience to lead a squad of Marines. I felt like he thought he was in Headquarters, and instead of listening to his instincts and his own common sense, he wanted to do everything by the book. He made stupid mistakes such as planning to set up an ambush where we faced each other on opposite sides of a road. We laughed at him.

Someone told Myers, "When the gooks come down the road and they get between us, not only will we shoot them but we'll shoot each other. Was this your plan?"

"Oh yeah, right," he said.

The platoon commander realized, as we did, that Myers didn't have the experience, and he was soon transferred out. Myers left the field, and that's when Sergeant Burris was introduced to Second Platoon. He looked like a heavy-duty weightlifter. He was built like the Hulk. He had huge shoulders, big arms, and a big chest. He was the first black man I met with a major chip on his shoulder, but he was not prejudiced at all. He hated everyone equally.

His looks were as threatening as any I have ever seen in my life. Even so, I was hoping he was a good leader like Jones, Malloy, and Muller. He walked over to the squad and said, "I understand you are a bunch of fucked-up sons of bitches. I'm here to square your asses away. You guys fuck up and I'll bust your fucking heads together. Understand?"

I couldn't believe my ears. Who the hell put this asshole in charge? They must have been scraping the bottom of the barrel when they got this jerk. I thought, *First Myers and now this asshole.* I shook my head.

He came right over to my face and said, "You have a problem with me?"

I felt so threatened that I didn't know what to say. I just shook my head at him and walked away. Every day for the next week it seemed to get worse. Burris was constantly yelling and screaming orders and threats.

PFC Harris came over to me and said, "I don't think I can continue another day. I always had this feeling like I was going to die, and now with this new sergeant, I feel like I'm going to crack. What do you think I should do?"

"You have to just take it like the rest of us," I said.

"What's it like being wounded?" he asked. "Did you ever hear about anyone who shot himself?"

"No, and don't get any stupid ideas," I said. "I know a lot of people feel the same way you do, but you just have to suck it up and stick it out."

"Would you shoot me tonight after dusk, during hole watch?" he asked.

I looked him directly in the eyes and said, "That's not a good idea, so forget about it and get it out of your head!"

"I just feel like I'm not going to make it home alive," he said. "I can't take it any longer. The thought of me getting killed or captured is overwhelming me. Plus, this damn sergeant is on my ass all the time, threatening me constantly. I'm going crazy, and I know it. Everyone's getting wounded and killed all around me. I can't take the snipers and the constant mortaring. I tell you, I can't take it any longer!"

"Why don't you tell the new platoon commander?" I asked.

"If that crazy sergeant finds out, what do you think my life will be like then?" Harris said.

"Things always have a way of working out," I said. "We have to let things take their course. You'll see."

We continued our sweep and set in near a small mountain range. It was after midnight, and I was standing our regular fifty percent foxhole watches. The evening mosquitoes were making their rounds, looking for a meal on a sleeping Marine. It was quiet except for a few crickets in the ground around us. I always used them as little sentries because if they went quiet it meant something disturbed them. The moon gave little light, so I was looking at the sky for shooting stars when I heard a loud *bang*! The entire line jumped forward and braced for a possible attack.

There was a lot of commotion in the hole next to mine. I went over to see what was going on. Harris was lying in the foxhole reaching for his leg while Bill Burgoon tried to stop the bleeding. Bill hastily wrapped bandages on his leg as I watched. Burgoon asked me to keep applying pressure on the wound while he ran to get help. Harris was shot center in the calf, and his bone was partially exposed. He screamed when I applied the pressure.

"What the hell did you do?" I asked.

"I messed up," he groaned in agony. "I tried to graze myself, but I didn't account for the recoil. I pointed the M16 at the fleshy part of my leg and when I pulled the trigger, the recoil kicked the barrel upward and into the center of my leg. At least I'm out of here."

Sergeant Burris came over and looked disgusted. A couple of corpsmen also came over. One gave Harris a shot of morphine while the other attended to his leg. Harris started to drift off into unconsciousness as the morphine filled his body with its pain-deadening power. A chopper was called, and before I knew it, he was on his way out of the field.

I glared at Burris, who was breathing heavily as he glared back at me. I saw the rage that was coming from him and wondered what the hell had caused him to be so mean.

I walked to my hole and sat there thinking that I, too, wanted out of the field, but I didn't want to shoot myself to do it. I couldn't stand being there either, but I had four and a half more months to go.

ON SEPTEMBER 29, WE returned to the ship for a well-deserved rest, but it wasn't the USS *Okinawa*. The *Okinawa's* tour was up. We were now going aboard the USS *Iwo Jima* (LPH-2). All the original old salts were now gone, and as a new squad leader, I was worried. We went through so many squad leaders, and I wondered if it was going to be my turn next. I had learned how to survive thus far, and just maybe I would be able to do the same for my squad. But then there was Sergeant Burris.

First thing we had to do was to retire all our ammo on the hangar deck of the USS *Iwo Jima*.

"*Okay*, Taylor, give it all up," said Burris.

I started with my eight magazines and ammunition from my jacket pockets, two seven-pocket bandoliers with twenty-eight more magazines of twenty rounds each, and four more on my cartridge belt. I produced an array of fifteen grenades from various places. In my pack I had ten cardboard boxes of even more ammo.

"Did you have enough ammo?" the sergeant asked.

Sarcastically and with a look of "don't be ridiculous," I retorted. "No! There's never enough ammunition."

I remembered when I first trained in Okinawa and had to decide which was more important, more food or more ammo. My ultimate answer was definitive—more ammo was now always the answer.

I was actually glad to shed that extra weight as I entered into the depths of the ship. This was our little haven from the VC, even though it was extremely hard to get around. It was a place of safety, sleep, and a little play.

When you put fifty Marines together in tight quarters after combat, you will find an abundance of activity. Varner went to his locker for his writing material. Eight guys walked naked to the showers. Nine went right for their seabags to fetch goodies like food, cards, or liquor leftover from the last time we were on the ship.

"Anyone for cards?" asked one of the Marines.

"When the hell do we eat?" another asked.

PFC Miller said, "Can I borrow five bucks 'til we get paid?"

I turned away immediately from that conversation, a smile on my face. Several guys plopped in their cots and crashed right there. Me, I just wanted a shower, but I wore a towel around my waist. I wasn't like a lot of other guys who didn't care about having their business right out there in public and weren't afraid to strut it.

Corralling a bunch of Marines on a ship in close quarters for almost twelve days, after being in combat for a month, often caused a lot of anxiety within the group.

The men I surrounded myself with were more like comedians than anything else. We told jokes, took ridiculous pictures, and snuck into every crevice we could find aboard the ship to get away from the different personalities. The others played cards for hours. A lot of fights broke out, especially when someone lost all his money. The word "cheat" would eventually come out, and the fight would begin. Nighttime was letter-writing time.

We were aboard the ship for a week, and tensions grew among the combat-ready group. For a myriad infractions, ten guys from our platoon had to go up to the company commander for "office hours."

When I heard about the Marines standing in line waiting for punishment, I had to do something crazy. I grabbed my camera and started on a trek to find the guys waiting for office hours. It was a Polaroid instant camera; it developed pictures within two minutes. I ventured to the hangar deck, where I saw what appeared to be supplies for the next operation in large crates off in the rear of the ship. Choppers were everywhere, their blades disconnected and turned backward.

Mechanics attended to their jobs, and the other personnel ignored my presence. I acted as if I had orders to do something important. I saw a Marine and asked him, "Where are the Marines who are having office hours?"

He said, "Right up those stairs over there on the other side of the bay. You'd better hurry up. They should get underway in about ten minutes."

I think he thought I was one of the Marines having office hours. At least he gave me as good a reason to be up there as any. I went up the steel ladder attached to the gray bulkhead of the ship. I entered the ship's door, and there was a long, narrow hallway. I heard some laughing and soft talking just a little way down the corridor. I proceeded down the hallway leading to the CO's office. At the end of a small, drab-gray hallway, six guys were standing in line.

"Smile, guys, you're on *Candid Camera*!" I said.

I caught them by surprise as I held up my camera for the shot. Immediately, two of them went into poses. One gave me the finger. Wakefield jumped into the center of the view and gave a peace sign with a big smile, displaying an unlit cigarette in his mouth. The others were not amused. The door opened, and a lieutenant took one of the guys in and then noticed me.

"What are you doing here?"

"I was told to find the men in my platoon," I said. "They have to be back for a meeting soon. The sarge was just wondering where they were."

He didn't see my camera. I sped out of there, real quick, and headed back to the squad bay where I passed around the Polaroid photo to everyone's amusement.

Life on the ship had just become better. No one had seen Sergeant Burris the whole time, and I was happy about that. The less I saw of that bastard, the better.

Someone from another platoon came over to our platoon's quarters and said, "I heard that Burris hit your platoon commander in the face. He was taken away in shackles and put directly in the brig."

I couldn't believe it. I wondered if he was messing with us, but we soon found out it was the truth.

Here we go again. I wondered who was going to be our new platoon sergeant.

CHAPTER

TEN

WE WERE ABOARD THE ship for a little over a week. During that time, Captain Reczek was promoted up into Battalion, and replaced by Captain Burleson. As far as we were concerned, Reczek was the best company commander in the battalion, so we had little confidence that his replacement could fill his shoes. It seemed that, as time passed, replacements just kept getting worse. Still, we were all relieved that our hated sergeant was no longer with us.

It was time for another mission. On October 9, an order was given for the platoon to meet on the hangar deck after evening chow. There were fifty of us gathered, milling around, when the new platoon commanding officer, Lieutenant Giesell, appeared. He was soft-spoken and not intimidating at all. He was a butter bar like Lieutenant Francis, but unlike Francis, he wasn't trying to win the Congressional Medal of Honor. I had the feeling this was his first command and that he was a little intimidated by it.

"Listen up, because I have some important information here, so let's gather around," he said. "We're going to the southern area of the Quang Tri Province where the Hai Lang Forest is located. Since our SLF came to Vietnam, this forest has been an enemy stronghold, and it needs to be rendered ineffective. This operation is called, Medina. The game plan is to execute the hammer-anvil tactic. Our battalion will be the anvil. We will set up our stationary positions as a blocking force. Two other battalions are going to be choppered to the west of the forest and act as the hammer, flushing the NVA toward us. We'll be waiting for them on the other side of the forest.

The lieutenant's last words were, "If you have any questions, refer them to your individual squad leaders. Steiner, you'll be the radioman for Second Platoon, and Weaver, you'll be the radioman for me. We'll assign a new platoon sergeant soon. Diss...missed!"

The meeting concluded abruptly, and there wasn't a peep from anyone. Many of the Marines just sat there in confusion, because we usually got to ask questions. This time, however, there were no comments or discussions.

Everyone departed in different directions. I stuck around and watched as Third Platoon got the news, but again there was no follow-up discussion about the operation. We were the blocking force for two sweeping battalions of Marines, period. As a grunt, I accepted the information, but as an experienced combat Marine, it felt incomplete. The new company commander and my platoon lieutenant were new, and they didn't allow us any questions as all the others in command had.

I was happy about the fact that, for once, we weren't doing the sweeping. I almost felt a sense of relief because we were going to be in set positions waiting for the gooks. How bad could that be? I envisioned the landing, moving into position, digging in, and just waiting. I was aware of the unknown, though. It could be deadly. I knew better than to get too cocky with my assumptions, but I deduced that if we were attacked, we could just call in artillery and air support and blow them away.

I saw Varner and Penny from Third Platoon moving toward me, talking about the meeting.

"That was a strange meeting," I said.

"That's the way the new company commander wants it to be," Corporal Penny said. "No discussion; just get it done."

I wondered if we had another know-it-all or was he a genius and we just didn't know it yet. Regardless, he was in charge because he was the new CO. We had lost a great bunch of leaders so far—Malloy, Jones, and Sutton—because they were either killed or wounded. I was happy for Captain Reczek that he was promoted, but I hated the thought of going on a mission without him. I always felt like he truly cared about us and he always seemed to be one step ahead of the enemy.

Dan Varner grabbed me and said, "Are you going to be around later when we can talk? I have some awesome news I want to share."

"Sure," I said. "How about just before they turn out the lights? I'll have a surprise for you too."

We left the hangar deck and returned to the squad bay, knowing our old sergeant was in the brig and was gone. He was another casualty of sorts.

I thought it was only fitting that I get the bottle of lime-flavored vodka that my sister, Bev, had sent me from home. I looked forward to sharing it with Varner. It was my last bottle of booze, but I decided, *What the heck.* Just then, Steiner happened by to get in his bunk.

"So, are you ready for the great news?" Varner later asked.

"Yeah," I said.

"I'm a father! My wife, Pam, had a baby boy, and I'm so happy! But I wish I was home with them right now."

Varner had been on the flight with me to Okinawa, Japan. He had the same amount of time left in his tour as I did. I handed the bottle of vodka to him.

"Congratulations, Daddy," I said, handing him the bottle of vodka.

I remembered when, on Operation Beaver Cage, he'd said, "Screw this shit," sat up with his legs crossed Indian style, and blasted away while enemy bullets thrashed the ground around him.

"You gotta be more careful now," I said. "Don't expose yourself so much."

He had a good slug of the vodka and squinted his face. He tipped the bottle up again, but took a smaller drink this time. Again, his face distorted. He closed his eyes, puckered his lips, and then coughed.

He shook his head a little, gave an embarrassed smile, and said, "Thanks Taylor. That was great!"

"What about me?" Steiner said, sitting next to us.

I handed Steiner the bottle. He guzzled it down pretty good, which was not really in character for him at all, so I grabbed my camera and took a picture.

"I wish I had a son or daughter. You are one lucky man," I said to Dan.

"I have so much to lose now and have an awful feeling about this operation," he said, shaking his head from side to side with an ominous look on his face. "I really don't think I'm going to make it home."

"What do you mean?" I asked. "You know we all feel the same way at times."

"No, Bill, I'm really serious! Since I found out about the baby, something just came over me. I feel like I'm not going to see him or Pam ever again."

"Dan," I said, "of course you would feel that way. You have so much to live for. As a matter of fact, I get that feeling too, but it always goes away."

"Really?" he said.

"Yeah, you can't be thinking that way going into the field."

He was so serious about his premonition that it actually made me start thinking about my own mortality. I looked over at Steiner, who was sleeping with the bottle still in his hand. It was half-gone. While I had been talking to Dan, he'd drunk half the bottle. I shook my head, grabbed my camera, and snapped another picture of him sleeping like a baby. I then asked one of the guys from the squad bay to take a picture of Dan and me. Then we all retired because the assault was scheduled to begin at 6:00 a.m.

THE NEXT MORNING, ON October 10, I found myself standing in line waiting to board the choppers to God only knows where. We were told that recon had checked out the area and it was clear, but we had to expect that we might get hit with mortars when we landed. Our new platoon commander, Lieutenant Giesell said, "We need to dig in the second we land."

My squad would be one of the first to take off and one of the first to land. As I stood there waiting in the drab gray hallway, I thought about the possibility of getting hit with mortars on the landing and I sure didn't like that idea. It would be pretty difficult to set up a perimeter while mortar rounds exploded around us. I was going to take his advice and dig a fighting hole for cover immediately.

We all moved closer to the ship's exit door, where we readied ourselves while the choppers warmed up. One of the Navy flight deck personnel, who wore a bright orange flight suit, gave us a signal to trot to the waiting chopper. I ran to the farthest chopper on the deck, the one that would be departing first.

Others piled into the chopper behind me. About twenty seconds later, the chopper's engine started its familiar roar. It started to shake before liftoff. I watched the gunner check his M60 machine gun. He pulled the bolt back and shoved a round in the chamber. The blades pushed a cool ocean breeze through the door. As the chopper lifted, I thought, *Here we go again.* The chopper bowed its massive head forward and we moved off to the Hai Lang Forest.

As usual, the choppers rose in unison. We climbed to extreme heights and the *Iwo Jima* slowly disappeared. I looked out the door and could see land in the distance. As we got closer, most of the men looked out the door of the chopper to have a sense of where we were. A couple of Marines had their cameras and took pictures, as if they were sightseers. Others may have wanted to remember the beauty or exhilaration of the moment.

We finally passed over the shoreline, which told us we were halfway there. As the ground passed under us, the terrain became a weedy landscape of rolling hills. Normally, we saw a lot of rice paddies and hooches, but this time it was different; it seemed barren, with large, round pools of water all over. As our altitude decreased, I could see the pools were actually large, water-filled craters from our B-52 bombing runs.

The pattern of craters was exactly like a bomb spread would be: in line, one crater a little left, and the next a little right. They went from the north to the south. This area had been blasted by high-altitude bombing. Each crater had rainwater in it. The water would have taken time to accumulate, so this event had to have taken place some time ago.

The choppers descended and then landed farther than normal from each other. The second we hit the ground, we dispersed in all directions and secured the landing zone for more incoming choppers. Recon had done their job well. We landed safely again, as there were no combatants at our rendezvous point.

We had landed on top of one of the large, rolling hills in the area. I wondered if this was good or bad. It could be good because we were on the high ground and able to see the valley before us. On the other hand, the NVA might have been able to see us from miles away and be able to report everything we did, as well as our strength by the number of choppers that landed. Perhaps the reason our officers thought we might get hit with mortars was because we could be seen for miles. A well-hid mortar team with a good spotter could easily target us.

"Dig in!" Lieutenant Giesell yelled. "We are expecting to be hit with mortars soon."

I looked around. Everything looked strange. The usual greenery wasn't present. Weeds and small, knee-high bushes were everywhere. The weeds were a lot like dried old brush. The ground was red and gritty, with small volcanic-type rocks laced in it.

I took off my pack and grabbed my e-tool with its collapsible spade-shaped blade. I adjusted the spade at a ninety-degree angle, like a pick, and then swung the shovel at the ground. I expected the blade to cut into the soil. Instead, it made a loud noise and bounced like I'd hit a sidewalk. What the hell? So I hit it again. *Bong* went the e-tool. I couldn't believe it. Now I understood why there weren't any tall trees or greenery. The ground was as hard as rock, and all I could see were these nasty-ass, stiff weeds growing everywhere.

"I said, dig in!" The sergeant yelled again at everyone. "We're expecting a mortar barrage at any second!"

I started whacking away, over and over, but after about fifteen minutes, I realized I was never going to dig in. Using all my strength, I had dug only nine inches deep. The next set of choppers was going to be landing soon, and I'd have to give up my hole and dig another one a little farther away. After a while, everyone realized there wasn't going to be much digging, but everything appeared calm. No mortars were coming in, so everyone became lax and milled around. It was unusual to see Marines milling around a fresh LZ.

It was already past 9:30 a.m. and starting to be another one of those hot days in Nam. Niederberger had already shed the radio and his flak jacket. He draped a green towel around his neck to absorb the accumulating sweat. Several flights of choppers would be coming in all morning long. For some reason, the landing was getting drawn out longer than any I'd experienced.

When the next set of choppers arrived, we had to expand the landing area to accommodate the influx of more men. It felt different than our previous landings—too lackadaisical, as if no one was in control. I decided to pay attention to my instincts, which were starting to indicate the operation was already getting FUBAR.

I heard the sound of a CH-53 chopper coming in. The CH-53 was the biggest chopper I'd ever seen. Underneath the chopper was a cargo net that carried what appeared to be extra supplies for our command group and Weapons Platoon. We had never utilized a CH-53 before. The new CO was apparently going all out for this operation.

In the end, the landing was uneventful overall. Several hours passed, and there had been no mortar barrage. We got the word to saddle up and get ready to move out. Weaver had the heavy radio on his back and had just sat down. He gave me a disgusted look. I shook my head, smiled, and extended my hand.

First Platoon moved out and took the lead. The company was told we were sweeping to the edge of the forest, but there was no forest in sight. It looked like we were in for one long forced march to our blocking positions.

My platoon, Second Platoon, moved out moments later. The CO and Weapons moved out with us. The CO was using an old, inaccurate map of the area. We were following what was supposed to be a main road marked on the map, but it was really just a large dirt path. My position in the march had me walking with Weapons Platoon. I hoped I would be able to stay along the path, but I gradually ended up in the heavy weeds off the right flank. While sweeping, I came across one of the large craters from the B-52 bombing run that we had seen from the air. The crater was large enough to fit a city bus in the middle and never see the top. We had to move around these obstructions, causing us to congregate dangerously close to each other.

About an hour into the march, we were still in the rolling hills. The valleys in between had more of that brittle, yet tough, weed growing everywhere. Every once in a while, we ran into another stretch of bomb craters moving off into other directions. The craters would fade into the distant countryside. Four hours into the march, we came over a hill and saw a small lake to the right. It was the first semblance of Vietnamese life, but it wasn't our destination, so we ignored it.

After another hour, we ended up on a small hill overlooking natural ravines that had more dried-out plant growth. I thought it was peculiar that a place called the Hai Lang Forest was so devoid of healthy foliage. There were really no trees to speak of; everything resembled more of a deserted landscape than anything I would call a "forest." This was to be our blocking position.

First Platoon had control of the northeast side of the perimeter. Third Platoon was left of me and covered the south and southwest side of the perimeter. As luck would have it, my proposed two-man foxhole would be connected to Third Platoon somewhere on the western side of the perimeter where the gooks would most likely be pushed by the other Marine battalions sweeping toward us. The rest of my platoon went off to my right and hooked in with First Platoon on the north side of the lines. Altogether, the platoons formed a complete circle, which would then give protection to the center where the CP was located, along with mortars. Given as many as a hundred and fifty men from three platoons, with two men in each hole, and holes as far as forty feet apart, the circle perimeter was enormous.

On our side of the lines, the first order of business was to decide where the machine-gun emplacements should be set in. Roger Bacon went out to set up fields of fire for the M60s. He was in charge of Weapons and had a talent for understanding machine-gun tactics. His job was to maximize the killing zones protecting the lines. Bacon had been with us since our first operation on Beaver Cage in April, when he was wounded and medevaced from the field. Lieutenant Giesell, my new platoon commander, assigned our holes and positioned them at the top edge of the hills. I felt very comfortable knowing that, from this vantage point, we could protect the ground in front of our hole as it sloped downward.

To my right were two foxholes, then a machine-gun emplacement where the hill extended in front of the lines like a finger. This was a perfect place to put a machine gun. Fields of fire were perfect for everyone on my right flank. To my left were Corporal Penny and another Third Platoon guy. All of us could look down the hill in front of us, having the high ground.

We were just waiting for the word to start digging, when the new company commander, Captain Burleson, came out to check the lines and started arguing with Lieutenant Giesell and our XO, Lieutenant Neuss. Bacon was there and was trying to get his point across about the placement of the machine guns. The new CO just walked away saying, "No," shaking his head emphatically side to side. I watched with a frown because I knew for a fact that Roger Bacon knew his shit but had no idea what we could expect from the new CO.

Sergeant Martinez told us to move away from the crest of the hill because it would make for a tighter perimeter. The new CO believed that the lines were too far apart and extended. I knew it was true that the lines were far apart, but it was also true we should never give up the crest of the hill. I believed it was a big mistake. I was glad I didn't start digging my original hole.

We faced the coming sunset. I looked to the hills in front of us, hoping there weren't any VC watching this fiasco play out. The sergeant told me to dig my foxhole away from the crest of the hill as the new CO had directed.

"What asshole made this decision?"

"The new CO made the decision, and I'm not countermanding it," Sergeant Martinez said. "We have to follow his orders. He said we were spread out too far apart."

I told him that it was insane. No one should ever tell us to set in away from the crest of the hill. It would take away our fields of fire and make it easier for Charlie to sneak up on us. The sergeant just walked away shaking his head and said, "I know!"

"Hey, Sarge," I called after him, "by the way, I know we're short on troops but I'm all alone here. You got someone who can stand watch with me? Sarge, you hear me?" *Holy fuck! What a nightmare this is going to be.*

My heart started pounding just thinking of the lunacy. We were being run by a bunch of rookies. This was Burleson's first day of command and his inexperience was showing. Jones, Malloy, or Pike would never have allowed this. But they were all dead and there I was, stuck with the insanity. My odds of making it out alive were dwindling.

I started digging my foxhole. The ground wasn't as hard as where we had landed. It was much easier digging into the red, hilly terrain. I made a strong parapet in front of my hole. All the dirt from my hole was put in front to act as a barrier for incoming from the front. I went in front of my hole and tried to memorize the area. I grabbed some of the surrounding brush and camouflaged my fighting position even more, especially the parapet. Once I felt confident that my position was safe, I decided to eat and get comfortable with my surroundings.

I opened a small can of bread. After removing the bread, I used the can as a stove. There was a large can of beans and franks in my pack, and I used a heat tab to warm my meal as usual. I went into my pack and retrieved a very small tin of cheese from one of my other meals and put it on the bread. When heated, it made a miniature grilled cheese sandwich. We had to invent ways of making meals taste good, and my ability to make unique dishes out of the same twelve C-rat meals was proud proof that I'd become something of an old salt.

We were always being inundated with new guys who were the replacements for the wounded, sick, and dead. One of these FNGs came over to my hole.

"Hey, I was just assigned to have watch with you," he said.

He didn't look like much—just a short, eighteen-year-old kid with bright green utilities that had yet to be sun-bleached from time in the field. Aside from being new, he was apprehensive as well. Apparently the sarge had heard me and sent a new guy so I could break him in. He looked at me in a shy way and said, "Are you Taylor?"

"Yep, what's your name?" I asked.

"Private Freeman," he said.

I could tell he wasn't sure what to do. He looked lost and confused. It was like his eyes were asking, *Where the hell am I, and what the hell did I get myself into?*

"Did you eat?" I asked.

"No, but I'm not hungry."

I shoved the last of my little grilled cheese in my mouth, dusted my hands, and then spread them out sarcastically over the fighting hole.

"Well, make yourself at home in my little Taj Mahal here in beautiful Vietnam," I said.

My flak jacket, cartridge belt, bandoleers, and my pack took up the entire space around the hole. He looked at me, not knowing what to do next. I laughed, slid into the hole, and started tossing my stuff aside.

"Hey, would you take a picture of me in the hole for the people back home?" I asked, reaching for my camera.

"Sure!"

I took my camera out of my pack and handed it to Freeman. *Click.*

"Thanks," I said.

He handed my camera back to me. I thought this would be a good time to show everyone back home how fucked up Vietnam was. So, I took a picture of Corporal Penny and the other Marine with him at the hole to my left; they were far away. Then I took some pictures of what I'd be looking at if we were attacked and how the CO had pushed us back and away from the crest of the hill.

As I viewed our new position away from the crest of the hill, I couldn't help but notice the high brush out front. My problem was compounded because we could barely see forty feet in front of our foxhole before the ground dropped out of sight over the crest. How could you defend a position like this? It would be even worse at dark. They could sneak right up the hill and crawl through the brush.

Freeman looked on and didn't say much. I knew he was scared and totally lost.

"Look," I told him. "I've been here a long time, and I've been through a lot. I know what I'm doing and if you listen to me, you'll be okay."

"Thanks," he said. "I needed to hear that. I'm really scared right now and I'm glad to be with you because it's my first day in the field."

"Stick with me. You'll be fine," I said.

I thought that I'd better not tell him my true feelings about being backed off from the crest of the hill. He was already too scared, and I didn't need to get him more upset than he already was.

IT WAS NOW PAST sunset, and the leftover rays of the sun were getting ready to leave us. No one checked the lines, and no one was reassuring anyone of anything. Again, I felt like someone was dropping the ball. Something wasn't right. I remembered there were a lot of new people on this operation, and I felt like no one was in command and no one cared. I told Freeman that we needed to set up our fifty-fifty night-watch schedule.

"It's 8:00 p.m. right now. We're up at 6:00 a.m. That gives us ten hours to share," I said. "Five for each of us if we work it right. I like getting three hours' sleep for my first watch. We have two more hours each to sleep and stand watch. I'd say, one hour on and one off after the three-hour watch. What do you think?"

I could tell from the expression on his face that he didn't follow, but he nodded anyway.

"Sounds perfect," he said.

I said, "Now, whatever you do, do not sleep on watch. There's no moon tonight, so you won't be able to see a fucking thing, but your hearing will take over. Remember to pay close attention to your hearing."

"I don't think I'm sleeping at all tonight," he remarked.

"You'll get tired, believe me."

He asked me if he could have the first watch.

"Sure."

I lay outside the foxhole and fell into a deep sleep. It felt like I had just fallen asleep when I was shaken awake by Freeman.

"I hear something," he whispered.

I jumped in our foxhole and listened carefully. I didn't hear anything at all. *God, this new guy has the jitters and it's 10:00 p.m.*

"Just keep a sharp eye out," I whispered. "It's okay for light animal sounds, but if you hear brush moving, definitely let me know."

At 11:00 p.m., Freeman again began pulling at my leg. I thought he was waking me because it was time for my watch to begin.

"I'll take it from here," I said.

"You know, I keep hearing something, but it wasn't loud enough for me to wake you. I just listened like you said. It's so scary because it's like being blind," Freeman said.

"If it's blind for us, then it's blind for them too," I said, trying to calm his nerves.

To my right, I heard the sarge. He had finally come around the lines.

"This isn't a social call," he said. "Our listening posts are hearing sounds out there. They're getting worried. They've been told to hold their positions and keep us informed."

"Where are the flares? Why aren't we getting any illumination?" I asked.

"The new CO doesn't want to give away our position," he said.

"What? Fuck that. We need to see in front of us," I said. "We're like blind out here. I won't be able to tell if they are crawling up on us."

"I know, but I have to alert the lines, so I have to go."

As fast as he was there, he was gone. I turned to get Freeman's attention, but he was already wide awake. Even in the dark, I could see that his eyes were wide open and full of fear.

"Get all your grenades out," I said to Freeman.

My survival mode kicked in. I had my grenades at the ready and placed them just behind the parapet in front of the hole. I straightened out the cotter pins so they could be easily pulled. In all, we had about fifteen grenades behind the parapet in a line. After about half an hour, we started hearing intermittent and obscure sounds from the depths in front of us.

"What do we do?" Freeman asked.

"Don't do anything," I said. "Just listen, for now."

We crouched inside our foxhole as if our lives depended on it. Every five minutes, we would both hear distant sounds: the faint and quick shuffle of dry bushes, the occasional snapping of twigs. This went on for two more hours. Still, no one was walking the lines telling us what was going on, plus we didn't have illumination.

Then there was a sudden loud whisper from out in the brush in front of us.

"Don't shoot," the voice said. "We're the LP. Don't shoot."

"What's the password?" I asked.

"Fuck, I don't know. Just don't shoot my ass," he said.

That was good enough for me. No Vietnamese ever talked to me like that before.

"Come on!" I said.

The two Marines came right to our hole, both terrified and out of breath. One of them proceeded directly to the center of the lines where the CO was located. The other stopped.

"There are so many fucking NVA out there you can't imagine," he said, catching his breath. "Too many to count! The gooks are all over the fucking place. It felt like there were hundreds of them all around me. We barely made it out of there alive."

He then ran toward the Command Post.

"Holy fuck! Get down," I said to Freeman.

"What do I do?" Freeman asked.

"Right now, nothing," I said. "Don't do anything. Are you locked and loaded and ready to fire your rifle? You have a round in the chamber?"

He checked his rifle and there was no round in the chamber. I shook my head.

"It's a good thing we checked," I said.

With a look of shock, he nodded his head in agreement. Both

of us put the safety lever in the firing position so we could fire full automatic into the enemy if necessary. It was completely dark.

"God, I can't believe we're not getting illumination," I said.

We waited in total darkness for what seemed to be hours, but in reality was only thirty minutes. *Boom* to the left, another *Boom* to the left, then right in front of us, *Boom*! Each explosion blinded us with light. I didn't think it was the Chicom grenades, either. I didn't understand what kinds of charges were being tossed in front of us. The Chicom grenades I had seen at night had sparks like a sparkler coming out of the handle. I was sure I would have seen the sparks in the air.

More explosions were being launched from somewhere over the hill and landing in front of us. Corporal Penny opened fire as did everyone to our left in Third Platoon.

Boom! Boom! Boom! Then there was another series of explosions in front of our hole. The gooks were trying to draw our fire to give away our positions. Sure enough, we could see Corporal Penny and the other guys' faces as they fired their M16s. I thought, *How stupid.* Each round out of the chamber lit up their faces, as if someone were holding a strobe light in front of them.

"Look at how those guys are giving away their positions," I said to Freeman. "Don't fire until we know they're coming and almost on top of us. That's when we will give it to them."

Then it went quiet again.

"Damn, I wish we could get some illumination," I said. "They're out there, and they're coming soon. I can just feel it. Remember, don't give away our position by firing."

"Okay," he said. "Okay."

The explosions started again. Third Platoon opened fire, giving away their positions as they had done before. The Marines to my left fired full automatic and then had to reload. I put my bandoleer around my chest and continued to wait. There was a brief lull on their firing when they reloaded. It was about 4:30 a.m. when the explosions intensified. Then all went quiet again.

"They're getting ready to attack real soon," I said to Freeman. "I'll throw the grenades in a pattern. Don't fire until they are right on top of us. Let them give away *their* positions."

This time the enemy threw Chicom grenades as they advanced. All along the lines to my left and in front, grenades exploded with a greater intensity to cover their attack. I felt it was time. I had my first grenade in my grasp with my finger on the pin.

Now! I said to myself.

I threw the first three grenades about ten feet in front of our hole. I threw another three farther, from left to right. The next four, I threw a little farther, and then the next even farther. I had several left and threw them in all directions. I threw them so fast that none of them started blowing up until I had thrown the last.

"Get down and cover your head," I said to Freeman.

They went off like crazy. The gooks in front of our hole had just walked into a minefield of explosions from our grenades. I felt no one could live through it. But then, maybe there was another group ready to advance from behind them. I took a glance at the hole to my left and saw all kinds of firing going on. I couldn't see who was who, and I didn't want to shoot our guys, either.

I said to Freeman, "Get down and get ready. There could be more gooks coming."

We waited about a minute, but no more NVA seemed to be coming at us. All the actions were now happening behind us, inside the lines. I realized the gooks had broken completely through the lines of Third Platoon. I didn't know what to do next. I couldn't really tell who was who. Our section of the lines was now quiet, but the NVA had steamrolled right over Third Platoon.

The NVA moved into the center of our perimeter. I could tell that large numbers of them had broken through because of the number of green tracers firing around the command post. The Marines shot red tracers, so red and green tracers flew in every direction. I could see men only for milliseconds at a time when the muzzles of machine guns flashed on them like strobe lights.

I told Freeman to stay in the hole and cover me while I crawled to Corporal Penny's hole to check them out. Freeman looked terrified as I crawled out of the hole. He kept his head down and had his M16 on his shoulder and pointed over the parapet, ready to fire. I moved on my belly toward Penny's hole. It was quite a distance to crawl, and I really didn't know what to expect. As I approached their hole, I could hear someone moaning. It was horrible to hear. I knew it wasn't going to be good. Green and red tracers were still flying in all directions from the command post. I peered slowly over the edge of Penny's hole, afraid of the carnage I feared I would see. Sure enough, one of the men was still alive. The other appeared to be dead and lying across the moaning Marine's torso.

I couldn't tell who was who. The moaning Marine had been shot in the jaw. He started talking incoherently. I couldn't understand a thing he was saying. I got into the hole and tried to see where else he was wounded. I had to lift the body of the dead Marine off him. The moaning Marine seemed to be hit everywhere but his main torso. In addition to the jaw, he'd been shot in the groin, shoulders, arms, and legs. I figured that the Marine lying on top of him had absorbed most of the rounds aimed in the hole, sheltering his main body.

"I'm here. It's Taylor," I said. "I'm going to get you out of here somehow."

As I looked up, other Marines appeared, offering assistance. I told one of them to get a corpsman and he raced off screaming. "Corpsman up! Corpsman up!"

But no one came.

We used all our strength to get the dead Marine out of the foxhole. We finally succeeded in also getting the wounded Marine out and laid him just outside. We stripped him down as best we could. I bandaged his face and yelled for someone to check the other Marine.

"He's gone."

"Well, we have a live one here," I said. "Let's get him bandaged up."

It was extremely dark, and none of us could see very well. I knew we needed a corpsman. We didn't carry any morphine or larger bandages. All I had were small bandages in my medical kit. Everyone tried to take care of the many wounds we could find. I counted about nine holes. No blood coming from his wounds meant he had lost a lot already. We needed to get him medevaced immediately. We were unable to wrap all his wounds because we didn't have enough bandages.

"Does anyone know who this is?" I asked.

"Yeah, it's Penny," someone said.

In the chaos, in the dark, and under all the blood, I hadn't even recognized him.

"Oh no!" I said. "Not Penny."

I tried again to assure him by mentioning his name when talking to him.

"I'm here, brother. I won't leave you, Penny. Just hang on!"

213

The Marine who went looking for a corpsman came back and said, "The corpsman was working on the officers who were wounded in the CP. Both the CO and the XO were hit. I think the XO's dead."

"Holy shit," I said. "Who's running the company?"

"I don't know. It's pretty bad at the CP. They called in for medevacs. I was told to tell you to bring the wounded Marine to the LZ over on that hill over there."

Freeman came over to the hole, and I felt a little apprehensive that there was no one watching for another attack, but I knew I was going to need help getting Penny to the chopper.

"Fuck it!" I said.

We still had our M16s and could defend ourselves if we had to. A Marine who came to give assistance had just checked the lines, so I asked him.

"Is Dan Varner okay? His wife just had a baby!"

"I don't know, but it doesn't look good," he said. "Every hole along here was overrun, and I think Varner was in one of them."

"Let's get Penny to the LZ," I said to Freeman.

One of the other Marines who were helping with our wounded said, "We have to get back and help the others. You two can get Penny to the LZ."

"Grab his feet and I'll grab his hands," I told Freeman.

I reached down to grab both wrists, but his left hand was shot almost completely off. I dropped his wrists and jumped away from him because I felt the raw meat slipping through my hands. I shook my hand in disgust to get his blood off. I couldn't believe I had totally missed that wound. I knew Penny was in real trouble because there was no fresh blood pumping out of his wrist at all. It was just red, raw meat.

There was no more firing going on, and I thought it was safe to move him.

"Let's get him going to the LZ."

I grabbed his two elbows and we both started moving down the lines. There was no one manning the lines at all. We walked down a ravine and up the hill the Marine had pointed to. I could hear the chopper coming, but there was no one else around. I yelled, and no one answered. I could hear the chopper coming in closer. I needed to get Penny to it right away. It was landing all right, but on a hill a little more than a football field away.

In the dark, we had wandered outside the lines. I needed to get Penny back on the right side of the lines and to the chopper before it took off. With a surge of panic, I took Penny up completely in my arms and carried him the rest of the way alone.

It was landing as I yelled, "Wait! Wait!"

I don't think anyone could hear me from the roar of the chopper's rotor. They were just putting the last of the wounded men in. I didn't think I would make it. I was gasping for air, ready to fall at any moment, and my back screamed out in pain. The adrenaline in my body was the only thing that kept me going. My screams caught someone's attention. I made it to the chopper just in time to load Penny aboard.

"He's critical!" I yelled to the gunner, gasping for breath. "He needs blood now!"

The chopper engine got louder, and debris blew into my eyes. I covered them with the crook of my right arm where my bicep meets the forearm. I was still holding my M16 in that arm as the chopper slowly moved up and away. Its tail moved up, the nose tilted forward, and then it disappeared almost immediately into the darkness—the familiar thumping of the blades fading into the distance.

Freeman had disappeared. I saw Arnold Ewings, and he told me it was his first day in the field. His orders were to help set up the chopper landing zone by using mounds of heat tabs he was able to scrounge up. He seemed to know where the CP was, and I was totally disoriented as to where I was or where I was going.

"Who did you put into the chopper?" I asked him.

"It was the CO," he said. "Burleson."

"Was he hit badly?"

"He was shot in the groin and was bleeding pretty bad," he said. "He was one of the first ones hit when they overran the lines."

"Anyone else get hit?" I asked.

"Yeah, the XO was killed."

"You mean Neuss was killed?"

"Yeah, they got in the lines and went straight for the CP. There are wounded and dead all over the lines."

We stumbled in the darkness among the overgrowth to what appeared to be the valley where the CP was located. I looked to my right and could see my hole from where I was standing. All the firing had stopped, but the scene in front of me was disorder and confusion. Marines were all over the place, walking in different directions. They were assessing who was in charge, trying to get a count of who was dead, and trying to understand where the NVA had come over our lines and where they had gone out.

To my front, I noticed three captured Vietnamese, along with one big-ass Chinese machine gun with a fifty-round drum attached.

"Holy crap," I said. "Look at the firepower they had!"

Just then I saw Bacon and Bum walking toward me, talking about the battle. They had both been in the center of the lines. Bum was a tall, thin Marine from Missouri who had been with us since Okinawa. His hair was wet, and dirt clung to the sweat on his face.

They both spoke in short, breathless bursts, each still jumpy with adrenaline. Bacon told Bum that he and the XO (Neuss) had argued with Captain Burleson about the vulnerability of the lines, but he wouldn't listen. Turns out, the NVA had broken through exactly where they had told him they would.

I interrupted them and said, "I was complaining about that too! Why didn't anyone send up any illumination, for Christ's sake?"

"I told him we should send up illumination for the lines," Bacon said. "He just kept saying that it would give away our positions. He flat-out refused."

All I could do was roll my eyes. Hell, Burleson joined us a few weeks ago, and now he was gone.

"Who the hell is in charge now?" I asked.

"God only knows," Bacon said. "I heard the platoon commander of Third Platoon is dead and First Platoon's Lieutenant is wounded. I think there's only one lieutenant left in the whole damn company and that's Lieutenant Giesell from Second Platoon. And he's brand new too!"

"You mean Giesell is the only officer left?" I said. "God help us, there is only one officer for Charlie Company. I better get back to the lines."

I went back to my fighting hole, realizing I had managed to escape death again. Freeman was already waiting there.

"Did you make it with Penny?" he asked.

"Yes, just barely," I said.

I hunkered down in the hole along with Freeman. We both tried to stay awake as it got closer to dawn. The lighter it got, the safer I felt . . . and the heavier my eyes became. By full daylight, I was in a dead sleep. I felt a kick from the platoon sergeant.

"Wake up Marine; we have patrols to go on soon."

I shook my head and got myself out of my stupor. I was curious to see what was in front of our hole. I jumped up and wandered out. Three dead NVA soldiers lay in front of the hole, full of shrapnel from the grenades I'd thrown. Flies were crawling in and out of orifices to plant their larvae. I also noticed blood trails leading back down the hill. *How long could my luck hold out?*

I took out my camera and took some pictures of the men lying there. *I got you first, you sons of bitches.* Truth be told, I was disappointed that there were only three.

Later some men from the CP came over, talking to each other. I went over to them and took their pictures as they looked at the enemy bodies. No one came over to talk to me about the evening before or how those enemy were killed. I thought to myself, *Who cares if they ask me. I survived again.* I walked away, back to my hole.

Dead Marines lay side by side a short distance behind my hole. Ponchos covered their bodies. I wondered if one of them was my good friend, Dan. I looked for some indication. I was hoping to hear that he was okay and that his son wasn't going to be fatherless. Then I recognized one of the deceased Marines as being taller than the others. His boots protruded from the bottom of the poncho much farther than anyone else's. I closed my eyes and put my hands on my face. I thought for a moment that maybe it wasn't him. I wanted to get up and check, but I just couldn't. I opened my eyes and peered through my fingers at the tall Marine.

"Let's get these bodies to the choppers," someone said.

A Marine walked over, grabbed the top of the poncho that covered the tall Marine and pulled it back. It was Dan.

I covered my eyes with the palms of each hand and cried.

I felt depressed and also angry. Though I had my eyes covered, my shoulders were shaking and tears streamed down the bridge of my nose. I wiped my eyes with the sleeve of my jacket and tried to regain my composure as Marines passed by. I thought about Pam, Dan's wife, and his baby boy. I immediately started feeling like I wasn't going to make it, just like Dan had felt the day before. I still had four more months.

How many more times do I have to go through this shit? Fuck, I hate this place. New officers who didn't know what the hell they were doing—they were putting us in danger all the time. Where was our Sergeant Stryker from the movie *Sands of Iwo Jima? We can't ever seem to get an edge on the enemy. We're losing this war.*

CAPTAIN RECZEK, WHO HAD been our company commander and had been promoted, came to our rescue. He volunteered to help Charlie Company until we could get new leadership. We sure needed him. All but one of the officers was gone, either killed or wounded, along with half of Third Platoon.

Two more days went by, and the enemy's dead bodies still lay in front of my hole. The daytime heat was over one hundred degrees. The bodies had started bloating and turning black. Flies and maggots now covered them completely. I walked over to the bodies every day and watched the flies crawling by the hundreds. The darkened and cracking flesh with ghoulish faces was slowly decomposing. Thousands of maggots infested each corpse, and the smell was nauseating.

A recon Marine came over to me and asked, "Where are the dead gooks?"

"Over there," I pointed to the front of my hole. "Right there, about twenty yards in front."

I was kind of proud that someone wanted to look at my quarry. He took out his KA-BAR knife, bent over, and reached toward the dead gook.

"Hey, what the fuck are you doing?" I yelled.

"I'm cutting off their ears," he said.

"The fuck you are!" I said.

"What's your fucking problem?"

"Those are my gooks, and you aren't going to cut off anything," I said.

"Fuck you!" was his reply.

I grabbed my M16 and put a round in the chamber so fast it startled me, and I pointed it at him.

"Leave him the fuck alone! He's my gook!"

"Fuck you, asshole. He's anyone's gook."

"That motherfucker is mine. Leave him the fuck alone."

He knew I was serious, so he stood up from the crouched position and put his knife away. He wasn't happy at all and walked away mumbling some derogatory stuff to himself. I was proud of myself at that moment. Freeman watched the whole interaction. He looked at me in wonderment, trying to understand what happened. Hell, I didn't know what had just happened or why I defended the bloating masses of decaying flesh. I just felt it was the right thing to do at that particular moment. I also remembered Operation Beau Charger where the First Battalion, Ninth Marines had desecrated NVA bodies. The NVA got their revenge on Operation Buffalo.

A FEW MORE DAYS passed, and it was my turn to lead a patrol outside the lines. I really didn't want to leave the safety of the lines. I felt like we were bait. I and my squad of eight men walked in single file with just flak jackets, water, ammo, and no packs. I decided to be point man because I knew how to spot an ambush better than anyone. I felt safer in front watching everything, and I knew better than to give commands and wave my hands. The enemy targets the leaders.

My senses were on high alert. A lone tree stood about five football fields away from the lines. It stood in the open terrain like the Eiffel Tower at the top of a hill. I headed directly for it, as we were told, but I didn't want to get too close because the tree was an obvious landmark and a probable target or hiding place. Just before the big tree, I noticed a B-52 bomb crater. I thought it might be a good spot to set up because it was a depression, and we wouldn't be exposed to gunfire. We could fight from within the hole, giving us cover if we ran into trouble, so we held up in the crater for about half an hour. After getting overrun on Operation Medina, Freeman was on full alert.

"Hey," he said, getting the team's attention. "I think I heard something."

We all jumped onto the perimeter of the crater facing the tree.

"Let's get the fuck outta here," one of the guys said.

"Yes, I totally agree with you," I said.

I noticed that the tree line went down into a ravine.

"They could be right over the hill, Taylor," one of the Marines said.

"I have a bad feeling about this position. I feel like we're exposed if we were attacked by a large force," I said.

"I heard something again!" the Marine at the perimeter said. He opened fire toward the location of the sound.

The rest of us immediately opened fire. A grenade was thrown from the patch of trees over our heads. It landed on the other side of the crater but rolled to the center of the crater. putting it in range of us all. It exploded, but somehow, we were all still intact.

"Keep firing!" I said.

I knew immediately that we were in the worst possible fighting position because if any more grenades were thrown at us, they would do the same thing.

I called the CP on the radio and they said, "Pull back."

What a relief to get that message. But how were we going to do that?

"Throw some grenades out in front of us to keep their heads down," I said. "As soon as they go off, we move out of the crater. We reset on the other side!"

Three of the Marines threw grenades, and we all ran in unison to the other side. This strategy worked like clockwork. No one was hit, and we were able to disengage from the contact. I was exhausted. It was now about one hundred degrees. I felt the sweat on my face and more running down my back.

We worked our way back to the lines as fast as we could. It was obvious that we returned much faster than when we went out. We approached the lines and gave the password "ghost," a reference to Halloween because it was October. We then worked our way to our platoon commander.

"Was anyone hurt?" Giesell asked.

"No, sir. We all got out in one piece," I said.

"How many were there?"

"I can't really say," I said.

The lieutenant asked if we got any kills. How many kills? From day one, they were always asking, "How many kills?" I hated when they did that. How the fuck should I know?

He said to me, "Battalion has to know how many kills and probables there were. Do you think you might have gotten one of them?"

To keep everyone happy I said, "Yes, one probable, sir. There were only eight of us, and I felt like we might be outnumbered. I knew we were in a bad position and needed to get out of there."

"Good job, Marine," he said.

I felt good to stay alive another day. The sweat was running profusely down my back. I felt like I needed to wipe it away. So, with my right hand I went under my shirt and I wiped the sweat away. When I looked at my hand, it was bright red with blood. *Fuck, I must have been hit by the grenade.* A corpsman was called.

He took one look at my back and said, "This guy needs to be medevaced. He's got shrapnel in his back."

The corpsman bandaged my back. The shrapnel was still in it, and it didn't seem to want to stop bleeding. He put a bandage all the way around my torso to keep pressure on the wound. Freeman got my pack from our foxhole and brought it to the LZ.

"I'll see you aboard the ship later," Freeman said.

"I sure hope so," I said. "Hey, Freeman, remember to keep your head down!"

"Will do," he replied.

A chopper was called from the helicopter ship, and I waited a half hour for it. The chopper landed, and C-rations were deposited on the ground, along with some other boxes. I climbed aboard and moved away from the door into the safety inside. I leaned my back against the bulkhead and felt a sharp pain. I had forgotten that I was wounded and realized I shouldn't put pressure on my back.

I didn't look out as we took off and the chopper climbed fast, exiting the area. The farther away I got from Vietnam, the better I began to feel. As the chopper approached the *Iwo Jima*, I saw the familiar white hospital ship shadowing her in the distance.

The wounds in my back started hurting for the first time. At first it was an ache, then quickly thereafter, a burning.

The chopper's blades roared as we landed, and I was met by two corpsmen who led me to a mini-operating room inside the ship. I had to take off my shirt and expose my dirty body. My arms were dark brown from the sun, and my back was totally white.

The doctor came over and cleaned the wound. The first thing he did was tell me that I was going to feel a sting from the shot to deaden the wound. I felt the sting of the needle, and then the pain was gone almost immediately. As he pulled the sharp pieces of metal out of my back, I could hear a *kerplunk* as each hit the thin, shiny chrome pan.

I asked the doc if I could have one of the pieces.

"Sure," he said, fetching one of the fragments for me.

I thumbed the flat piece of metal between my fingers and considered just how lucky I had been. My second Purple Heart. Would the next one send me home or put me in a body bag? Four and half more months seemed like a long way yet to go.

CHAPTER

ELEVEN

I WAS IN SICK bay for two days and was released back to active duty without restrictions in time for Operation Granite, which was set to attack the communist base camp called "114." The four companies that made up our battalion were going to be split up for various operations in the DMZ. Our mission was to help out Fourth Marines again. We actually never located the base camp, but we did manage to kill seventeen enemy soldiers. Unfortunately, three Marines were sent home in body bags.

I had always wondered how the enemy knew we were coming and was able to get out of the area. There had to be a leak some- where. Some of our Marines had friends in other units. These men would brag about how they had Vietnamese cleaning ladies, cooks, and barbers for practically nothing in terms of cost. As fighting men, we surmised that the VC could have infiltrated the rear area using our friends to obtain information. As often happens in war,

VC women sometimes used sex as a way to get information and pass it on to the opposition leaders.

Granite came to an end near Camp Evans.

Our new orders were to spread out and move to the northwest toward Dong Ha, searching for Charlie. We were going to check villages and suspected ambush locations along the way. For the next five days, it was the same old thing. We walked in dried rice paddies, through tree lines and, of course, checked villages the entire way. Charlie was out there all right, because we received periodic sniper fire. It was on one of those sweeps that my hypervigilance noticed movement on the ground in front of me. It appeared to be a snake heading directly for me at full speed. As it bolted for me, I noticed it was banded yellow and black and was seven feet long. Marines knew it as the "two step," because of the belief that if the snake bites you and releases its venom, you take two steps and you die.

This damn thing was five feet away when I lowered my M16, about to pull the trigger. The snake appeared to be attacking me but actually was retreating to a hole in the ground at my feet. While the danger was real, it was over in seconds. But at that moment I feared again for my life.

We arrived in Dong Ha City and reconnoitered the area to the east. Our march went all the way around the city and finally ended up in a barren piece of land alongside a red dirt road heading north. The orders were to wait for trucks that would take us to Con Thien. While waiting for the trucks, my platoon was uncommonly quiet. We had been through many arduous days of constant sweeps, and we were not looking forward to going to the DMZ again.

Bill Burgoon and I made eye contact, and Bill cracked the mischievous smile everyone knew him for. He gave me a little nod and started to mime a situation. With his right hand, he pretended to hold a piece of thread. He put the end of the make-believe thread in his mouth to wet it and then straightened out the tip. With the other hand he held up an invisible needle. Yep, he was now trying to thread the needle. He tried several times, but of course it wouldn't go through the eye. He put the end of the thread back into his mouth to tighten up the tip with more saliva. Everyone started watching as he pantomimed this struggle.

He pulled the thread through the eye and then tied a knot with the two ends. I smiled at him and nodded back as if to say, "I understand." More men started watching and wondering how it was all going to play out. Bill took the needle and stuck it in his right index finger. He squinted his eyes at me as if to say, "Boy, did that hurt!" He pushed the thread through his middle finger, then his ring finger, and finally his pinky. With a smile, he pulled the imaginary thread and all his fingers slowly closed. He loosened the thread and they spread out. He did this action five times and everyone started cracking up, which drew the attention of more men.

I, of course, didn't want to be outdone, so I got out my imaginary thread, threaded my needle with ease, and smiled at him as if to say, "I can do this better than you." I also threaded my fingers, but I had a different plan. I pretended to stick the needle all the way through the palm of my right hand to the other side. As I pulled the string, I made a fist. I then held out my arm and pretended to stick the needle and thread through my bicep. As I pulled the thread, my arm bent at the elbow to flex, showing off my big bicep muscle. As I pulled the string tighter, it flexed my muscle harder before his face. He smiled at me and nodded. More Marines ambled over to our little gig.

Bill took his thread and needle and stuck it through the palm of his hand and made a fist. He came over to me and put the string through my nose. He pulled the string and mimed punching me in the nose. About twenty guys who were all around us roared with laughter. After threading my hand to make a fist, I put the needle under his chin and pulled it out. I pulled the string and, of course, my fist hit him with an uppercut. He shook his head to recover from the artificial blow.

Bill, not to be outdone either, got his needle and created the fist once more. He stepped close to me and looked me up and down. His eyes stopped at my crotch. I shook my head in a plea for mercy. I put my hands together as if to say a prayer. He put the needle through my crotch and pulled the string. By now there was a growing chorus of chuckles from the crowd and a rising moan of sympathy for my doomed crotch. When he pretended to hit me, I bent over in a mockery of excruciating pain. Everyone exploded with laughter. We were totally out of control. That drew the attention of one of the officers and a sergeant, who came over and yelled, "Break this fight up!"

Realizing his error, he screamed some orders, "Okay ladies, saddle up! We're headed to Con Thien and the DMZ."

What a spoiler; just when we really got things going. I can say one thing: Bill and I took the edge off the platoon that day. Everyone talked about it for days.

WE WERE TRUCKED NORTHBOUND, about two miles from the DMZ. Con Thien, which means "The Hill of Angels," rests on higher ground and overlooks the entire area, especially the DMZ. This base was designed to give artillery support to the area, and it allowed us to run patrols to and around the DMZ. Con Thien also helped stop the infiltration of the NVA into the south. The previous battalion had been whittled down to half their strength from recent fighting. They needed some relief, and we were the guys who had to take their place.

It was our job to run patrols and stand watch. Night watch was extremely boring. A soldier sits for hours on end, staring into the dark and waiting for what he hopes is nothing. One can never tell what is going on at night. The enemy moved at night, and we moved during the day. One evening, while I was standing watch on the perimeter, it was so hot I had no problem staying awake. I was trying to picture what Charlie was up to out there beyond the perimeter. Was he close or was he going to probe our lines tonight?

I heard what I thought might be the sounds of rodents from the trash piles, or was it a gook? I listened carefully. What I was thinking was that I didn't want to die, so I forced myself to stay awake. As my mind wandered, I heard a faint sound of jets flying very high in the sky. I was used to standing watch and hearing the sounds of the immediate area. The jet engines were so distant I was surprised I heard them at all. It kind of reminded me of Operation Buffalo when the B-52s came in.

Without any warning, I could hear a faint whistle. It became louder than any whistle I had ever heard and closer than any B-52 strike I had ever heard. Then, *wham, wham, wham*! Huge explosions erupted, one after another, over and over and over again. The sky lit up like daylight in a strobe of explosions. I jumped in my foxhole. I couldn't believe I was so close to a B-52 strike. It was as close as anyone could ever get without dying. The entire line went on alert.

Bill Burgoon was with me and yelled, "What the hell was that?"

"It had to be a B-52 strike in the DMZ," I said.

If there were any NVA anywhere near us in the Z, they had to be dead. The massive power of those bombs was unlike anything I had ever experienced. To this day, I can't believe how accurate they were. Then again, were the bombs off course and were we lucky not to get hit?

THE NEXT DAY, THE new company commander said, "Pack 'em up. We are headed to another base."

The entire company, about two hundred and fifty of us, was sent on a forced march to another base between Con Thien and Gio Linh, which is all a part of the famous McNamara Line. The base we were going to protect was called A-3. It was another hilltop, about the same distance as Con Thien from the DMZ, yet closer to the South China Sea.

We were going to be on the high ground overlooking the DMZ. I expected the landscape at A-3 to be like that of Con Thien, but the area was totally void of all trees, grassy fields, or anything resembling normalcy. It looked like one big, long, red mud hole. The ground had been trampled down from soldiers and tracked vehicles. There were bomb craters everywhere. Put all that in a blender, throw it out there, and that's what was in front of us. Everywhere we looked was nothing but desolate land. We were relieving the men who needed a break from the action they had been through over the previous few months. They looked worn out and yet had this smile of relief on their faces as they left. Their tour at A-3 was up for now, and they were moving on to something— anything other than this.

Our platoon moved in single file north along the lines and ended up with squatters' rights, two men to each hole. The Marine who was leaving my assigned hole said, "Man, you can have this place. It sucks real bad."

"What do you mean?" I asked.

All he could say was, "You'll soon find out." He walked away, shaking his head with a snarly look on his face. Then he turned around and said it again, "You'll find out real soon."

That surely didn't seem like a good omen to me. Our battalion had previously been in this general area on two operations before: Beau Charger and Buffalo, both of which were horrible battles with hundreds killed on both sides. Nothing grew here anymore. The area had become a constant battlefield since we left the previous July.

I remarked to myself, *It couldn't get worse than this.*

Then it started raining.

Every day became worse than the day before. I felt I was in a personal hell. The monsoon had come to our part of the world. To make things worse, we were hit by North Vietnamese mortars three times a day. They hit us morning, noon, and night. Occasionally, they would target choppers coming in with supplies.

It became a game for all of us. A chopper would appear. As it approached, it hovered about six feet off the ground, and the crew would start throwing off our food and ammo in midair. The choppers would land only to pick up the wounded or for passengers coming or going. As it took off, the first set of mortars would start coming in. "Could the chopper leave the area before being hit with mortars?" was the game.

We spent almost an entire month at A-3, enduring the worst conditions imaginable. It literally rained every day for a month. For days, we were wet and shivering in the freezing cold. We would freeze as if we were in Chicago during the worst winter, because we were wet for weeks on end with no way of drying out. Using our helmets, we bailed water out of our fighting holes daily. The lightest rain would be a heavy misting; the worst would be a full downpour.

We heard that we were going to get something special on Thanksgiving Day, which was on November 23. A chopper came in with extra C-rats. It wasn't able to land because of mortars exploding in the center of the lines. The helicopter gunner kicked out the extra food from about the height of a three-story building. I watched as the cases of extra C-rations crashed to the ground and broke open. Cases of food were strewn everywhere. From the cover of my hole, I shook my head in disappointment.

Finally, after a full month, the rains stopped about as quickly as they had started.

We were told that we were no longer a part of Special Landing Force, Alpha. I believe command knew we'd had enough. We reverted back to being an ordinary battalion of Marines. I wondered if this was good or bad news. Was it going to be easier, or were we jumping from the pan into the fire? After all, First Battalion, Ninth Marines wasn't on SLF when they were wiped out in the DMZ back in July. I wondered if we were going to stay there in the DMZ or go south.

We found out we were leaving A-3. Another company of Marines came in and took it over. We ended up sweeping in an easterly direction toward the South China Sea. I wondered if we were heading for another highway to load onto trucks or walking to a base camp. Again, we never knew anything. Bill Burgoon kept me smiling, as I did him. What a great guy and such a great sense of humor. Bill and I were the best of friends.

We could see jets diving north of us in the distance, dropping bombs and napalm. Bill said to me, "Hey, Taylor, check out the jets!"

"Yeah, some poor suckers are getting hit pretty hard," I replied. "I heard that a recon unit was out there and getting hit quite a bit. They probably ran across some NVA regulars and are pounding the shit out of them."

"I hope First Battalion, Ninth Marines isn't getting hit again," he said.

We walked for hours. On the first leg of the sweep, we were on flat, hard ground with brush and bushes everywhere. There were also tree lines in every direction. We walked through a tree line and ended up in a small clearing. The ground was spotted with little discolored craters everywhere. I thought it might be from a mortar barrage. It must have been a pretty intensive onslaught, because the craters were so numerous. As I walked, looking at all the craters, there was a huge explosion somewhere to my right followed by a bloodcurdling scream.

I got down on one knee and heard several Marines yelling, "Corpsman up!"

Smoke billowed from the next tree line where the explosion had taken place. Someone to my rear yelled, "*Stop! Nobody move!*"

Everyone stopped dead in his tracks. It was Sanders who was yelling.

"Damn it! *We are in a minefield!*" he yelled.

Immediately we all looked around at our feet. Holy crap! I was terrified. I could hear more Marines screaming, "Corpsman up!" Everyone was afraid to take another step. Three guys had got it with a bouncing betty mine. One Marine was definitely dead, and the other two were badly wounded.

The platoon sergeant yelled, "Everyone back off and trace your steps backward if you can!"

There were nine of us out in front, in the middle of the mine-field. I turned only my head, surveying the ground around me and unsure of what to do. I'd never been trapped in a minefield before; hell, I didn't even know they had them there.

More than a dozen men were thirty yards behind me. The ones who were just entering the minefield backed out easily, but I would have to retrace my steps about fifty yards to get out. Some Marines were close enough to me that if any one of them set off a mine, I could easily be hit with shrapnel. I looked behind me. I could faintly see the footprints I had made. I slowly turned myself around, twisting only on a single foot. I made the maneuver, but not without almost losing my balance.

Okay, now to get my ass out of here.

I looked for traces of footprints and tried to approximate the length of my last steps. I also looked for telltale signs of what I thought a mine might look like. I knew I had to walk slowly, keep my balance, and just retrace the way I walked a few minutes ago. No wonder there were so many craters in the ground. They were detonated land mines. I couldn't tell where the minefield ended or began, but it didn't matter. I couldn't assume anything. I slowly walked step by step back to where I'd started. I could see other Marines in the tree line watching us. Just one step could be my last.

In some cases, I could not see any trace of the step I'd taken before, so I had to guess where I probably would have stepped. I looked hard for any little indication. Step by step, I slowly moved toward safety. I got closer and closer to the tree line, which looked as if it was the end of the minefield. One by one, we each moved back. I finally crossed into the tree line and looked back at the Marines who were still in the field. Freeman, who was extremely slow, froze dead in his tracks. He had come a long way since his first day the month before, when we got overrun.

"I'm going to get it. I just know it," he cried. "I'm surrounded by mines. I'm going to step on one of those bastards, I just know it."

"Don't worry, Freeman," The sergeant yelled to him. "We all just did it. You'll be okay; just follow your steps like we did."

"I lost track of my steps!" Freeman said. "I don't know where the hell to step!"

The sarge calmly said, "If I have to, I'll come out to get you, so don't worry."

"No, *no*, Sarge. Then we'll both get it if one of them goes off."

"See? You said the word 'if,'" the sarge said. "Just take a step where you think it's safe."

Everyone was frozen still and quiet, watching Freeman. I had my fists clenched in the air in front of my chin. Freeman took a deep breath and moved his foot slowly to a spot in front of him. He closed his eyes and applied pressure to his foot. To his relief, he didn't die. He took the next step and started to feel more confident. He took another step, and another, and another. Finally, he entered the safety of the tree line. Relief and embarrassment crossed his face. Freeman had survived being overrun on Medina and now a mine field.

"Right on brother," I said.

I had broken the ice, and everyone slowly started moving out to the right side and away from the area. We walked until about noon and into an area of rolling hills—more like tight, rolling hills. The valleys in between each were small, only about fifty yards across. We could see the change in plants, too. The area reminded me of far Southern Illinois, near Kentucky. I remember visiting family there and walking in the backwoods. I had hunted for small game and remembered how easily the game could hide and escape my advances. I started to become concerned.

What if we get into one of these valleys? How easy it would be to kill all of us. I would rather be on the upside shooting down, I thought, *than down below with no place to retreat.* I stayed high on the hills whenever I could.

The word came down that we were stopping for lunch. The sergeant said, "Get out your grub, find a place to rest, and make sure you dig a foxhole."

I was beat from the long sweep. I didn't see anyone digging a foxhole. Sweat poured off my brow. I had a green towel around my neck to keep the sweat from flowing into my green jungle shirt and flak jacket. There is nothing worse than getting a rash from the rubbing of wet items against the body.

I had gotten my pack off and was starting to open it when a couple of artillery shells screamed over our heads, crashing into the trees and hills east of us, about fifty yards away. I was on the ground and covering my head before the rounds hit the ground. The next few hit all around us. I thought some of the guys had to be hit for sure because none of us had dug holes. As fast as the rounds came in, it was over.

We speculated that the gooks had an artillery piece set up somewhere to the north of us on the other side of the DMZ. Then again, it might have come from our own base at Con Thien—our own artillery. I saw a small depressed area and dug a quick hole next to where I was eating. About thirty minutes later, lunch was over. No one had been injured in the barrage. We were lucky that time. The orders were given to saddle up and move out.

We kept sweeping eastbound, and we soon emerged from the hilly area. We had to have walked at least twenty miles before we set in for the night. The company of about two hundred men started to mark off the lines in a circular pattern, with the command post in the center. The sarge helped with setting up the fields of fire. I was given a hole to dig on the north side of the lines. I started digging while waiting for someone to be assigned to help.

The sarge came up with a short, stocky black kid and said, "Hey, Taylor."

"Yeah," I said.

"Meet Taylor."

"What?" I asked with a curious look.

"Bill Taylor, meet Billy Taylor," the sarge said, and walked away, laughing.

It was a big joke. All the guys within earshot were laughing. They had put the new guy with the old salt.

"My name's Billy Taylor," the new recruit said.

He seemed like a really nice kid and spoke in a shy and soft manner.

Huffman was in Machine Guns and in the foxhole right next to us. "Hey, Taylor," Huffman yelled.

"What?" both of us replied in unison.

He fell back on the ground, laughing his ass off. "I figured you both would do that," he said.

The other gunner had just lit a cigarette and was laughing so hard he dropped his shovel. He managed to grab his cigarette before it fell out of his mouth. Then he fell in the half-dug foxhole, still holding his cigarette, laughing uncontrollably.

Billy and I dug our foxhole together and broke out some C-rations. I showed him how to make a homemade stove. Once that was done, I broke out a heat tab for the food.

"So, where you from, Billy?" I asked.

"I'm from Mississippi," he said.

He was about five feet, one inch tall and very black-skinned. He seemed good-natured, and I had an immediate sense that we were going to get along well.

Billy asked, "You've been here a while, huh?"

I loved his Southern accent too. "Yeah," I said. "I've been through a lot and have only three more months to go."

I told Billy that I'd started a short-timer's calendar. He seemed interested, so I showed him. The calendar was actually an outline of a naked woman. Her outline was covered with squares and rectangles with numbers in each. Of course, the last three numbers were two circles on her chest and number one on the crotch for when my tour was over and I was going home.

"Whadaya think my chances are of makin' it out of here?" Billy asked.

"You have a long way to go, so just don't do anything stupid and don't volunteer for anything," I said. I could hear Pilgreen's words echoing in me. "You'll get killed faster than anything by volunteering."

"Thanks, I'm glad we're together. I actually feel better just talking to you," he said.

I acknowledged the same to Billy.

At dusk, the sarge came over and said, "Taylor."

We both popped our heads up.

"No, I mean Bill."

We both laughed again.

"Okay, the old salt."

"What's up, Sarge?" I asked.

"We need someone to lead one of the ambush patrols north of the lines tonight, and you're the one. You have the most experience."

"No problem, Sarge," I said. I looked over to Billy and said, "See what happens? And I didn't even volunteer."

"See you later," said Billy.

Ambushes are actually a blessing most of the time because we usually get more sleep. Regular watch is fifty percent on watch and fifty percent off, every night. When you're on an ambush, twenty percent is on watch, and eighty percent is off. It's like being able to sleep almost the entire night—that is, if Charlie doesn't mess with us.

I hadn't been on an ambush in over a month and looked forward to a good night's sleep. I started to pack up and move out to the CP. Before I left, I told Billy, "You take care now, you hear?"

"I'll see you when you get back," Billy smiled, waved.

"You bet."

I went to the command post. About twenty-five other Marines were there. Our lieutenant came over and said, "Okay! Here's how we're going to do the patrols. Wakefield, you and the others go about five hundred yards south of here. Take a look at the map. Simpson, you work your way covering our western flank. Bacon, you cover our eastern flank. Taylor, you take your men out to the north. All of you set into some good positions for an effective ambush. We know the NVA are running at night, and just maybe we can pick off a few."

It was 6:32 p.m. *Click, click.* I unlocked and loaded my M16 rifle.

"Does anyone have any questions?"

"Should we take our packs?" someone asked.

"No. We need you to be light and tight if you need to get back. Set out as soon as we finish here. Make sure you tell the lines you're leaving. The password for coming back is 'starlight.' Don't forget it! Taylor, your call sign on the radio is 'buster.'"

About ten minutes later, we were outside the lines heading north in a single file. We moved slowly, stumbling our way through high weeds to an area of trees and a path.

I said, "Perfect place for an ambush. Good place to set up!"

Cover was perfect, and there was a path at which to aim. We set in on line so we could fire in any direction. Our flanks were covered naturally with heavy foliage. As an experienced soldier, I set up the watch to maximize coverage and get us some well-deserved sleep. Each man would spend one watch for one and a half hours. My watch was in the early morning, the hardest part as well as the most dangerous. Charlie liked moving around at three or four in the morning.

Once in position, each of us settled in. No packs to worry about. Some took off their cartridge belts and flak jackets. I told everyone to set their M16s on full automatic and keep a couple of grenades handy just in case. Each man on watch had to watch the radio and listen for our call sign, buster. The radio was on low so as not to alert any gooks in the area. I listened carefully to get a feel for the surroundings, and then soon fell into a deep sleep.

I woke to the sound of a huge explosion that had gone off directly south of us. Then there were five more in quick succession. *What the hell?* Everyone was awake immediately. One more hit, and then, as quickly as it started, it ended.

The radio traffic erupted with emergency communications. Our lines had been hit with artillery. *Those fuckin' gooks,* I thought. *How did they zero in on us so perfectly?*

I asked the radioman for a report. "They're calling for medevac choppers. It sounds pretty bad! Damn!" he said.

Twenty minutes later, he said, "The CO is calling in all the ambushes."

"Okay, pack up. Let's go!" I said.

The radioman eyed me with a serious look and said, "One other thing."

"What?" I asked.

"They think it was friendly fire."

"What the fuck? Is everyone ready? Stay alert!" I said. "We don't need any more mistakes tonight."

As we approached our lines, we heard, "Halt. Who goes there?"

"It's starlight; we're the ambush coming in."

"Come up slowly," one of the Marines said.

We entered the lines in a single file and ended up grouped together by the Marine in the foxhole.

"Where is the CP?" I asked. By then, it was dark and I couldn't really tell.

He pointed straight to his rear and to the right of where we walked in.

"Anybody hurt?" I asked.

"Yeah, but I don't know any particulars."

"Okay, thanks. Let's go," I said, and we moved toward the command post.

The CP came into view after about fifty yards. I saw a few small, homemade tents, some foxholes, and a number of Marines buzzing around. Seven Marines stood and looked down, with three corpsmen bending over.

I approached the Marines and asked, "Where's the captain?"

That's when I saw what everyone was looking at. One of the Marines was talking to the medevac chopper on the radio. A wounded Marine lay on the ground, his entire face blown off. I couldn't believe what I was looking at. There was no discernible face at all. I could hear him breathing with a gurgling sound from what appeared to be where his mouth used to be. The gurgling was horrendous. He was struggling to breathe with every breath. There were two smaller holes in the center of the face where his nose used to be, and blood bubbles were coming out as he exhaled. I couldn't believe anyone could live in that condition.

"Oh my God!" I said. "Who the hell is that?"

One Marine said, flat-out without any hesitation, "That's Billy Taylor."

A rush of blood filled my face, and my heart started pounding. I put both hands to my face as tears started welling up in my eyes. I flashed back to our last words together.

"See you when you get back," he had said.

My fond farewell from Billy was never going to come true. I asked one of the Marines around us as the tears broke and ran down my face, "What happened to him?"

"The first round hit directly in front of his foxhole. He was sitting up on the topside of the hole when it hit, blowing his face completely off. He didn't see it coming!"

I had dug that foxhole, and if I hadn't been called to go out on the patrol, my life would have taken a different path. Was this just random luck? Again? I was starting to get the feeling that some sort of divine intervention was at play.

I had to walk away because I was in the way of everyone working on the young Marine. I was stunned. Overwhelmed with sadness, I fell to my knees and covered my face with my hands so no one else could see how hard I was weeping. I couldn't hold it back. The captain saw me and came over.

"Find a place to camp out in the lines," he said. "If we need you, we'll call for you."

"Captain," I said.

"Yeah."

"Was that our own artillery?"

"Yeah," and he walked away.

I dug an exceptionally deep hole that night and curled into a fetal position at the bottom.

CHAPTER

TWELVE

THE NEXT DAY, WE walked to the ocean and then headed north along the beach. It was one long walk and it took the entire day. Thankfully, there was no resistance along the march.

Our unit arrived at a newly built base called Charlie 4 (C-4). It was located on the South China Sea, about four miles south of the DMZ and about six miles north of where the First Amphibian Tractor Battalion (First Amtracs) was stationed. The base was designed and built by the Seabees, and you can bet your last dollar they built it well. The Seabees brought in long, heavy-duty timbers and bulldozers to build several bunkers. They built them strong enough to take a direct hit from North Vietnamese artillery. The monster wooden beams were set into rectangular buildings and roofs. The bulldozers moved sand over and around the newly built structures. They pushed mounds of sand around the perimeter of the lines to create a defensive wall for the Marine positions. Also added to our arsenal were two M48 Patton Medium Tanks. The bulldozers built defensive positions in strategic areas on the lines for the tanks. Not to be outdone, the Seabees also built a chow hall, latrines, and a command post bunker.

The last piece of the puzzle was that thousands of sandbags had to be filled and laid around every structure. Of course, it was our job to complete this task. We ended up on sandbag duty every single day.

Our main job was to provide security and stop the infiltration of the NVA into the south. Our company was put under the direct command of the First Amphibian Tractor Battalion, stationed at the mouth of the Cua Viet River. We were to be in control of the entire coastline all the way to the DMZ. First Amtracs had a 105 mm howitzer battery at the Cua Viet River to support us if needed, about two miles away.

When the platoon walked into the new base, we were introduced to my new squad leader, Corporal Marvin Smith. He had all the good qualities of all the other squad leaders, and I recognized he could very well be the best squad leader I would ever have. He was from Suffolk, Virginia. He was a thin, black Marine who stood five-foot-ten. He was smart and the type of man who took leadership to new heights by actually listening to our experience. Corporal Smith, or "Smitty" as we'd come to call him, didn't just give orders; he was right there with us. I liked him immediately. After all the crappy leaders I'd been through, I knew I was finally going to be proud to serve with this one. My confidence about making it out increased considerably.

It was sometime during the first week of December 1967 when we arrived at C-4 and set in the lines. Small fighting holes were already in place. All we had to do was pick our spot. With only three months left in my tour, I wondered if C-4 was going to be my last duty station. I had my short-timer's calendar and was anxious to continue using it, counting the days I had left.

The company had three full rifle platoons and a Weapons Platoon. We had two sets of mortar teams in the center of the lines within circular sandbagged pits. One pit was for the larger 81 mm mortar, and the other was for a set of 60 mm mortars. The perimeter of C-4 was such that all three platoons took turns manning the lines. Every third day, a platoon would go on an area patrol around the base. The other platoons would be working for hours filling bags full of sand and then laying them in line, covering the bunkers. Every platoon had its own bunker. Each man had a spot to sleep and store his gear.

There were latrines in various locations, and the worst duty of all was burning the shitters. Every day, someone had latrine duty. Under each toilet seat was half of a fifty-gallon drum filled with diesel fuel. The drums had to be pulled out and set on fire once a day to rid the area of the waste.

Mass was held almost every Sunday, and I acted as an altar boy for the services because I figured when I died, at least I would do so in a state of grace. We usually had about twenty or so men attend, and all were invited to receive Communion no matter what their faith was.

It took a short time to settle into our new home and then we began running patrols in the area. Halfway to the DMZ was an abandoned village. We had relocated many village people in June on Operation Beau Charger. The huts were gone, but the infrastructure of the area was still in place. The telltale signs that someone had once lived on and managed the property showed everywhere. We ran regular patrols to the abandoned village every day initially, but they were uneventful, and we never took enemy fire.

As more weeks passed, however, we started receiving sniper fire and then mortar fire from the area to the north on a daily basis.

To our west was an open area of sand that gave the appearance of a desert. There was a Buddha praying area a little north and in the middle of that barren landscape. Rolling sand dunes went from C-4 and continued north close to the DMZ. Units of NVA started to contest the area and knew they had some leverage due to their proximity to the DMZ. To our east was the South China Sea. It was a great natural barrier, but unfortunately not for recreation. The NVA were close, and no one wanted to get killed over a swim. To our south were several more vacated villages. There was a large ville approximately a mile and a half south, close to the Cua Viet River. That ville was considered to be friendly.

I had to run a patrol south of our base. The captain gave word for me to come to the CP and go over the plans for the patrol.

He said, "There has been a lot of activity with small NVA groups infiltrating from the DMZ. We don't know what's going on. See if you can get a feel for what's happening. Travel south of C-4. As you know, there shouldn't be any people in the area directly to the south of us. I want you to proceed to the large village to our south. From there, hike to the ocean. Scout along the shoreline and back to C-4. Keep in radio contact the whole way. Move along as fast as you can, but check things out and be careful. We're not really sure what's out there."

As I moved out to gather my squad, I noticed a couple of prisoners. I thought it would be interesting to check them out. I stopped to look at them and asked one of the guys interrogating them, "What's up with them, and how did we catch them?"

"They walked into one of our ambushes, just walking along without a care in the world."

The prisoners appeared to be about twenty-five years old. Judging their ages proved to be difficult. All South Vietnamese had to carry ID cards. When we checked their ID cards, they never looked like the ages stated nor did they look like their pictures. Some looked like they were young, but their IDs showed they were older, or the other way around. Both prisoners were wearing civilian clothes and their hands were tied behind their backs.

"What were they doing?" I asked.

"They said they got lost and wandered too far north. When they arrived at the ocean, they followed it south, and that's why they were caught."

"Why don't you believe them?" I asked.

"They were wearing three sets of clothes," the interrogator said. "We caught them at night wearing black pajamas. Under the pajamas were civilian clothes, and under that, NVA uniforms. Here, look."

He showed me all the different clothes that were still on the prisoners.

"What did they say about the NVA uniforms?"

"They said they found them!"

"Yeah, right. They're the enemy," I agreed.

"We're flying them out to Headquarters for interrogation. Let's see if they can get anything out of them."

I continued to our bunker, where I met the rest of my squad.

I said to the men, "We're traveling light. Bring plenty of ammo; we'll need it out in the field. If my calculations are correct, we should be back about three or four this afternoon. We have to check a ville about two miles south of the base near the coast, and hopefully home at four." I asked, "Any questions?"

Bill Burgoon asked, "What is the actual objective of the mission?"

"The CO wants some eyes out there, and then report what we find when we get back."

There were only seven of us. We never could get enough Marines to fill a squad of fifteen. Time was of the essence, and we needed to get moving.

"Is everyone ready to go right now?" I asked.

"No," was the answer by all.

"Let's meet up here in ten minutes. Get everything you need, go to the crapper, and the sooner we leave, the sooner we get back!"

About fifteen minutes later, we were ready. I set up a single-file patrol out the east gate and started south, finding paths along the way. About a quarter-mile south, we entered the first ville. I remembered clearing it back in June. It was now abandoned, strange, and devoid of farm animals. The hooches seemed to be protected by overgrown tree limbs and brush. There were no women and children around, plus there was no sign of movement from the hooches. All around were small, unattended, square fields where crops once grew. The fields hadn't been worked in a long time, and they were overgrown and neglected.

We approached the first hut. I wanted to do a complete search of the ville. As we approached the hut, a small Vietnamese man came out, very humble. He bowed with his head and his hands in a prayer position, fingers facing upward. He took me by surprise. I hadn't expected to see anyone there. What the hell was this guy doing here? The ville should have been abandoned. I wished I had brought an interpreter along.

He was rambling on and on.

"Con-cook," I said, which means ID card.

He either didn't understand me or was reluctant to give it to me. I wondered if he was just ignoring my directions.

Very forcefully I said, "Con-cook, con-cook!"

The man finally retrieved his ID. There was a picture, but it didn't even look like him.

"Check out this guy's hooch really well," I said to Foster. "Keep an eye on the perimeter, so no one sneaks up on us. I'm going to look around. Make a special effort around the fences and especially by those dilapidated empty pig pens."

I entered the hut and looked around. There was a bamboo basket turned upside down. I kicked it over and found an NVA uniform inside. Over in the corner behind a chair were black PJs. He was wearing civilian clothes. Nothing indicated that this guy was a farmer. I looked at his hands and they were smooth, certainly not the hands of a farmer.

I said to Burgoon, "Grab him and tie his hands behind his back and bring him along."

Burgoon tied his hands, and we moved along to the next hut. There was another man, and he also appeared to be older than the age on his ID. This guy didn't look anything like his ID either.

"Search his hooch too, and the surrounding area."

Sure enough, we found an NVA uniform and black PJs. Still no weapons though. Upon questioning him, he knew a little English. He said the NVA uniforms are everywhere. They needed the clothes to stay warm at night, and that is why he had the pants. He said everyone had black PJs and NVA clothes, but I never saw NVA uniforms lying around on my patrols before.

"Tie his hands and bring him along," I said, not buying the story, and I told Burgoon to watch him closely.

We went on to the next hooch. Another guy came out. There were still no women or kids. I checked his ID. He did look like his

ID, but his birth date gave him the age of forty-nine. He didn't look a day over thirty.

"Anybody find any PJs or uniforms?"

"No," they said.

Just then, the captain's radioman called us. The captain wanted to know where we were. I told him I had two prisoners and I was still in the first village. The captain was agitated.

"Why aren't you farther than that ville just south of us?"

I told him, "Things just don't look and feel right here, sir."

"Fine. Just get your asses on down to that big ville and get back here. I want a report!"

I looked at the third guy, trying to figure out what to do with him. Yeah, I wanted to take this third guy, but I already had two prisoners. There were only seven of us, and we still had a long trip ahead. One more prisoner would have been difficult to maneuver, to say the least. I decided to let this one go because we needed to get moving. After all, we didn't find any NVA uniforms, and his ID seemed to check out. There were other hooches I wanted to check, but I had to follow orders. I felt rushed and uncomfortable about leaving. All of us moved straight south. Rushed by the captain, we walked in the open and spread out instead of using the tree line for cover.

The prisoners, with their hands tied behind their backs, slowed us down.

"Move them along," I told the guys. "Keep spread out."

Three hundred yards to the right and left were tree lines. We walked directly between them. It was the most direct and fastest route to the next village. Sniper fire erupted from the tree line to our right. We all got down. Some of the guys opened fire on the tree line.

"Hold your fire! Anyone know where the fire is coming from?" I looked around. "Anyone hit?"

"No," Burgoon said. "They're all shit shots, whoever they are!"

"We can't go in the open anymore," I said. "We have to work our way to the tree line to our left."

The sniper stopped firing.

"Okay, you two guys with the prisoners move out about sixty yards and stop. We'll cover you the entire way. Then you cover us and we'll go about a hundred yards, sit down and cover you, leapfrogging to the other tree line."

I figured the farther away from the snipers, the better. We did the maneuver and it worked perfectly. We got into the tree line and used it for cover all the way to the big village. I thought, *God that was too easy. We sure were lucky.*

About 1:00 p.m., we entered the farthest village. I saw about fifty villagers, mostly men. We walked directly to the center of the ville. I thought to myself, *Shit! Why the hell are we fighting this war and all these able-bodied men are here, living out their lives while we are fighting for their country?*

A delegation of four older Vietnamese men came over to us, very friendly and bowing all the time. One spoke pretty good English. He sat with me and asked if we needed anything.

"Can we eat right here in the safety of your village?" I asked.

"Oh yes," he said, bowing his head. He asked who the men were that we captured.

"They are our prisoners. I didn't like their ID cards and they were in a restricted area," I said.

The ville was bustling with activity. The English-speaking Vietnamese elder asked where I was from and thanked me over and over for fighting for his country. He bowed his head many times. I asked him for water. He had one of the other men take our canteens and fill them up. The head villager offered to take the prisoners off our hands. He took his right hand and motioned his index finger straight across his throat as if to say, "We'll kill them for you."

I shook my head no.

He insisted, "NVA number ten," and motioned again indicating that he would kill them.

"No," I said. "Don't worry about it."

I radioed our progress to the captain. The captain wasn't there, but the radioman would give the message to him. We finished our lunch, packed up our weapons and prisoners, and then began our way back, using the shoreline. Anderson led us out of the ville, and none of us looked back.

We headed northeast until we saw the South China Sea. It was an hour and a half from the village, and we came across a blown-up French Catholic church. No one was around. It was really hot, and one of the guys asked to take a quick break.

"Sure," I said, "I'll call in our position and give a sit-rep."

My curiosity got to me. I walked over to the bombed-out church. There was a partial roof. The front door was gone, but all the sides were still intact and there were some French words on the walls. I knew the French had taken Vietnam as a colony and the missionaries had built churches throughout the countryside. Since the French were kicked out at the battle of Dien Bien Phu in 1954, the missionaries had been either kicked out or killed. I wondered what had happened here. I found a bench and rail, and knelt to pray. My prayers were for everyone. For the Marines, the people of Vietnam, the missionaries, and especially for my safety in hopes my tour would be over and I could go home to my family.

We were going to be a little late getting back, but at least we were safe again this time.

We still had a little farther to go, and all were truly tired. At the end of the hump, we entered C-4 through the same gate we left from. The guys and I walked over to the CP bunker.

"I have two prisoners, sir. I'm not sure if they are the NVA or Cong."

"Okay," the captain said. "Leave the prisoners with the guards at the entrance."

"Do you want my report?" I asked.

"Yeah, sure! Go ahead," he said.

The captain seemed to be preoccupied with maps, radio chatter, reports, and other officers talking all around. One clerk was typing something on an old typewriter. I commenced to tell the captain about the ville just south of us. I tried to tell him about my concerns, the sniper, and the ville with all the people, but he was distracted.

"Yeah, yeah, anything else?" he asked. "Did you see any NVA?"

"Well, I ..."

The captain got interrupted again. He turned away, talked a minute, looked at a map, and noticed me out of the corner of his eye still standing there.

"Was there anything else?" he asked.

I asked, "What about the prisoners?"

"We'll take them off your hands and fly them to Da Nang to be interrogated," he said.

The captain turned away, and I took that to mean it was the end of the patrol. I felt bad about the prisoners. Why couldn't we interrogate them here, and if they were okay, just let them go? I wondered if they would be beaten. *How are those prisoners going to get back home if they are released in Da Nang?* It felt so unrewarding and so incomplete and confusing. Was I bringing more misery to the people here? I'd seen so much misery since I got to Vietnam. I walked out and returned to the bunker for a rest before going to the lines for night watch. No sleep again that night.

I HAD ARRIVED IN SOUTHEAST Asia at the beginning of February 1967. My first R&R was in December 1967. I had been in combat situations for eleven months straight before I was able to take my first R&R. I was handed my orders, and they read, "You will be boarding a plane in Da Nang and then fly on to Cam Ranh Bay, Vietnam. From Cam Ranh Bay, you will then board a TWA airliner to Bangkok, Thailand for five days." After five days of R&R, I was to come back the same way.

I spent five days in Bangkok, Thailand. It was over in the blink of an eye. I returned to Vietnam via a four-engine prop plane, flying over Cambodia back to Cam Ranh Bay Airfield. I sat by a window looking out. The wing was forward from where I was sitting, and I had a good view of Cambodia. How scary to think that the land below was more dangerous or worse than Vietnam.

Halfway over Cambodia, I heard a big bang from the outboard engine on my side of the plane. Oil gushed on the wing and flames erupted from the engine. I witnessed the entire episode unfold before my very eyes. Great, I made it through eleven months in Vietnam just to die in a plane crash in Cambodia. There must have been some kind of fire suppression system in the engine, because white foam sprayed over the fire, putting it out. The propeller was dead, except for a slow spin created by the wind blowing against it.

The pilot got on the PA system and said not to worry—they had everything under control, and the plane could fly on two propellers if it had to. We were assured there wasn't any kind of problem. As we glided in for a landing at Cam Ranh Bay in South Vietnam, I could see we were coming in from the east and over the South China Sea. I could see the waves of the ocean getting closer as we descended. Finally, the runway was in view. Several vehicles were standing along the edge of the runway: huge fire trucks, ambulances, and all kinds of emergency vehicles. They followed us down the entire runway until we stopped. Slowly, the plane taxied to the terminal. A crew brought the movable stairs, and we deplaned. All the emergency vehicles were on the other side of the plane, and I realized I had just dodged another bullet.

I made my way to the inside of Cam Ranh Bay Airport—not a large airport by any means, just a two-story building that housed the arrival and departure of mostly military people. There were a few civilians, and I thought they might be contractors. I caught a plane for Da Nang, where I was to catch a helicopter to the Cua Viet River before taking an amtrac back to my base near the DMZ.

When I arrived in Da Nang, I looked around to catch my bearings. I overheard someone saying something about the fact that Bob Hope was coming the next day to entertain the troops. I realized that the only ones who would be lucky enough to see Bob Hope would be the guys in the rear. It takes ten logistical and support personnel to support one combat soldier in the field. All the area infantry units would be in the surrounding hills and fields protecting the Bob Hope Troupe and soldiers.

Then a great idea hit me. I would just catch a chopper the next day, after the show. Why shouldn't I go see Bob Hope? Given the distance between Cam Ranh Bay and C-4, I was pretty confident that nobody would know any better. So I left the airport en route to where the show was being held. The showing area was huge. The seats were in place and slowly graded up a hill.

Looking around, I saw a chow hall and next to it, a big, beautiful USO building. I couldn't believe how well the soldiers in the rear lived. I went inside, where they served good old American food. There were places to sit comfortably and write letters or just stretch out. I saw a bin loaded with letters from the folks back home who had written to random servicemen. Any serviceman could take whatever he wanted. In another corner was a bunch of Christmas decorations and small Christmas trees. I figured after the show I could return here and pick through the Christmas stuff and bring it to C-4 and the DMZ. I would make sure the guys in Second Platoon had the most. The thought of actually bringing Christmas to my platoon made me happy.

I ended up staying at the USO until it closed and then I wondered where I would sleep for the evening. I decided to go where the show was going to be and placed myself on the first seat, front row. I slept there all night long, and no one bothered me. Early in the morning, people started to gather to take advantage of the best seats. Soldiers sat next to me and crowded me like crazy, but I wasn't moving an inch. A couple of them told me to move over and, of course, I just shook my head with a cocky look. No one was going to get me to move from that seat.

Hundreds of soldiers filled in all around me and all the way back up as far as I could see. To my front, there was an area roped off for special seats. I figured all the officers would get the best seats in the house. I was wrong. They started bringing in wounded and sick soldiers and placing them there. About an hour before the show, it was a packed house. Hundreds of people were talking, and there were all kinds of noises everywhere, especially backstage.

About then, a bunch of MPs started roping off the section where I was sitting. They took the rope up ten rows behind me and across the entire bench where as many as twenty-five men could sit. The MPs told everyone to get up and move. The groaning started. It wasn't fair. All the good seats were taken, and we would have to move all the way to the back.

The MPs said, "Tough fucking luck. Now get the fuck outta here."

They pushed everyone out, but I just ignored the order. Finally, one of the MPs came over and said, "Get the fuck out of here."

I shook my head and said, "I'm not moving. Who is this area being roped off for?"

The MP smiled and said, "Officers-only area."

"Why the hell didn't they rope this area off before everyone sat down?" I asked.

"Officers don't have to give a shit. When they tell us to rope off an area, we do it," he said.

I shook my head and said, "I'm not moving."

"We'll just see about that," he said.

He went over and talked to some boot lieutenant. This squared-away Army lieutenant walked over and read me the riot act.

I said with a look that could kill, "I'm not moving. I slept here all night so I would have a seat, and I'm not moving."

It was getting close to showtime, and finally a colonel walked up. "What's going on here?" he asked.

"Sir, he refuses to follow a direct order to move," one of the MPs said.

The two MPs grabbed both my arms. I was holding my M16 and getting ready to fight both of them.

"What's your problem, Marine?" the colonel asked.

I said, "Sir, respectfully, it's not fair. I've been fighting with Charlie Company 1/3 for eleven months straight and wounded twice. I happen to be in Da Nang on travel orders to go back up to the DMZ after the show. Every one of these soldiers are rear soldiers. I may be the only combat soldier here besides the wounded. I slept on this seat all night, and I plan to defend it with my life."

"Son, this is one battle you can't win," the colonel said. "I'll tell you what, soldier, how about if I move you to where the rope ends right behind you. You can sit in the first seat, but eleven rows back. I'll make everyone in that row move over for you."

Wow! Talk about dodging a bullet. I smiled and said, "Yes, sir! That would be perfect!"

I moved, and everyone had to move over for me.

I watched Bob Hope, Barbara McNair, Miss World, and the beautiful Ann Margret. We went crazy for Ann Margret! God was she sexy. What a great show it was.

When the show came to an end, the entertaining guests and troops sang "Silent Night." Thoughts of home entered everyone's mind and how wonderful it would be with family. There wasn't a dry eye in sight. Tears were streaming down my face.

Finally, the show closed, and the men dispersed in every direction. I went directly to the USO club, where I picked up letters to servicemen, a Christmas tree, and a plastic bag full of decorations. It was quite a load, to say the least.

I made it to the Cua Viet River by helicopter and then caught an amtrac to C-4. I couldn't wait to see all the guys and tell them the stories of my adventures in Bangkok, of the beautiful women I met there, of the USO show, and about Ann Margret.

All the guys were standing just outside the bunker when I arrived. As I approached, they seemed eerily silent.

"Look what I brought!" I said excitedly.

I held the small Christmas tree, bulbs, and tinsel in both my arms and stood there expecting a better greeting than I got.

"What's wrong?" I asked.

Bill Burgoon looked at me and said, "Smitty's dead."

I dropped everything I was holding.

"What happened?"

"Our squad was sent on a patrol by the new lieutenant and sergeant. We were told to go west by that Buddha altar and then sweep north in the sand past the washout toward the DMZ. Charlie was waiting for us. We got within sixty-five yards of the tree line and that's when they opened fire. Everyone hit the ground and no one was injured at that point, but they had us seriously pinned down."

Visions of Operation Cochise and the tree line flashed through my mind.

"Smitty had a forward observer with him who called in an air strike. Weapons had two machine gun teams with them for support. Guns were laying down a good suppressing fire to Charlie's left flank. Smitty lifted his head one too many times and got shot in the neck. We couldn't stop the bleeding, and he bled to death right in front of our eyes. The F-4 Phantoms were making their approach. They weren't the usual Marine Corps jets going east to west. These were Air Force jets and were making a north-to-south run. This put them on a path for the gooks but on us also if they released the napalm too late. One of the Phantoms released its canisters of napalm a little too late, and they landed near the machine gunners, one of which was Ben Westerman, and some of the guys in our squad. They were all hit with napalm. They were screaming in pain. They all lived, but some of them got burned up pretty bad. The corpsman patched them up as best he could. We fell back here to C-4, and they took Smitty and some of the wounded out on choppers."

I was stunned and in disbelief. I had been away from the unit for only nine days, and Smitty was gone. Best squad leader I ever had. I wondered why the new platoon sergeant, Staff Sergeant McCarthy, hadn't been out there with them.

Had my R&R not been deferred for so long, I would have been in that battle. Having dodged the bullet yet again, I was tempted to believe that the good Lord had my back, but the DMZ was only a short distance away and there's a reason some grunts called it the "Dead Marine Zone."

LIKE CHESS PIECES ON a board, the NVA had been successfully infiltrating to the south by walking along the ocean. C-4 was built to stop that infiltration, so it became the goal of the NVA to get rid of our base at C-4.

It was our duty to sweep north toward the DMZ. We would rotate one of three platoons to sweep along the coast. The sweeps were uneventful at first, but the NVA set up snipers on the north side of a washout that we called Little Ocean View. It was a natural obstacle, devoid of any growth. Monsoon rains washed everything out to the sea through this opening. On both the south and north sides of the washout were thick brush where enemy could easily conceal themselves.

The NVA snipers' mission was to stop us, and they did. After a week of sniping, they also started to mortar us at the washout every day. We, in turn, would mortar them back. It became a daily stalemate. Every day, we had to march up that beach to Little Ocean View knowing they'd confront us there with mortars. We would hear the *bloop* sound in the distance, and then I would take cover in the same spot. It was insanity—repeating this combat daily. Nobody on our side had gotten hurt yet, but we couldn't seem to put an end to it.

On January 10, 1968, I dove into my usual sand depression for cover, just like I had done a few times before. The mortar tubes sent their projectiles toward us. About twenty rounds landed seventy yards south of us and stopped. I knew the NVA were adjusting their fire and another volley would be coming soon. I heard the *bloop* and in my mind's eye, I imagined the actual mortar shell that came out of the tube and pictured it clearly, heading directly for my head and blowing me to a million pieces. Mortar rounds were now hitting all around me, and I began screaming and crying to God right there in my hole.

"Please Lord, save me. Don't let me die! I promise I will go to church every Sunday for the rest of my life. Please, please Lord, save me!"

The mortars stopped immediately.

Some people might say that I was saved at that very moment. I had never been totally sure there was a God until then. My life had changed forever.

CHAPTER

THIRTEEN

IT WAS ABOUT 4 P.M., and none of the guys from my platoon were standing perimeter watch. We had eaten lunch a couple of hours earlier at the bunker chow hall named after Smitty. A newly posted sign at the entrance of the bunker read, "THIS MESS HALL IS DEDICATED TO THE MEMORY OF CORP MARVIN SMITH, CO. C, 1ST BN, 3RD MARINES."

The word was that our platoon commander, Lieutenant Rogers, wanted to talk to the platoon. I hoped we weren't being called for another work detail of sandbag duty. It wasn't our turn to go out on the daily patrols until the next day.

I didn't know half the men in the platoon. I had given up trying to remember their names at that point. It seemed as soon as I got to know someone, he would be ripped away. Our lieutenant had been with us for only thirty days at C-4, and this was his first command as a platoon commander. Captain Osgood was our new company CO, and Captain Dockendorff was the XO under him. Captain

Osgood was young for an officer and looked more like a movie star—thin and muscular, with a five o'clock shadow on his face.

He gathered us to the side of the bunker, near the entrance. One by one, the platoon members showed up. The new guys arrived with flak jackets and M16s, ready to go. I showed up in my worn, faded utilities, as did some of the other salts. Some of the new guys sat on the edge of the huge sandbag bunker that was at least twenty-five feet high. Another bunch stood by the entranceway. Others sat or stood on the sand in front of the bunker.

Our new platoon sergeant, Staff Sergeant McCarthy, who had been transferred in from another outfit, stood next to Captain Osgood. McCarthy was somewhat of a hard ass. I wondered if there was a reason why certain people needed to act that way in Nam. My thought was that they must be overcompensating for some weakness they had.

It had been hot, and the noon heat was beginning to dissipate.

"Well, men," Captain Osgood said, "Your new platoon commander, Lieutenant Rogers, and platoon sergeant, Staff Sergeant McCarthy, will be leading you on a night patrol up close to the DMZ. I'll be in radio contact with your platoon commander at all times. You men know that there's been a lot of infiltration from the North Vietnamese lately, coming down from the DMZ. The area north of us has been unstable, and we're not sure what's going on. One prisoner, captured the other day, admitted that he was an advanced scout for a North Vietnamese regiment sent down from the north to recon our area. As you are aware, our company has been getting hit daily on our sweeps moving north toward the DMZ. It seems as if the NVA are building up to something. When we hit them back, they retreat back north and over the DMZ and we fall back to C-4. It's going to be Second Platoon's job to set up a platoon-sized night ambush and catch them before they set up. We're going to catch them in the open as they come down from the DMZ."

I sure hope they know what the hell they are doing, I thought to myself.

I felt sick to my stomach. Staff Sergeant McCarthy was new to us and untested. Captain Osgood used to be a platoon commander. He had recently been promoted to captain and company commander. On top of it, rumors were circulating that our new staff sergeant, McCarthy, had been kicked out of some other unit and they sent him here to redeem himself. *Here we go again.*

Staff Sergeant McCarthy was too wild and crazy with us, like with what happened on Christmas Day when Smitty was killed.

As I was thinking in a world of my own, Captain Osgood began talking and said in a loud voice, "Taylor will be the point man for this movement." I snapped back to reality. "We're going to set up three different squad ambushes. Lieutenant Rogers will set them up once you are out there. If you want to stay alive, follow and listen to Taylor." He pointed to me. "He's been here longer than anyone in the platoon."

As a matter of fact, I was the only man left from the training in Okinawa, from Second Platoon. I was a little embarrassed to be singled out that way, but it also felt good to finally get acknowledged after all my months in country.

"Second Squad, Taylor's squad, will be the first to move out, followed by Sergeant Hill with Third Squad, and then First Squad. Machine guns and rockets will be trailing at the end. Are there any questions?"

"Sir, we've been getting hit every time we sweep north toward the 'Z at Little Ocean View. Is it possible they could be waiting for us on this night patrol?" Weaver asked.

"Not likely. We know the gooks retreat to the shelter of the 'Z after we hit them. We think they are coming back at dawn, and that is when we expect you to hit them. Staff Sergeant McCarthy and Lieutenant Rogers will be taking you out and, as I said before, we'll be in radio contact with them. Niederberger, you will be the radioman for Staff Sergeant McCarthy, and Weaver, you will be radioman for Lieutenant Rogers."

"Sir, I have a question," Niederberger said. "As long as I have been here, we've never gone out and set up such a large night ambush after dark."

"I know," the captain said. "This will be the first time, but it's important we set up the ambushes and catch them red-handed before their snipers, mortars, and machine guns are set up. We'll move out just as it starts to get dark. It won't be a good idea to take a lot of heavy gear. Load up with ammo and one day's food. Make sure you eat dinner because it's going to be a long night out there."

Everyone got up and headed in different directions. I just sat there and thought, *How are we going to do this?* I had swept in platoon and company movements during the daylight hours. I had set up ambushes after dark. We never had sent an entire platoon on a nighttime patrol, let alone set up a platoon-sized ambush after dark. I wondered how this new gung ho sergeant and new lieutenant were going to pull it off. I didn't have a lot of confidence in them or their plan.

The bad stuff was supposed to be behind me because we were no longer on the SLF. It appears this was wishful thinking on my part. I thought to myself, *This is going to be a scary night from the start. Oh my God, I'm such a short-timer too.* It felt as if I had gone through all these months of hell just to be killed at the end. I knew it was true that I was the best one to lead the platoon, but I hated it all the same.

Closer to dusk, everyone gathered at Second Platoon's bunker where we had had the meeting earlier. Both my canteens were full. I made sure I had plenty of M16 ammo. I always carried extra hand grenades, but this time I limited myself to ten. I carried a light pack on my back with extra ammo and enough food to last an entire day. After all, the NVA might not be there at all . . . but I knew that was probably a hope and a prayer.

The sergeant told me to move out. Niederberger followed just behind him with the radio. Staff Sergeant McCarthy instructed me to go to Little Ocean View a half mile away, where we would wait for a few hours of darkness to pass. We would cross it later in the evening.

I headed for the C-4 gate with McCarthy and the rest of the platoon filing behind me. It was starting to get dark. The gate faced east toward the ocean, where it allowed the amtracs a direct way into the base. The gate was just wide enough for tanks or amtracs to get through. Barbed wire wrapped around both sides and was secured heavily to poles in the ground.

As we went through the gate, I noticed the sky was clear and the moon was out and almost full—great for seeing where we were going but also easy for the gooks to see us. The white sand was everywhere. Bushes and trees seemed to be abundant. It was my job to slowly move through the maze of underbrush, trees, and small hedges toward Little Ocean View and the DMZ. The trees resembled thin spruces. Many looked malnourished. They were definitely not beaming with life, but large enough to obscure our view of the ocean.

The sand made it difficult to walk to Little Ocean View. The landscape had mounded-like hills within the tree line but was flat against the beach. The overgrown, deserted rice paddies that were about one hundred yards from the shore gave little cover. I didn't want to get caught in those open areas for sure.

There were about forty of us in a long line, everyone closely following each other. Each squad would have about twelve to fourteen men. Everyone was keeping to his training and walking quietly and cautiously. I felt pretty confident we would make it to Little Ocean View without a problem because, in the past, we had never caught hell until we were at or just over Little Ocean View.

After moving for quite a while, I knew we were getting close to our first objective, but I had become a little disoriented with the darkened surroundings. I started moving more slowly and watchfully as we proceeded. I could see in the sergeant's face that he was irritated at me because I wasn't following his time line.

"Why the hell are you so fucking slow?"

"I'm just being cautious," I said.

"Well, move it!"

I'm not walking down the street somewhere in the States, I thought. His lack of seriousness about our movement proved to me that I was again in a dangerous situation. We had just started the ambush movement, and he must have been nervous as hell. The farther away we got from C-4, the harder it would be for us to get help. There was no way I was going to lead us into an ambush.

About an hour into the night march, we came up to Little Ocean View. Now I knew exactly where we were and how far we had come. It wasn't far from where snipers would usually start shooting on our daily sweeps.

Staff Sergeant McCarthy said, "Hold here for a while, and we'll move across a little later."

He got on the radio with the new lieutenant at the end of the column, and filled him in on our progress. The word was passed down the line to set in until two or three in the morning and stay alert for any movement.

One of the new guys took out a smoke and started to light it up, and I rushed over to stop him.

"Are you fucking crazy? You're going to have to wait until we find a place to sit and get under your poncho. Then and only then do you smoke."

Where the hell are these new guys coming from? I thought.

I looked across the long washout and began to realize there was danger in this move. I said to the sergeant, "All of us will be in the open with no cover when crossing the washout. I know the moon will be setting, but we'll all be in the open. They could still be in positions over on the other side."

The sergeant said to me, "This is where I intend to cross, and that is exactly what we are going to do later tonight."

"That's just too dangerous," I said.

"I'm not going to argue with you," he said as he turned away and moved back in the formation.

I looked across what seemed to be a long abyss. The washout was wider away from the ocean to our left than to our right. I pondered on what to do as I looked across the open area. I came up with a perfect solution for me to feel better about the move.

Later, the sergeant came back and said, "It's time to move out."

"Sarge, let me do a quick recon across that opening," I said. "I'll crawl over to the other side and check it out. If there is no one there, we have nothing to worry about. One person may not be seen crossing the opening. If I prove it's safe, then we can all move out somewhat confident that we won't get hit. What's worse, me taking a few minutes to check out the other side or getting ambushed here in the open and getting guys killed? The safe thing would be for me to check it out first."

The sergeant thought for a second and said, "Okay. Hurry! It's already getting late, and we're supposed to move out. The CO's on my ass to move out as it is. I'll get on the radio and let the lieutenant know what's going on."

I left my pack and cartridge belt with Burgoon and started to move across Little Ocean View. Slowly, I crawled forward for about ten to twenty yards and stopped. I worked my way, crawling up farther in the open space of the washout. I figured it was about sixty yards across, but it felt like a hundred miles. I knew I could be seen, but the moon was starting to set. I was hoping I could go fast and stay low, stopping periodically so I wouldn't become obvious to anyone on the other side. Once I made it to the halfway point, in the middle of the washout, I knew the remaining thirty yards would be critical, but I also felt that I could make it. It was better than having the whole platoon caught in the middle of the opening, including me.

Slowly, I moved, then stopped and listened. I didn't hear a thing, so I crawled like an alligator with my head down, getting as close to the ground as possible. I couldn't help but get sand all over my M16. I tried to keep it out of the sand, but that was impossible.

I stopped to listen again. I still didn't hear anything, so I moved again very fast and then stopped as suddenly as I started. Sand was in every crevice of my uniform, but the adrenaline was so high I ignored it. I was close to the other side now. I listened closely again and didn't hear anything.

I moved ever so slowly to the edge of the other side of the washout. There was a six-foot embankment of slanting sand to the top, where brush and a tree line stretched the entire length.

Again, I listened very closely, and this time I heard someone laughing.

Fuck! No one laughs by himself. What the hell?

I tried to determine how many there were and how they might be set up. Then I heard three, maybe four, voices.

Now what do I do? Attack them?

I couldn't throw grenades because I hadn't brought any. Attack them with my M16? I still had to make it back to the platoon. If I did something, I wondered if it would compromise the mission.

What should I do? God, what were you thinking, Taylor?

There were a lot of people talking low and laughing. I knew I couldn't stay there. The sergeant was going to be wondering what the hell was going on. I decided the best idea would be to pull back and call in artillery from the Cua Viet River or mortars from C-4.

So many things could go wrong if I acted independently. *Definitely, go back and notify the sergeant.* I pushed myself away from the edge. I realized they were not aware of my presence because they were still talking and laughing. I scurried back across the washout as fast as a lizard running for cover over the sand. I started to tell the sergeant what I discovered, but he chewed my ass out about taking as long as I did.

"We have to get moving right now," he said.

"*No fucking way*! The gooks are already here!"

I pointed across the way.

"They're set in the tree line," I said. "We need to call in mortars or artillery to knock them out."

"Artillery! What the fuck are you talking about?"

"Sarge," I said. "We need to do this. Call back to C-4 and get us some support!"

The sergeant looked like he didn't know what to do, or maybe he didn't know how to call in a strike. I could see the indecision on his face. I felt he was being pressured to set the ambush, but the gooks were already there waiting for us.

The sergeant argued with someone on the radio. He came over to me and said to get down. "First amtrac at the Cua Viet is going to hit them with arty from the river base."

I was so happy to hear that we were going to do the right thing. We waited and waited to hear the artillery coming. It seemed like about thirty minutes later when we heard the first whizzing of a large projectile going over our heads. *Great*, I thought. *Finally, they're listening to me.*

The first round went so far over the spot where I heard the gooks it wouldn't even have woken them if they were sleeping. It took a while for the sound of the explosion to come back to us. The next two rounds were in the exact same spot.

"They only sent three rounds, and they totally missed!" I said. "We need to adjust the fire. They weren't anywhere near where I spotted the gooks."

The sergeant looked at me with hatred in his eyes.

"Get moving across that washout," he said.

"No fucking way!" I said. "You want to kill everyone, you lead them across!"

He said, "You are going forward, and we're going to set up the ambush. We're behind schedule, and we have to get moving."

"If we cross here, we're all dead," I said. "I think if you want to set up the ambush, we need to move east toward the ocean where the washout narrows. The ocean will be about forty yards across to our right flank. The only other thing to worry about is in front of us and to our left flank."

"Okay! Just move out," Staff Sergeant McCarthy demanded. "We need to get this outfit moving and cross Little Ocean View now."

I learned later that the lieutenant had decided to move First Squad with one machine gun team straight west. This was contrary to what we had planned in our platoon meeting. He moved parallel to Little Ocean View, near the Buddha altar in the sand dunes and away from the washout. The lieutenant was then nowhere near our objective. He didn't even cross Little Ocean View at all. Apparently, the lieutenant thought he could monitor the night patrol from the safety of the island tree line and stay away from the gooks I'd discovered.

Jimmy Hawkins, in machine guns, went with the lieutenant. As they traveled out, Jimmy saw that his gunner, an FNG, was scared shitless, so when they set in at the tree line near the Buddha altar in the sand dunes, he tried to calm the FNG's nerves. He opened a can of C-ration fruit cocktail, which was a prime pick among C-rats, and offered some to the new guy.

Jimmy grabbed his poncho, and pulled it up over his shoulders as the new gunner took a few bites of the fruit cocktail.

"You want a smoke?" he asked and the boy nodded.

Jimmy took the can and spoon from him, set them aside, and motioned for him to come closer.

"Come here," he said. "Let me show you how we do it here in Nam."

Under the poncho, in the glow of his flame, he was pleased to see the kid's nerves had settled, at least a bit.

I LED TWO SQUADS in a single column east toward the ocean, one man behind the other, along the washout. I finally reached the spot that was best to cross Little Ocean View's narrow passage. There was a cool, thick mist heading inland, which would be to our advantage as we crossed the narrow opening by the ocean. There weren't dunes where we crossed. One by one, we crossed the washout as the sound of the ocean waves splashed ashore, covering the sounds of our movement. Once across, there was a small dune to our right rolling in the direction I was moving. To my left the rolling dunes continued throughout the area. It seemed I was on a path between the dunes.

The wet mist continued to blow in as thick as a cloud, and we were soaked. The moon had set, and I walked slowly, regardless of what the sergeant said. It was 4:30 a.m., and I knew for a fact the gooks were there! The men behind me were close to each other. The mist was so thick and it was so dark that some of the men were holding onto the man in front of them so as to not get lost. Machine Guns still followed in the rear. Our Marine training was at its height, because no one made a sound as we walked.

It seemed like I saw a gook in every crevice I came to. I saw a depression, and thought that would be a good place for a gook to hide. I'd check it. Good. Nothing there. I saw a piece of plastic lying against a sand dune and thought a gook could be under it, sheltering from the mist. Nope. The plastic was just lying randomly on the ground. *Why were they at the washout and not here?* I kept asking myself.

The sergeant became very agitated at me, the farther we went. I couldn't care less and knew to be more cautious. I was following a narrow path. We were passing a rice paddy to our left but, then again, it looked like it could be a cemetery. *How appropriate*, I thought. I could hear the ocean waves, but the dune blocked the view.

We finally got to a spot where our platoon's Third Squad was going to set in with Machine Guns. Sergeant McCarthy called the lieutenant to let him know. McCarthy seemed to get even more agitated as he talked to the lieutenant. Everyone in Third Squad took positions quietly.

Now only my squad was left. We continued to our ambush site even farther north and west. Third Squad stayed in place and continued setting in while our last gun team and the rest of the men spread out.

McCarthy said to me, "Move out."

Fuck it, I thought, trying to get my mind to realize where my squad should set in.

About this time, back near the sandy flats and by the Buddha altar, Lieutenant Rogers was still with First Squad. He looked with his starlight scope and saw about a hundred NVA walking on the edge of the tree line directly opposite of the area I was in. The gooks were heading toward Little Ocean View. He decided his squad of only fourteen men should attack the NVA. Jimmy Hawkins, an experienced machine gunner, tried to stop him.

"Sir, we can't do this," he told the lieutenant. "It's crazy. They have the cover, and we'll be in the open. There's no moon. We can't see a damn thing. We don't know where anybody is. It's a death wish for all of us!"

Maybe Lieutenant Rogers wanted to prove himself and go for glory or maybe Captain Osgood had told him to attack, but luckily, he finally agreed with Hawkins and decided against it.

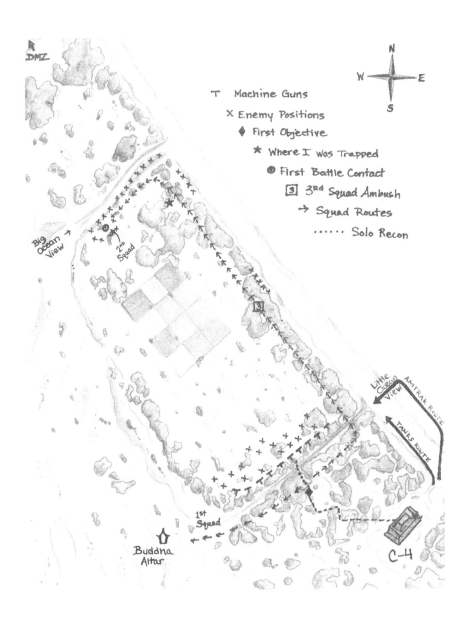

I WAS MOVING TO our ambush site. It was about five in the morning and dark as hell. I noticed that Staff Sergeant McCarthy wasn't saying anything anymore and guessed he'd finally realized the seriousness of our situation. The alarm was ringing with fury inside my head. What was driving me was pure adrenaline and caution more than anything else. All my training instincts were in place.

I finally moved to a point where the northern path toward the DMZ ended. There was a huge sand dune in front of us, twelve feet tall. I had to go left and move away from the ocean, or right toward the ocean. Toward the ocean wouldn't be the best place to set up the ambush. That was when I looked down at the path I would have to take. On the ground in front of me, I spotted an obvious sign that we were in big trouble. My heart started pounding hard and I got down on one knee.

"What's holding you up, Taylor?" McCarthy snapped.

I pointed to the ground.

"Look!"

"At what?"

"The sand is pure white."

"Yeah, so what?"

How was I going to explain that when I graduated from high school, I had moved into an apartment by the beach? We would go down to the beach at 4 a.m. and walk to the shoreline of Lake Michigan. As we walked on the beach, we could see a trail of pure white, dry sand footprints against the wet sand. I explained to the sergeant that the white sand was the tracks of the NVA, but he couldn't see it.

"All night long, the air has had a mist and moisture," I said. "The moisture settled on the sand, turning the top layer dark. This path is two feet wide—pure white sand, not dark brown. This means a whole shit load of gooks just walked down this way not too long ago."

Looking at the bright white sand next to the dark sand, it was so obvious to me. I told the sergeant the gooks were already here and set in.

"Right here on this very path, right here," I said, pointing down the path.

"Get your fucking ass going down that path!" McCarthy said.

"Fuck no!" I said. "We're going to walk dead into an ambush."

"If you don't go down that fucking path right now, I will cite you with cowardice in the face of the enemy! Either move out or get to the back of the squad and you'll have office hours when we get back."

I thought for a second and realized that if I let anyone else lead the squad, we were all going to die for sure. So, I moved out, slower than I had gone previously. It was at least 5:30 in the morning, and I walked and watched for any kind of movement. Everyone was extremely quiet. We moved slowly, but still nothing. We were about a city block from where we had turned west, and I noticed another piece of plastic sheeting lying across as if it was stuck in a couple of trees from the wind or maybe, just maybe, a gook could be using it to keep the moisture off, like we do.

Slowly, I walked up to the plastic as my chest pounded. The safety was off my M16. I was on full automatic, with a round in the chamber, and I pointed it to the opening at the side of the plastic. As suddenly as a bird startling me, a gook stuck his head out of the plastic and started speaking Vietnamese to me. I noticed another gook next to him, sleeping. I opened up on him and the other guy in the hole, emptying my M16, all twenty rounds.

"Ambush right!" I yelled.

With all my training and without thinking, I automatically put another clip in my rifle and ran another round in the chamber. The entire squad got down. No one did anything, including the gooks. It was like everyone was in shock and hoped this wasn't happening. Maybe that was the end.

Not a chance. A grenade was thrown at us from our right. It looked like it was moving in slow motion.

I could tell it was a Chicom grenade. Chinese Communist grenades were like the German potato masher grenades of World War II. They had hollow wooden handles with a grenade head. The handles were used as leverage to throw long distances. To arm the grenade, one pulled a brass ring, which was connected to a string at the bottom of the handle. The grenade was thrown in a high arc from not far to our right, slowly turning through the air, with sparks spraying from the handle. It was like watching a Fourth of July sparkler spinning toward us.

As I dove to the ground, the grenade exploded and the concussion hit me immediately with such a huge force that I felt myself being lifted a couple of inches off the ground.

I grabbed the sergeant's shirt and said, "Fuck, I told you they were here! What do you want us to do now?"

That is when the firing commenced from an AK-47 at our right flank. The squad returned fire with all M16s blasting. Bullets flew in every direction. Then, as fast as it started, the firing stopped—another lull in the action.

McCarthy said to me, "Pull back to where we dropped off Third Squad. Tell everyone to pull back."

I crouched as low as I could and ran down the line telling everyone, "Pull back and follow me!" I repeated this to everyone in the line as I hurried down the path from where we had just come. After all, I was the one who had led the way to where we were. Who knew the way out better? We all needed to get the hell out. I assumed everyone was following, because there was no more firing. I got close to the turn where I saw the white sand, so I stopped and turned around. There was only one guy behind me, another FNG.

"Where the fuck is everyone?" I asked.

"I don't know," he said.

I saw that the terrified Marine didn't have a rifle.

"Where the fuck is your rifle?"

He stood there with a look of horror on his face and said, "I dropped it."

I took a deep breath, grabbed a grenade from my belt, handed it to him, and said, "At least now you have something."

I had to ask myself, *What do I do now?* Do I go back to where the squad was and bring them back, or should I go back to Third Squad and bring them up? I was the only one who actually knew the way to where my squad was located. I had on-site info about what happened. Then I heard a lot of firing from my squad, which I knew was now pinned down. I moved swiftly back to where Third Squad was set in.

Coming up on Third Squad, I said, "Don't shoot, it's Taylor!"

"What the fuck is going on out there?" asked one of the Marines. "Where is the rest of your squad?"

"We were ambushed!"

I saw the squad leader talking on the radio. I assumed he was talking to Captain Osgood, the company commander. Osgood's instructions to the squad leader were to get back to where my squad was trapped and help pull everyone back.

"Taylor, what happened?" the squad leader asked.

"We walked directly into their lines and an ambush, just like I told that fucked-up sergeant we would," I said.

The captain was on the radio with Third Squad leader, Sergeant Hill, arguing with him. I could hear him saying, "I know there are a lot of them here, sir. Yes, sir. I know, sir."

He was going back and forth with Captain Osgood. He was looking for another answer from Osgood, looking for another approach to this disaster in the making. The CO was yelling into the radio at him. Osgood instructed him to get up to where Second Squad was trapped. It was about 5:45 a.m. now.

Hill said, "Okay Taylor, take us to where your squad is."

"Yeah, let's go," I said.

I took point and started on the perilous march back to my trapped squad.

"Let's move out," someone whispered.

Third Squad started moving north, following my lead. I was moving along fine until I noticed that first light had arrived. The sun wasn't up yet, but the predawn light started to get me confused about the exact route I had taken. Shadows I had noticed before had disappeared, and everything was different because of the light. Nothing looked familiar.

I came to a split in the path. It was difficult to remember if I had gone left or right. I took a path that went right, and it wasn't long before I realized I should have gone left. This new path had started to take me gradually away from where my squad was pinned down.

I got on the radio and asked Niederberger, "Where is your location? I'm bringing Third Squad up."

"We're over here on your left, see me?" he said.

I looked to my left and there he was, waving his hand at me from about a block away.

"We are on our way," I said.

I couldn't go directly to the trapped men. There was a clump of bushes and debris on my left. It was thick enough that I thought we might get stuck in the underbrush. I continued on the white sand trail and approached the tall dune where I had to go left, directly toward my trapped squad. Just as I approached the dune, I saw an NVA soldier's head pop up over the top to look at us. I immediately opened fire at him and yelled, "Ambush forward!" I turned around and started running away from the sand dune while yelling to everyone, "Find cover, fast!" I had walked us directly into an ambush.

I jumped into a small depression, and I could hear bullets going over my head from every direction and hitting the sand around me.

A bullet hit the ass of one of the men. "I'm hit," he yelled.

Another of the men got it in the arm and the leg and began yelling also, "I'm hit."

All the men were now on the ground around me, and it seemed that every one of them was screaming, "I'm hit! I'm Hit!"

There were so many bullets flying that I couldn't believe I hadn't been shot yet. I had to find shelter. Marines were scurrying everywhere like roaches looking for better cover. My current position became too exposed, and I needed a place to set up a base of fire. It sounded like someone had thrown a brick of firecrackers at us and they were exploding and flying everywhere. We were all flat to the ground. Bullets skimmed the backs and legs of many of the Marines. Some were hit two to three times.

I saw a small bomb crater a short distance away. I didn't think I could possibly make it, but I knew I was in the worst possible place in the open. Bullets were still flying all around us, but then I noticed a very small reduction of fire. I thought the gooks might be reloading or looking for new targets. With my chest pounding and with all the intensity I could muster, I scrambled to the bomb crater, expecting to be hit at any second. It seemed like it took minutes, but actually, it took only seconds until I slithered into the sandy crater.

Oh my God, how did I make it? I knew I had to keep firing to keep them off me. I poked up my head and saw the gooks everywhere. Some were running, and some were hidden behind sand hills. Gooks were falling, being hit from the Marines returning fire. Machine guns cracked in loud bursts all around. Even though I knew the sounds of the gooks' guns from ours, I couldn't tell which were ours and which were theirs because there was so much of it going on.

I started looking for targets or anything immediately threatening. I saw one gook with a pith helmet lifting his head over the dune. He shot and then lowered his head. I took a bead on where his head had lifted. I remembered Harvey being hit in the head on Operation Cochise, and now it was time for my payback. I aimed, knowing he was going to lift his head again. He did, but I didn't shoot. *Damn*, I said to myself. *If he lifts his head again, he's mine.* The gook popped his head up again, and I slowly squeezed the trigger the second he aimed his AK-47. His helmet went flying, and I saw his hands and head fly backward.

I saw another gook trying to flank me to the right by the ocean and I went full automatic on him. He fell.

I thought it was strange that the last burst was about half of what it should have been. I got back down in the hole. I had a horrible feeling. Keeping my head down so no one could see me, I took out the clip from the M16, and there were still rounds in the clip.

Holy fuck, my rifle jammed.

Too much sand had gotten into the chamber. When I fired full automatic to kill the last gook, sand must have melted inside the chamber. The very next round stuck and froze in place, not ejecting from the rifle. The following round came up from the clip and then got jammed into the spent cartridge shell. The only way to clear the rifle was to break it all the way down.

No, no, no, I thought. *Not now!*

I pulled out my KA-BAR knife and a grenade and put them at my side for protection. Frantically, I disassembled my M16. All kinds of fire continued to erupt all around me: machine guns, automatic rifle fire, explosions, plus AK-sounding weapons and M16s. I had to keep a cool head to survive. We were all stuck everywhere. I suddenly felt a stinging in my left bicep. Blood was oozing from it. The Chicom grenade from earlier must have gotten me.

My squad was still sitting out there about a block away, firing at the gooks who were moving in on them. Anyone who moved was shot, NVA included. I felt good when I heard our machine guns ripping away from Third Squad.

Taking apart my M16 was not a fast process. First, the clip with the rounds came out. The button to unlock the inside mechanism needed to be pushed. I bent the rifle into two pieces. The piece that is attached to the barrel has an injector piece, which I pulled out and then the bolt followed. Once all the inner parts were removed, this exposed the chamber where the shell casing had gotten stuck. I put the cleaning rod together by threading the three smaller pieces into one long rod. Then, like with a flintlock from the Revolutionary War, I rammed the rod down the tip of the barrel to kick out the old shell casing. Once it was out, I set the ramrod down, put the bolt and injector piece back, folded the rifle back together, pushed in the locking pin, put the clip in, and pulled the injector handle back to put a round in the chamber. I popped my head up and looked for something to shoot at. *Bang!* Another gook went down.

One round shot, and the rifle jammed again. I got down and started all over.

I broke down the rifle one more time, and then sent a round into the chamber. I put my bayonet on the end and just hunkered down. I couldn't be caught with my rifle broken down, because I knew at any moment a gook would pop up at the top of my position and kill me before I could put it back together. I would be giving away my position every time I popped up my head. So I lay down and pushed against the wall of the crater with my M16 to my chest and bayonet ready. With one hand grenade within reach and a round in the chamber, I waited for what I thought would soon be the end of my life.

CHAPTER

FOURTEEN

I DIDN'T KNOW IT then, but I would later learn that when I had brought Second Squad up, passing Little Ocean View, we had been so quiet that we walked right past a large group of gooks who were set in on the ocean side of the sand dune. We had passed on the other side of the same dune without them hearing us. They might have been sheltering their bodies from the mist, waiting for daybreak. Now, Pat Blakely and his gun team, who were coming to our aid, were running straight into them.

Blakely was attached to Third Squad at the end of the column. He had been following us until he was instructed to set in. When Blakely and his gun team heard the gunfire breaking out, they sprang into action to help us out. As I was running for cover from the ambush, they were running headlong into the group of NVA regulars at the sand dune we had just passed.

As Blakely approached, a gook just stood there watching them, apparently thinking his gun team was a friendly unit of their own. When Blakely was only a few feet away, the gook suddenly realized his mistake and began to take aim. Those were the last seconds of his life. Without hesitation, Blakely opened, full automatic. He had stumbled on the enemy point man, the first one in the NVA's line along the ocean, right where I thought they might be. This meant that two of our three squads were now completely surrounded.

LIEUTENANT ROGERS HAD TAKEN First Squad out by the Buddha altar, out of touch with the rest of his platoon. The lieutenant's position was clear away from the battle, and the sand island gave them good cover. They were not in the open. The only problem was his cover was almost a football field away from where Second and Third squads were. Osgood, the commanding officer, was on the radio with Lieutenant Rogers, furiously chewing him out for not following the original plan. He urged Rogers to get back with the other two squads and, if he had to, lead a charge across the dunes and come to our rescue.

"Get ready, men. We are going to attack," Lieutenant Rogers said.

Jimmy Hawkins again warned the lieutenant that it wasn't a good idea, but the lieutenant jumped up and started the charge.

Just as they entered the open dunes, a hundred NVA opened up on them in a horrific scene of carnage. Lieutenant Rogers was the first one to get hit. Everyone else was down within seconds. The sounds of AKs and light machine guns were deafening. Deadly accurate crossfire was hitting them from the entire tree line. The gooks had had all the time in the world to set up their fields of fire, and they exacted a punishing blow to the Marines of First Squad.

Wounded Marines were everywhere. Out of a squad of fourteen, only four men were not hit.

Jimmy and his new gunner were still safe. They opened fire on the tree line in front of them. The other two Marines covered the other two routes to their sides. Everyone was trying to help the wounded and did what they could, when they could. Rogers and his First Squad were in the open now, with very little to conceal them.

There was still predawn light, and Hawkins and the new gunner feared for their lives. The young gunner said, with a puzzled look on his face, "I'm only nineteen years old. What the fuck am I doing here?"

"Right now, you be fightin' for your life," said Hawkins. He understood they were caught in a well-executed ambush.

They were surrounded, and the gooks were closing in on the sides of the dunes. They were trying to pick off the Marines with individual movements from all sides. Jimmy directed the M60 into the tree line, where most of the fire was coming from, and watched the other two avenues that were wide open. He was trapped, but dead set on knocking off as many of the gooks as he could before they finished off the squad. Still, Jimmy fired in short bursts with the M60, conserving ammo for the long fight ahead. Between bursts, Jimmy encouraged the wounded to fight alongside the nonwounded with esprit de corps. The NVA never took prisoners; we *all* knew that.

Gooks were hiding in bunkers everywhere. We had walked right into the middle of a sophisticated ambush. The problem was the gooks hadn't expected a full platoon of Marines, complete with M60 machine guns, to set up an ambush in the middle of their own ambush and in the middle of the night. They also might not have realized that an entire company of experienced SLF Marines supported with tanks and amtracs would be forthcoming.

Our platoon was disbursed far apart, which made it harder for the gooks to get to us. You might say we had set up the makings of three ambushes in different places. Ironically, they were far enough from each other that our fire didn't affect the other Marine ambushes, but they were deadly enough to pick off the gooks who tried to flank or surround any one group. Now if we could only hold our positions until we could get reinforcements.

The enemy had been caught totally off guard. Still, they were shooting from behind the sand wall to the north of us and from the tree line along the ocean to the east.

The hundred NVA that were now engaged with First Squad had actually been coming down to reinforce the ambush site against the Marines at Little Ocean View. They intended to get more men into the heart of the battle. Their true original goal was to set a trap and kill the Marines who were expected to come to the aid of the ambushed Marines. They hadn't expected to run into First Squad along the way, so many of them were now engaged with First Squad, who were still in the open and trapped.

Once the enemy reinforcements had set in at Little Ocean View, my platoon was totally cut off from our base at C-4. The NVA had now set up at least six machine-gun nests on the north edge of the washout where I had heard the enemy at the start of our patrol. The ultimate trap was now set. Marines coming from C-4 to help my platoon would run headlong into the wall of machine guns, and any trapped Marines who tried to retreat to C-4 would have to pass the wall with the guns at their backs. If anyone was able to get past the enemy barrier at the washout, there was still a good chance of being hit by one of their scattered positions throughout the area.

EARLY IN THE INITIAL fight that started at 5:45 a.m., Ed Niederberger was radioman and still trapped with my beleaguered Second Squad. He was in contact with everyone by radio, and that was a real plus. He had the presence of mind to assess the situation. At the point Staff Sergeant McCarthy gave me the order to pull back, Niederberger was on the radio with the CO. By the time my squad started to move out and follow me, they had to stop because they were receiving enemy fire from various directions. Ed got down and took a head count before continuing. After the head count, he knew that four men were missing from the squad. He realized that I wasn't there, as well as the FNG who'd followed me. Bill Burgoon and Staff Sergeant McCarthy were also missing.

It was 6:00 a.m. at this point. Niederberger knew he could not continue to pull back, so he told everyone to lie prone.

"Just stay down," he said.

Niederberger learned from his radio that Osgood was coming with reinforcements. "Help is coming, men. You need to just hold on," Osgood had told him.

Ed Niederberger started to develop a plan to find the four missing men. Out of the clear blue, he heard Bill Burgoon yelling for anyone in the squad to help him.

"Lie still, Bill," he yelled back. "Help is coming!"

Several attempts were made to move into a position to help Bill, but any movement drew fire from the surrounding gooks. Apparently, Bill was hit in the legs with a blast from one of the AK-47 rifles that opened up on us when I had stumbled upon the gooks in the hole. The gooks were everywhere, and Ed's team received tremendous fire because they were in the open. So Ed was keeping everyone low to the ground. He didn't want to get anybody else hit, so he set the men toe to toe in a circle. Joe Benedict, who'd been in country for only two weeks, was lying next to Ed on his left.

Gooks ran around the circle of men to get into a better position. From there, they shot rounds and threw a few grenades. Ed knew they had to keep their heads down. If they moved, they most likely would be hit.

About an hour passed, and the gooks targeted Bill's calls for help. They threw several grenades at Bill, and one landed extremely close to him with a huge explosion. Shrapnel tore into his back and peppered all the way up his side. Ed continued to talk to Bill and to reassure him, but there was little more he could do because anyone who moved at all would receive fire. The squad was zeroed in, and there were more gooks than Ed had originally thought.

Captain Osgood, our company commander, remained in radio contact with Ed. This gave Osgood a picture of what he was up against.

Ed knew Osgood well enough to call him Skipper. This is a term of respect for a Marine infantry captain. "Skipper, we are totally pinned down and surrounded," he pleaded. "We need immediate support and medical. We have several wounded and one critical. I'm not sure we'll be able to hold out much longer, but we'll give 'em hell if they try and get us, sir!"

"You're doing a great job, Ed!" Osgood reassured him. "Just hold out. First and Third platoons are mustering right now, and we'll be there shortly. Where's your platoon sergeant?"

"Sir," Ed said, "I have no idea where he is."

"Okay, just hold out. We'll be there shortly."

AT 6:30 A.M., OSGOOD started to put his plan together. Third Platoon was assembled and getting ready to move out of C-4 with two tanks. Also part of the plan was to get Lieutenant Higgins, Third Platoon Sergeant Bonnie, and Sergeant Art of Weapons Platoon together at the command post. These men were the best in the company and were not yet in the fight.

By about 7:00 a.m., Osgood called the First Amtracs Battalion based at the mouth of the Cua Viet River. He asked for the Amtracs to bring reinforcements, more ammo, and medical supplies, and then to assist with medical evacuation.

Amtracs immediately gathered about fifty men and supplies. Ammunition was loaded into one of the amtracs. A group of corpsmen put together a trauma team to stabilize the injured and developed a plan to medevac as many as they could in another amtrac. A group of five amtracs in all were hastily put into action by 8:30 a.m. Reinforcements boarded the other amtracs, and help was on its way.

It was a twenty-minute drive along the coast to C-4 where First Platoon was manning the lines. Osgood had the amtracs' Navy reinforcements unload at C-4, so his First Platoon Marines could take their place and be sent into the fight. Cooks, office personnel—hell, anybody they could possibly scrounge up at C-4—were gathered to bolster the platoon.

Lieutenant Rogers, who was with First Squad trapped at the Buddha, kept radioing for help. They were stranded, and many were wounded. He insisted on them being the first to be rescued. Meanwhile, Ed radioed the Skipper that he was holding out and keeping the gooks at bay.

WHILE THE NAVY REINFORCEMENTS were taking First Platoon's places on the lines, the Marines of Third Platoon were massed on top of the two tanks and heading out.

Some Marines opened the gate to let out the tanks, but in their haste, they failed to pull back the main gate far enough. One of the tank's tracks got snagged in barbed wire and almost tore off the gate and post. It took about fifteen minutes for it to be cut and freed. It was now about at 9:00 a.m., and critical minutes were ticking away.

Once cleared, both tanks headed toward the ocean and made a hard left turn to go north along the coast toward Little Ocean View. Of course, this was the trap the NVA had hoped for. Just maybe their plan could work. The entire time we had spent building C-4, the NVA were designing a way to lure the Marines out of it. The NVA knew we would call in for reinforcements. After annihilating the reinforcements with machine guns, mortars, and artillery, they could attack and crush the remaining forces at C-4, finally wiping out the base that had blocked their infiltration route to Quang Tri.

The gooks had six concealed machine-gun bunkers on the north side of Little Ocean View, waiting for the reinforcements. Many of the bunkers were totally camouflaged. The NVA used downed trees, and some had roofs over their heads for camouflage. Individual soldiers were also waiting in spider holes surrounding the machine guns, creating crossfire. Their plan was to lure the Marines into Little Ocean View's washout clearing. Once they were in the open, they would cut the Marines to pieces. They suspected tanks would be coming, so they placed mines along Little Ocean View's washed-out area where they suspected the tanks and amtracs might go.

The tank crews were expected to go the route of least resistance and move toward the washout at Little Ocean View. Before reaching

Little Ocean View, they paused long enough for the Third Platoon to disembark and spread out. The tanks then continued forward and started running into small arms fire. The gooks had set up small ambushes on the way to Little Ocean View, hoping to catch some of the oncoming Marines in the open. The enemy was everywhere, and the tanks were having trouble finding targets because the gooks were so well-hidden. Of course, the tankers were also afraid of firing and hitting one of our own. There was also the threat of RPG rockets to worry about. The rockets were capable of knocking out a tank as they did in July on Operation Buffalo.

The tank commander, not able to find targets said, "Fuck this!" He popped open his turret so he could man the mounted .50-caliber machine gun.

"Sir, don't do that," one of the men in the tank warned him. "It's too dangerous!"

"We can't hit what we can't see," he said. "I believe this is what Patton would do."

He continued out of the hatch just far enough to grab hold of the machine gun and took a direct hit to his head. His brains splattered and flowed down the side of the tank in a pinkish and red mass. The tank commander fell straight back down the opening—the crew frozen with disbelief at the sight of his lifeless body. He had been the best tank commander in the unit.

"The CO is hit. He's hit!" one of the tank men yelled. "We have to pull back and regroup. We've got to get him some help now!"

The leadership of the tank crew broke down. The tanks were out of the battle almost as fast as they were in it. Both retreated toward the rear, still being harassed as they reversed.

Meanwhile, Sergeants Art and Bonnie, who had disembarked from the top of the tanks, were setting their men into firing positions wherever they could. Marines were all over the place, as was the enemy. There was no order to the battle. Men hunkered down wherever they could because all hell had broken loose on them.

Lieutenant Higgins called back to Osgood and told him that the tanks had pulled back. Osgood couldn't believe it.

"Where are the tanks now?" he asked.

"Sir, we really don't have any contact with the tanks at all anymore," Higgins said.

"Hold on!" Osgood told him. "First Amtracs is here and they're getting ready to move out of C-4. First Platoon is coming with the amtracs and with more ammo in just a few minutes. Hang in there; support is on the way. I've also called up for some air support. As soon as possible, we'll start air operations. We can't give you any close air support, but we can at least keep them from bringing in reinforcements from the DMZ."

Just then, mortars started rolling in on the stranded Third Platoon, one right after the other. They were missing their target for some unknown reason. Maybe their forward observer didn't have a clear sight as to where to place the mortars, or they were firing at pre-assigned coordinates. Then again, maybe they were just guessing.

Meanwhile, Ed Niederberger, who was monitoring everything on the radio, continued to yell out to the wounded Bill Burgoon. "They are coming, Bill. Hang in there!"

I COULD HEAR ALL the firing coming from Little Ocean View. Then I could hear Vietnamese voices toward the ocean. I hoped they wouldn't discover my location. The gooks did not yet realize I was in the crater. They were moving up to Little Ocean View to support their machine gunners. I then heard a lot of firing from what sounded like a battle taking place. I couldn't tell what was happening. I was waiting to be overrun in my concealed crater.

"I'm not going to be taken alive!" I kept saying to myself.

More firing came from where Ed was, but again, I didn't want to give away my position. What could I do anyway with a jammed M16?

Ed stopped hearing back from Bill Burgoon. He called out for him several more times, but there was no longer a response. He looked at his watch and noted for the record that it was 10:30 a.m. when Bill must have passed away.

So far, we had held the gooks from overrunning us for six straight hours. Ed turned to Lance Corporal Joe Benedict, directly to his left.

"Joe, I think Bill's dead," he said.

"Those damn bastards!" Joe said and then, in his peripheral vision, he caught a glimpse of an NVA soldier that had been edging closer toward them.

"Hey, Ed, do you see that gook to my left?"

"God, yes!" Ed said to him.

"Shoot him!" Joe retorted.

"No, you shoot him," he said, his eyes already on another possible target.

The gook raised his head again, and they both fired.

"Looks like we both sent him to Buddha," Ed said.

The gooks were moving to the left and right of Ed and Joe's position to have the advantage of a good shot. Every time the gooks got up, Ed and Joe would lay into them. Ed and Joe had stopped all the efforts to shoot at them, or so Ed thought, but the enemy was slowly getting closer. About 11:00 a.m., Ed heard a sharp, loud crack go right by his head and then heard Joe exhale deeply.

He looked over and saw that Joe's head was down. He called out to him, but Joe didn't answer. He rolled Joe over and saw a single bullet wound to his upper body. He surmised that Joe had taken a sniper round that was aimed for Ed's head. Joe started to come around and asked for water. Ed knew from his training that it was bad to give someone with a gut wound water. He tried to make Joe as comfortable as he could. He would now have to cover his own position, as well as Joe's, to stay alive.

I was still in the crater waiting for the enemy to come for me or stumble upon me by accident. I could hear someone in the distance calling for help. I thought it could be one of the guys stuck out with Niederberger. I wondered who it was or whether it was a trick to get someone in the open. I remembered that trick from watching the World War II movie *Sands of Iwo Jima* with John Wayne. In the movie, someone kept calling the sergeant's name, "Stryker!" Was the voice a trick to get us out in the open?

I was determined to survive the day. I kept my head down, and all I had was a single round in the chamber of my M16. I wanted to be one hundred percent ready to fight, even if I only had one round and a bayonet. I remembered that the gooks torture Marines, so I was determined to go down fighting. Mortars were going over my head. There was firing everywhere around us. I knew I had to remain calm and ready for anyone who might cross my path. I heard the sound of mortar rounds leaving the tubes—*Bloop, bloop* sounds, one after the other. I wondered if they were aiming for us. The mortars hit south of me, and I assumed they were directed at the Marines who were coming to help us.

Three amtracs had left the safety of their base at the Cua Viet River Basin at about 8:30 a.m. and had swept along the ocean at breakneck speed. They left a trail in the water at the beach, rushing north toward C-4. They were loaded with fifty men because it was all that First Amtracs could spare. The amtracs arrived at the gate of C-4 about 8:45 a.m. and immediately rushed inside the fortress. Once inside the gate, they opened their large ramps to allow the men to exit. Men from First Platoon lined up, ready to board in their place.

One of the men waiting to board the amtrac was Private Ryan Connors, who had gotten to C-4 that very day. He hadn't had time to put away his personal gear. One of the sergeants directed him to go directly to the line of Marines waiting to board the amtracs.

"You're in Guns now," someone told him as he hurried to the waiting Marines. "Here are three boxes of belt-fed M60 ammo."

He took the three boxes and then struggled clumsily to figure out how he was supposed to carry the three heavy boxes along with his rifle and pack. On top of everything else, his bladder was painfully full. In all the chaos, he hadn't been able to find an opportunity to piss. Connors just kept following everyone's orders. The FNG asked one of the Marines where the toilet was, but it was pretty far away, and the Marines were already inside and climbing on top of the amtracs.

First Amtrac's reinforcements took over First Platoon's positions. Fifty Marines in total from First Platoon and a few other Marines they were able to scrounge up boarded the amtracs. The Marines who had already got on top extended their hands to help others climb aboard. As soon as all the Marines were aboard the three amtracs, the roaring of their engines gave a sound of loud urgency to their task. The tracks turned, digging large grooves into the sand. They raced their engines and rushed, one at a time, out of the gate, all moving in line eastward toward the ocean. Once at the beach, they made a ninety-degree left turn toward the north and the sounds of the action in the Little Ocean View area. The Marines on top of the amtracs could hear the firing coming from the men of Third Platoon who had been riding on the tanks earlier. They were now trapped, and many lay wounded. The closer the amtracs got, the louder the sounds of gunfire became. Just as they arrived at Little Ocean View, the first amtrac in line hit a mine at the water's edge. It exploded with a frightening and unexpected plume of black smoke and debris.

The Marines were ordered to dismount. They jumped off the amtracs and ran inland, looking for cover anywhere they could find it. Some of the Marines went into bomb craters, others behind dunes, and still others were able to find only trees for cover. Private Connors, the new guy, not wanting to piss in his pants, jumped off the amtrac on the ocean side using the huge metal monster as cover from all the insanity around him. He immediately unbuttoned his utility pants and relieved himself. Once his bladder emptied, he grabbed the three cans of ammo on top of the amtrac and ran around its rear into the dunes. He took shelter behind a tree and then saw a machine gunner laying down fire on the enemy. He found a place next to the gunner. When he looked up to see what was happening, he saw a gook jump up and run to a different position. Connors didn't fire on him. The new Marine was confused and disoriented. Not knowing what to do, he just laid on his back in the hole with the three containers and his M16 at his chest.

The gunner looked at him and screamed, "Start firing your M16, you son of a bitch!"

"I can't see anyone," he said in a nervous voice.

"You best find a target, or you'll be the target!" the gunner said.

The best thing the Marines had going were the amtracs. The remaining two amtracs approached the trapped Third Platoon and continued a little farther north up the coast. They ended up on the north side of Little Ocean View. When Ewings and the other Marines got off, they secured the beach and helped lay down suppressing fire so other Marines could disembark. They had completely surprised the enemy with this maneuver. Ewings and others ended up securing the ocean flank of the enemy.

First Platoon was engaged with the enemy machine guns at Little Ocean View on the south side of the battle. Third Platoon and the amtracs had enough men to secure the ocean flank of the enemy on the east side of the battle. This eventually led to the dismantling of the entrenched enemy's positions. The strategy of the NVA was to overwhelm the reinforcements with machine guns at the washout. But the reinforcements landed along the coast and took positions on the beach. On the west side of the battle, the NVA were being machine gunned by our squad at the Buddha. Our guns now rained machine-gun fire from three sides.

Just when we thought we had them licked, enemy mortars and artillery started hitting the Marines all over the battlefield. The explosions intensified. The NVA artillery was firing at us from over ten miles away, somewhere on the other side of the DMZ. The artillery they were firing was much more powerful than the mortars, but the explosions were hitting where no one was positioned. Still, the sounds of the incoming rounds became scarier by the minute.

I lay in my small depression of sand and could hear the rounds going over my head and then explosions to my south. I noticed jets flying overhead. But they weren't coming in and bombing the gooks we were fighting. Our positions were just too close for that kind of air support. I could hear huge explosions to the north by the DMZ. I thought, *At least the jets are giving them hell*. It also occurred to me that if the gooks retreated, they would be looking for good places to hide like the crater that I was already in.

Maybe our guys aren't coming at all. What should I do if they can't get here?

I was afraid to take a look for fear of getting shot in the head. The firing around me had slowed, and I thought maybe I was the only Marine left alive in my squad. I thought maybe if darkness came, I could crawl out of there and still make it back to C-4.

I was to find out later that Captain Osgood had asked for the air support, which was the two Phantom jets that flew overhead. They were sent to seek out possible enemy reinforcements coming from our north. This turned out to be a smart choice because the jets did indeed report finding a substantial number of troops crossing the Ben Hai River on their way south toward us. I shudder to think where I'd be now if they hadn't stopped them with their 500-pound bombs.

At the same time, the USS *New Jersey* battleship had steamed at full speed toward our positions along the South China Sea. It was the only active battleship and had arrived just in the nick of time. I heard the *New Jersey* fire her sixteen-inch guns and the rounds exploding on the other side of the DMZ. The ground around my crater shook from the salvos.

Back near the Buddha statue, Lieutenant Rogers and most of his men were wounded from his fumbled attack. Much of the radio traffic was filled with his demands for him and his men to be rescued first.

We really needed the tanks to get back into the fight. Captain Osgood got ahold of the new tank commander and directed him to resume where they'd left off. He told the new commander, "We have Marines getting killed up at Little Ocean View and more stranded to the north."

Even though First Platoon had inadvertently flanked the NVA by the ocean with the amtracs and were in good positions to contain the enemy, the NVA's machine-gun emplacements were too well-hidden and difficult to take out. The Third Platoon still received heavy machine-gun fire. This caused another stalemate.

Ewings had exited the amtrac with his team, and was using his M16 to help keep down the heads of the enemy soldiers around him. Marvin Jackson, a thin, black Marine from Detroit, Michigan, was in a fighting hole in front of him at least thirty yards away. Jackson jumped up and started to run, zigzagging like crazy toward Ewings's position. Ewings thought he must need ammo, or maybe someone was wounded. Jackson dove into Ewings's hole. So many bullets were flying that Ewings couldn't believe Jackson hadn't been hit.

"Hey, man, you gotta smoke?" Jackson asked. "I'm so nervous I just gotta have a smoke. I can't take this shit any longer!"

Ewings took a pack of Chesterfields out of his pocket and handed it over.

"Thanks, man!" Marvin said, with a big smile and an expression of sincere gratitude.

Then, just as suddenly as he had arrived, Jackson jumped up with the pack of Chesterfields and zigzagged back to his last position, still somehow not being hit.

Ewings couldn't believe what he had just seen. Jackson was literally dying for a smoke.

The tanks finally returned and moved up to where Third Platoon was holding their positions in front of the enemy machine-gun nests. Sergeant Bonnie, who was in charge of Third Platoon, told the tank crews that at least five to eight machine-gun bunkers were spread out along their front trying to mow down the advancing Marines. The tanks opened fire on the area but, just like the first tank commander had experienced, they couldn't see anything to shoot at.

Sergeant Art looked around and saw a few mortarmen and ordered them to open fire on the bunkers in front of them. The mortarmen knew it was impossible to shoot mortars in the traditional way straight overhead. The gooks were too close for mortars. Sergeant Art yelled at them to take some initiative and figure it out.

The mortar team came up with a plan to fire the projectiles like a rocket. They took off the base plate and put the bottom of the tube against a tree, angling up. They dropped the mortar in the tube to have gravity take it down to ignite it, and just as it hit the bottom of the tube, they pointed the tube in the direction of the bunkers. The mortar shell came out like a rocket from a bazooka. The round hit a tree exactly where a machine-gun emplacement was firing from. Damn if it didn't work like a charm!

Sergeant Art had trained his men well, but not all of the machine guns were up front firing at the gooks. He yelled for Ken Burkitt, who carried the new lightweight LAW rocket, to find the other machine gun and get it up front. Under fire, Burkitt got up and started moving to the rear. Along the way, he ran across two new draftees who'd been newly assigned to the platoon. They had the machine gun, but had no intention whatsoever of getting into the fight. Burkitt ordered the men to take the machine gun to Ron Asher.

"Hell no, man!" they both said in unison. They wanted nothing to do with the Marine Corps or the war.

"You think I'm crazy?" one of them complained. "A guy could get killed out there."

"Hey man," the other said. "No fucking way am I going to move from where I'm at! My mama didn't raise no fool."

It was not the time or place to berate the young Marines, so Burkitt just snatched the machine gun from the two, moved forward under withering fire, and gave it to Asher. As soon as he'd handed over the gun, there was a huge explosion and Burkitt was thrown on his back, his entire face covered with an instant gush of blood.

"I'm getting too fucking short for this shit!" Ken yelled.

"Corpsman up!" someone else yelled.

Doc McAteer came over and pushed Burkitt and himself as low to the ground as he could. He looked over Burkitt and said, "You have shrapnel in your left eye and nose." Doc stopped the bleeding and wiped Burkitt's face, then helped him to the amtrac that was now being used for triage. It was Burkitt's third Purple Heart.

THE TWO TANKS MOVED parallel to Little Ocean View to help get the wounded lieutenant and men from First Squad. The stranded squad was still all the way to the west side of the battle-field by the Buddha, where our platoon lieutenant was pinned and demanding help. The view from inside the tank was obscured, and they had orders not to open the turret hatch and expose themselves to the fire outside. As they passed the line of bunkers, the tanks opened fire with their M60 machine guns. The men just fired at whatever looked suspicious. The NVA were hiding well and kept down. One of the tanks ran over a mine, which threw the tank crew into confusion. Disobeying orders, one of the tank crew members got out of the tank to assess the damage, but it wasn't severe enough to stop the tank from continuing on to retrieve the survivors of First Squad near the Buddha.

Sergeant Bonnie, seeing the tanks moving away and firing at the bunkers said, "Fuck this shit, being pinned down. I've had it."

Bonnie had a flair for being different. He'd gotten so fed up with his jamming M16, for example, he started carrying a Swedish K assault rifle. With the tanks' M60 machine guns keeping the enemy's heads down, he saw his opportunity. Sergeant Bonnie picked up an M60 machine gun, with its metallic split-link belt of bullets running down its side. He started attacking the bunkers alone, one at a time. He charged directly toward the first machine-gun bunker that was straight ahead and, as he got to the top of the enemy bunker, he opened fire. The three NVA soldiers lying in position there didn't have a chance. Bonnie had eliminated them with about fifteen rounds.

He received fire from his left flank from another NVA soldier, swung his machine gun around, and killed him too. Again, he kept firing full automatic bursts from the hip, exactly like out of a Rambo movie. Sergeant Art was watching Sergeant Bonnie and saw a VC scout wearing a blue-green silk shirt to Bonnie's right. Bonnie opened fire on him, and the gook flew backward as Bonnie's rounds ripped into his torso. The impact of the machine-gun bullets, hitting the scout over and over, sent his shirt flying off his body and into the air. Sergeant Art watched the VC scout fall to the ground and his shirt flutter down slowly from above him. The surreal image of that shirt drifting down, as if in slow motion, burned into his brain.

This was the turning point for the battle, but neither the gooks nor the Marines in the fight realized it yet.

The two tanks reached the squad trapped in the open area near the Buddha altar. The men were still pinned down, but the tanks positioned their sides to cover them until they got aboard. The whole time, the tanks' machine guns rained tracer bullets on the gooks in the tree line. The wounded Marines were carefully loaded on top of each of the tanks, and then the tanks retreated directly back to C-4. As soon as the tanks unloaded the wounded, they returned to the battle with a new fervor to eliminate the gooks. Their next run would be easier because they were now more familiar with the terrain.

Meanwhile, the Marines who had come up with the amtracs had been taking fire the entire time. They were in the fight of their lives, with a flow of wounded being shuttled back to the safety of the medical amtrac. The amtracs had become staging areas for the corpsmen treating the wounded. Doc McAteer was there, giving life-saving medical treatment. One of the Marines actually died, and McAteer brought him back to life using CPR. That Marine needed to be medevaced right away by helicopter to the First Amtrac base at the Cua Viet River medical facility, where doctors were waiting. Every time an amtrac was loaded with the wounded, it would close its huge front door and take off southward through the shallow water along the shore. When it arrived at C-4, another amtrac would take its place, bringing valuable ammunition, food, and medical supplies to the fight.

It was now closing in on two in the afternoon. It was over one hundred degrees, and the full sun was beating down on me. I had been baking from dawn to two in the afternoon with no shade. There were just a few drops of water left in my last canteen. I nursed every bit I could get out. It had been eight and a half hours since I fired my first shots. I could hear a lot of machine guns blazing away at the enemy. It was starting to sound like we might be getting an edge. I felt like it might be okay to peek out and see what was happening. Then I thought, *If it's our guys, they may think I'm a gook. If it's the gooks, they'll try to kill me for sure.*

Nope, I'm keeping my head down.

I wanted to make it out of that hole and to go home. If I died there in Nam and I never had children, it would have been like I had never existed. There would be nothing left of my essence to say that I had ever been alive.

I reminded myself to stay alert and be mindful of all my ears could hear. My eyes were plastered to the top of the cresting sand, waiting for the unexpected at any moment. I kept a close accounting of all the defensive weapons next to me. I had my hand grenade cotter pins unbent in the easy-pull position. I had two knives, my bayonet, and my KA-BAR. The bayonet was attached to the top of my rifle. If I needed a knife, I could use the KA-BAR, which was good for hand-to-hand combat. The KA-BAR was rusty and worn, but sharp as hell. I had taken off my flak jacket and cartridge belt in order to move faster if I had to.

I had survived twelve months of hell, for what? Just to die here at the very end? Who suffers the least? Is it the guy who dies at the end of his tour or the guy who dies right away? I figured it would have been better to have gotten it a long time ago. At least I wouldn't have suffered through all the terror and horror for months on end.

Something has to happen for me to get out of this mess.

I found myself wondering who I had listed as the beneficiary of my $10,000 life insurance policy.

At least that would be a lot of money for someone.

Was it my sister, Bev, who I left it to? I couldn't remember. Sweat ran down my face. I was getting uneasy lying there and had to move around, but at the same time, I didn't want to give away my position.

God, it's hot.

More artillery went overhead. It felt like it was theirs.

Yep, explosions to the south.

I wondered if Burgoon and the rest of the platoon were still alive. I didn't hear any more firing from them.

Where are the gooks hiding?

My mind was wired hot and racing nonstop.

The tanks were now sitting directly in front of the first machine-gun bunker in Little Ocean View. It was time to take them out. Marines gathered behind the two tanks for cover as they rolled forward with their .30-caliber machine guns blazing. They paused to fire their 90 mm gun, point-blank, directly at the bunkers.

When the cannon of a tank fires, the sound is deafening. A big plume of white smoke comes out of the barrel while, inside the tank, another high-explosive round is immediately inserted into the chamber.

The gunners of the tanks looked for the next target to let loose their explosive fury. The tank to the west was ordered to take out the west flank, so they both focused their fire at the west side, along the tree line where the hundred gooks had set in. One of the tanks made a hard ninety-degree turn and attacked down the westerly tree line. The other tank attacked directly in front of the machine-gun nests. Marines following behind the tanks went after the spider holes.

The Marines started receiving accurate artillery fire from the DMZ. The NVA must have realized they were in a do-or-die situation. They knew the tanks were coming for them, and they had no choice but to call artillery on their own positions. The Marines ran for cover, but the tanks didn't stop at all. The gooks got up and started running back toward the north. It was going on 3:00 p.m., and the tanks, plus Lieutenant Higgins's efforts, had finally broken the back of the NVA.

I could hear the firing and the Vietnamese yelling all around me. I popped up my head and there were about twenty of them already passing me and running like rabbits—running for their lives, some without their weapons. Shit, they were everywhere and were getting away.

I took aim at one of them and squeezed off my single round. I have no idea if I hit a damn thing. The gook was there and then he wasn't. I didn't know if he got away or not. I heard artillery from our guns going overhead north, silencing the NVA's artillery. Then the USS *New Jersey* blasted away, hitting artillery sites wherever they were spotted. Helicopters were going overhead, ripping away with their miniguns and rockets at the fleeing enemy. As the helicopters flew overhead, the minigun shell casings fell all around me. I saw the tank point its barrel directly at my own trapped squad and Ed Niederberger.

Shit, I thought, *they are going to open fire on my squad!*

Ed stood up, waving his helmet in one hand and yelling into the radio receiver that he held in the other. He was too far away for me to hear what he was saying, but it was the right thing because the tank didn't fire on them. The tank approached them, and Ed, along with the rest of my squad, were able to get behind and follow the tank for cover. As the tank progressed, Ed helped load wounded men on top. Then he and another Marine carried Bill Burgoon and Joe Benedict from the battlefield to an amtrac that had just arrived.

Third Platoon Marines came up, and they noticed I was a Marine. I had been worried they wouldn't recognize me out there on the wrong side of the battle lines. They ran right past me, chasing after the NVA. I felt a strong sense of relief to see our guys.

I had made it again.

There I was, standing in the sandy crater, starting to feel safe again. I began looking for another M16 rifle. After climbing out of my position, I was immediately surrounded by several Marines who followed behind the first wave. A corpsman came over to me and asked about the dried blood on my left arm. I told him about the grenade that went off. In the mayhem, I had forgotten all about it. After what I had just been through, I shrugged off the wound as insignificant. The corpsman put a dressing on my arm and ran off toward Niederberger, where several other corpsmen had gathered to treat the other wounded. I felt as though I were in a dream world, wandering around looking at the dead that surrounded me. I really didn't know what to do with myself at that point. Everyone who needed tending to seemingly had been.

This must be what it feels like to win a battle.

Yet, I felt sad and empty inside. I heard the sound of an amtrac moving north along the beach and then watched it making a hard-left turn and coming onto the shore a hundred yards away. The front of the amtrac came down. Men poured out and spread out as if they had specific tasks.

I then saw Staff Sergeant McCarthy, the sergeant who had led us into the ambush. *What the hell was he doing on the amtrac, and where the fuck did he come from?* I kept asking myself. *What the hell's going on?* I couldn't believe my eyes. I saw Niederberger walking along with the corpsmen carrying two of the Marines from our squad who were killed. Two other Marines followed them. I didn't know who was dead, and I didn't want to walk over there to find out. I just watched as they loaded the bodies into the amtrac. I heard screaming from Niederberger and one of the other Marines. They were yelling profanities at Staff Sergeant McCarthy.

Without hesitation, Niederberger threw off his radio and jumped at the staff sergeant right in front of everyone. The other Marine jumped in too, both landing punches as hard as they could. It took about eight Marines to pull them both off. A high-ranking officer came over to see what was going on.

Then the officer started yelling at the staff sergeant also. McCarthy tried to get a word in edgewise, but the officer wouldn't have any of it. He kept screaming directly in his face. He pointed to the amtrac. McCarthy, with his M16 in his right hand, slowly walked into the amtrac with his head held low. The officer then went to Niederberger and the other Marine. Both of their hands were pointing and waving. I heard Niederberger say the words "son of a bitch."

The corpsmen loaded the wounded into the amtrac, and the door closed abruptly. I heard the large roar of the engines as it struggled to back up from its position. The tracks spun in the sand, driving the huge amtrac into the surf, and then turning it around to go back down the beach. It shifting into gear and sped off, taking the wounded and the staff sergeant back to C-4.

Everyone was standing around. I saw an M16 that one of the wounded had left and grabbed it, throwing down the one I had that jammed. It was after three o'clock in the afternoon. All the wounded and dead were removed, and any weapons left from the battle were picked up. The Marines who had chased the NVA were filtering back to our position. I said to myself, "*Well that's that. It's over.*"

That statement couldn't have been further from the truth.

I heard *bloop* sounds coming from the north. The NVA were back and sending rounds raining down on us, showering us with shrapnel as they exploded. Our mortars started to return fire. I heard the order to pull back toward Little Ocean View. I said to myself, *"What the hell is this?"*

We had finally kicked the shit out of Charlie and taken the real estate he was holding, and now we were retreating and giving up the same positions that so many fought and died for? We're just giving all this real estate back? It felt wrong. At least in World War II when we took the real estate, it was ours.

One thing I did know for sure was that the North Vietnamese would come back for their bodies. My attitude had changed since I first arrived in Vietnam. A survival of the fittest had set in, and I'd had enough. I pulled out my hand grenade, pulled the pin, and shoved it under one of the dead gooks before I left. As long as that body rested on that spoon, it wasn't going off—a trick I had learned from them. When they came back to get that body, there was going to be another fatality on their side. I saw Niederberger as we started pulling back.

"What the hell were you doing?" he asked.

"I'm just taking care of some payback," I told him.

The mortar barrage lifted, and we checked to see if anyone was missing.

No one was taking charge. Niederberger had the radio and was talking to the captain and the commanding officer. I looked around the sand for my gear and equipment. It wasn't much, but I didn't want to leave anything behind. I started retracing my footsteps to where I'd been pinned down and found my gear.

NORTH VIETNAMESE BODIES WERE everywhere and, of course, the booby-trapped body. The walk to Little Ocean View was about two football fields away and was uneventful. We dug holes for night, and C-rations were delivered. I was finally going to get something to eat. I tore into the box and retrieved a can of Beef Spiced with Sauce, which was one of my favorites. I saw Niederberger again on the lines. I scrambled over to him. I wanted to know what had happened to the squad where he had been pinned down. I was sure he wanted to know what had been going on with me.

"What is the story on that idiot, McCarthy?" I asked him.

"He's in the rear, and I would think he's facing disciplinary action and Lieutenant Rogers is too." he said. "Both are being transferred out immediately."

"You know they almost got us killed!" I said to Ed. "I kept telling McCarthy about the danger signs I saw, but he ignored all the warnings and wouldn't listen to me. So, where the hell was he during all the fighting?"

"I don't exactly know how he did it, but he ended up back at C-4 just after we were hit."

"He what?"

"You got it," said Ed. "He must have run all the way back after the initial hit."

The look on my face must have been shock. My eyes and mouth were wide-open.

I said to Ed, "Wonder what's going to happen to him?"

Ed said. "I talked to the Skipper, and he felt they should be put up for a court martial. Looks like they lucked out, because the Battalion relieved them from duty here and they are being transferred out. Only God knows where they are going to end up."

I said, "I'm a short-timer, Ed, and I sure would like to get the hell out of here."

He gave me a nod, and I could see from the expression on his face that he was adding up in his mind how much time he himself had left. Ed had arrived in our outfit in August, after Cochise. He'd been in country for only five months. He had eight more to go.

It started getting dark and we had foxhole watch, two men to a hole. A bunch of FNGs were brought up to replace the wounded and dead Marines. We didn't have enough men even with the FNGs to stand the lines. The FNGs had never stood hole watch, so they took one older guy out of each hole and added a new guy in to give him some experience. I got this little black kid, with glasses that were like coke bottles. I stood first watch for two hours, and he couldn't sleep at all.

I kept telling him to get some sleep, and all he could say was, "I'm scared."

"Marine, we're all scared," I said.

"Really?" he said back to me.

"Yep."

I don't think it helped him at all. When it was time for me to sleep, he kept waking me up saying, "I think I hear something."

I would get up and look and listen carefully. No, I didn't see or hear anything but normal noises. I said to him, "Don't worry, we're all scared, especially when we just get here."

"No, you don't understand. I can't see anything," he said.

"What?" I asked in a soft whisper. "What do you mean you can't see anything?"

"I don't know what it is; I just can't see anything, especially at night."

"Let me see your glasses."

He handed me his glasses, and when I looked at them, I said, "Fuck! Why did they even send you out to the field?"

"I just followed orders," he said. "I can't see a single damn thing, and I'm scared as hell. Look at my hands shake."

He might as well have been sitting on a jackhammer, they were shaking so bad. I wasn't going to be able to go back to sleep, so we stayed up talking all night. About one o'clock in the morning there was a huge explosion from where we had had the battle the day before.

Looks like they came for the bodies.

Only God knows how many of them came down to retrieve their dead. They sure had their work cut out for them. Knowing they were out there kept me on full alert, realizing that at any time they might try to overrun us. I let the kid fall asleep that night. He wasn't doing me any good. I wasn't about to trust him with my life at that point anyway. I knew only one thing: the kid shouldn't be in the field.

Sunrise came on, and another platoon came out to take over our positions. We pulled out and moved back to C-4. When we got back, I was exhausted but hungry. I went to the bunker and dropped off my gear before going to the chow hall for something to eat. After eating, I went back to the bunker and lay on my cot and thought, *I will never forget January 19 ever again in my life.* The second I closed my eyes, I fell asleep.

CHAPTER

FIFTEEN

WE WERE TOLD THAT the Vietnamese Tet New Year celebration was to begin on January 30, 1968. We'd be on full alert and would not be taking any chances.

The day before Tet, our platoon set up fields of fire on our perimeter. Each tank was parked in a crucial location and had flechette rounds in its arsenal of shells. If we got hit and the NVA attacked, the tank would lower its huge cannon and shoot a flechette. Thousands of small, metal arrows would fly out in all directions, killing everyone and everything in front of the tank. We placed interlocking fields of fire with 80 mm mortars and preset coordinates. The Cua Viet River amtrac base still had its 105 mm howitzers that fired in support from several miles away. We had just received new electronic equipment and night vision binoculars. The new equipment would indicate the enemy's position and strength if they tried to overrun us. They didn't want to mess with this battalion of Marines anymore.

The next day was quiet at dawn and Tet was uneventful for us, but we heard that the NVA had taken the town of Hue and the new SLF Alpha Marines were there fighting to take back the city. Hundreds of NVA soldiers had filtered in from the Ho Chi Minh Trail and the DMZ. SLF Alpha, as well as other Marine units in the area, were getting creamed.

Five days later at 10 a.m., our lines spotted a large group of NVA marching in a distant tree line directly to the west of us. It was easy to see them because up to the tree line the terrain was all sand. We were curious about the unit and watched them in the distance. They were trying to infiltrate swiftly into the south, using the tree line for cover.

Puffs of smoke began to appear at different locations in front of the NVA unit. A firefight began to erupt. We wondered who it was. Captain Osgood came over to my position and looked out with his binoculars, watching the battle unfold.

"Recon ran into about a hundred NVA regulars trying to bypass C-4," he said. "They're calling in naval gunfire right now."

The sound of naval guns came from the ocean. We could actually see the huge shells going over our heads. The fast pace of the rounds created a whistling effect. My eyes gravitated to the sound, which sent chills up my spine. The first volley hit short of the tree line, and then the recon team adjusted the fire five hundred yards farther north and west, which was right on the NVA as they were fleeing back toward the DMZ.

Recon called, "Fire for effect." This means for all guns to fire several salvos.

Thirty to forty very large-caliber shells roared over our positions from the ocean, three to six rounds at a time. They destroyed the tree line. All that was left was smoke where the trees had been.

The naval guns finally ceased fire, and later we heard the recon team was safe. About twenty dead NVA were lying around where the Navy guns had struck. Most of the others were able to get back across the DMZ, we assumed. I was sure many who crossed back had to be wounded.

The captain was still next to me, still watching through his binoculars.

"By the way," he said. "Remember the prisoners you captured in December in that ville where you ran your patrol?"

"I sure do, sir. What about it?"

"The village you went into had been taken over by NVA regulars earlier that week. The entire village was under the control of the NVA. Small groups of two to three men were trying to bypass C-4 and build up their numbers. That's why we kept getting so many prisoners filtering from the north. They were staging in the ville to our south. Eventually they moved out and are now in Hue for the Tet offensive."

He lowered the binoculars and looked at me with a smile.

"I'd say you are one of the luckiest Marines I ever met," he said. "You were dead in the center of more than a hundred NVA soldiers, with their men as your prisoners. I guess they didn't kill you because they knew that if you turned up missing, we'd come looking for you. That would have blown their plan for Tet. They were willing to surrender your prisoners to stick to their plan."

I remembered how anxious the elders had been about getting my prisoners, purporting to want to kill them. The NVA sacrificed the men I held. I remembered being upset about the men in the village not being in the Vietnamese Army. Actually, they *were* in the Vietnamese Army. They were in the North Vietnamese Army.

EARLY THE NEXT MORNING after the NVA had been caught in the tree line, our platoon swept along the ocean to see if the NVA was lurking north of our base at C-4 again. I had only two more weeks left, but I was haunted by thoughts of Rangel, Pilgreen, and many others I'd known who were hit or killed in their very last weeks in country. We had to go back to Little Ocean View, which by now might as well have been hell itself. It's where the gooks liked to set up ambushes and mortar the hell out of us, where Smitty was killed, where machine gunners were accidentally napalmed, where the battle for C-4 had taken place, and where I hid alone in the crater with my jammed M16 anticipating the end of my life.

I dreaded the thought of going out there on another patrol. I couldn't shake the dark premonition that when I had escaped that place I'd left some kind of hole in the fabric of the universe that fate needed to fill. Little Ocean View was drawing me in one more time to take me forever.

Our new platoon sergeant sent a Marine to come get me. I stood in front of the new sergeant and waited for my patrol instructions.

"Taylor, you're going home on the next chopper out of here," he said. "Get your gear. You're leaving in a few hours."

I wondered if I'd heard him correctly.

"I've got two weeks left," I said, then quickly back-stepped. "How did I get out two weeks early?" I asked.

"Your third Purple Heart came through from the last battle," he said.

I didn't even know they had put me in for one.

I stood there with my mouth wide open as it slowly began to sink in. Then it hit me, and with tears welling up in my eyes, I yelled aloud, "Yahoo! Shit, I'm going home!"

I went around and took some final pictures with the men at C-4 who would have to carry on the war without me and then gathered my gear for transit to Quang Tri where the rest of my gear had been transferred from the *Iwo Jima.*

As my last duty in Vietnam, I had to turn in my M16 rifle and ammunition before boarding the chopper leaving from Quang Tri to Da Nang. I was as happy and cocky as a Marine could be. With a big smile, I handed my M16 to the butter bar lieutenant.

He looked on a list and said very arrogantly, "This isn't the rifle we issued you."

The smile immediately left my face.

I said, "I know it isn't, but what difference does it make?"

He looked at me and said, "Well, we're going to have to charge you for the M16 we issued you."

As fast as I could move, I grabbed the rifle out of his hands and said, "Then I'm keeping this fucking one."

"Give that back to me, Marine!" he said.

"No fucking way!"

He started saying something about how he was going to have me put in the brig for insubordination.

"Fuck you! You son of a bitch," I said.

We were into it pretty heavy when a captain came over.

"What the hell is the problem here?" the captain asked.

The lieutenant started to talk, but I didn't give him a chance to get a word in edgewise.

"Sir, I've been in combat for thirteen months, and my no-good, piece of crap M16 constantly jammed on me in battle after battle," I said. "I had to get a working rifle and grabbed what was available. Now this fucking asshole says I have to pay for my original rifle."

I continued my rant, but the captain could see I was turning red. This was going nowhere. He put his hand in the face of the lieutenant and moved his face close to mine and said very slowly, "Go home, Marine!"

My heart was pounding out of my chest. My temper had gone through the roof. I wondered where that extreme rage came from. I'd been totally out of control. I had transformed since joining the battalion in Okinawa. I had no passiveness anymore.

I grabbed my seabag with all my gear, and I got on the next helicopter to Da Nang. I then boarded a jet to Okinawa for staging, and then the next flight to the continental United States. My seabag was secured, and finally I boarded TWA Airlines heading back to "the world."

As I walked down the aisle of the jet, I couldn't believe there were round eyes (American women) as stewardesses on the plane. They were beautiful and kind. I couldn't remember the last time I had seen an American woman. I sat down near a window behind the wing and looked out at the Orient for the last time.

Tears streamed from my eyes as I thought about Corporal Penny, Bill Burgoon, Bill Benedict, Sergeant Jones, Staff Sergeant Malloy, Sergeant Pike, Dan Varner, Billy Taylor, Marvin Smith and all the other guys who had died. I tried to name them each in my head, but there were so many I couldn't remember all the names.

I closed my eyes and drifted off.

We landed on a beautiful day in sunny California. I followed the crowd of mostly servicemen down the aisle and then down the stairs outside onto the tarmac. When I reached the ground, I stepped out of the way of the crowd and dropped immediately to my knees. I bent over with my hands against the warm concrete, and I kissed the ground.

EPILOGUE

AFTER FIFTY YEARS, I'M still dreaming and thinking about all the men who fought and died in Vietnam. I believe we had good intentions but found out that people will fight to preserve their way of life against all odds. My life has changed forever. It's a part of me and ingrained in my psyche. The names of my brothers resonate in me, and they are bonded in my heart forever. They live as long as I can keep their memory alive.

I came home to a country that hated me as a soldier. It was the first war that was broadcast into the American living room. Over TV dinners, American families witnessed the reality of war, and many began to doubt our mission in Vietnam. The media sensationalized atrocities of the war, and blame for the whole damned thing somehow landed on our shoulders—the shoulders of the individual American servicemen. That we were spit on and called "baby killers" is no myth. Perhaps worse was that our service was largely ignored. It was almost twenty years before I was ever acknowledged for what I did over there, and other veterans I know have waited even longer.

I was asked to reenlist and go back to Vietnam, but I couldn't go back. I wanted to stay home and forget all about the nightmare I had lived. Of course, now I know that is impossible. It is impossible to forget. And for all those who died there—hell, for all those who served there at all—we should *not* forget. We must never forget.

I ended up meeting Dan Varner's son. He joined the Marines and served with honor. I talked to Staff Sergeant Malloy's son and was able to tell him stories of his father. I met Bill Burgoon's mother and brother and slept in Bill's room, which had not been changed since the day he left for the war.

Many of the men mentioned in this book are still alive, and we meet once a year at the Third Marine Division Association Reunion. John Steiner came to the reunion but was unable to stay because it brought up too many horrible memories.

The men from our battalion all came back different. A lot of them became policemen to satisfy their adrenaline urges. Others took to drugs and alcohol. Their families could never understand why they took that road, but I know why. They had to stop the painful memories of combat. Some gave into their PTSD rages and went to jail.

Most don't understand the veteran because he will never let you in. Maybe this book will shed some light on why so many veterans never fully made it home, mentally.

By the time the war ended, more than 58,000 US servicemen had been killed. Our objective was to stop Communism and help the South Vietnamese people, but we didn't stop Communism and pulled out leaving tens of thousands stranded. We left the south with military equipment but stopped all funding. The VA is only now starting to really help veterans, fifty years later.

Was it worth it?

IVAN HIESTAND JOINED MY platoon after the Battle of Cochise. He was the Marine who was shot by a sniper after being in Vietnam for only one month. We finally met again when both of us were in our seventies. We shared our stories of that fateful day, and I wrote down the stories he told me. Just two weeks after our meeting, I was saddened to hear that he had died. Ivan wrote a poem while in Vietnam just before he was hit. His brother, Terry, gave it to me at Ivan's funeral. I'd like to share it with you now.

ALL IN VAIN

It's quiet tonight on this lonely hill,
The guns are hushed, and the men lie still.
There lingers a silence beyond all compare,
The smoke from the battle looms in the air.
Today they fought, these daring young few,
Today they died for me and for you.
They were your sons, Americans all,
From all races and creeds, they answered the call.
And what, may I ask, did you do today?
You rioted and protested to get your way!
You burned your draft cards to prove us wrong,
You shouted protests to a doubting throng.
You murdered to silence an innocent voice,
Yet here men died, for they had no choice.
For these heroes it's over, there is no more pain,
Let us all pray to God that it wasn't in vain.

Pfc. Ivan G. Hiestand
Charlie Company, 1st Battalion, Third Marines
Vietnam, September 13, 1967

GLOSSARY OF ACRONYMS
AND TERMS

Atropine
Used in Vietnam as an antidote to nerve gas

Amtrac
Armored Assault Amphibian Vehicle,
which moves on land and water

ARVN
Army of the Republic of Vietnam, name given
to identify South Vietnamese soldiers

Battalion
Consists of a lieutenant colonel and three
companies or 729 Marines

B-52 Stratofortress
American long-range, high-altitude, subsonic, jet-powered strategic bomber

Bouncing Betty
An anti-personnel mine that shoots a projectile into the air to create maximum casualties

Butterfly Mine
A small anti-personnel mine usually attached to bushes, causing smaller wounds

BLT
Battalion Landing Team helicopter and amphibious assault infantry battalion, about one thousand men

C-Rations
A case that held twelve different meals in small boxes. No other meal choices were available to servicemen in the field

Charlie
A derogatory slang term for Vietnamese guerrillas, reported as Victor Charlies or VC

CO
Commanding Officer, officer in charge of a company, battalion, or regiment

Company
Consists of a captain, lieutenant, and
three platoons or 243 Marines

Corpsman
Navy medic attached to the Marines
and respected by all Marines

Division
Consists of a major general (two-star) and
three regiments or 6,561 Marines

Engineers
Men trained in explosives to detonate mines,
used in construction and demolition

Esprit de corps
The personal ties between a Marine and the Corps

Fire Team
Consists of four Marines: a corporal and three other Marines

Flak Jacket
Ten-pound jacket worn by Marines, which
deflected shrapnel but not bullets

Flank
To the immediate left or right

FNG
Fucking new guy

FO
Forward Observer, an officer experienced in calling in air and artillery strikes

FUBAR
Marine acronym for "fucked up beyond all recognition," pronounced "foobar"

Gook
Derogatory term for North Vietnamese or Viet Cong

Halazone
Military canteen water purification tablets

Hard Core
Complete loyalty and self-sacrifice to the cause

Howitzer
An artillery piece that sends various-sized projectiles that explode

Huey
During the war in Vietnam, the newest, fastest helicopter made by the US

Intel
Short for "intelligence"

KIA
Killed in action

KP
Kitchen police or kitchen patrol, a dirty job given as punishment for a minor infraction

LAW Rocket
Light anti-tank weapon, like a small but powerful bazooka used against bunkers

LCM
Landing craft mechanized, a small landing craft large enough to hold a tank and or troops

LP
Listening post that is at least fifty yards outside the lines and manned by two troops

LPD
Landing platform dock, a large ship with a ramp doorway in the rear for loading amtracs

LPH
Landing platform helicopter, aircraft carrier facilitating helicopter attacks from the sea

LZ
Landing zone

Mama-san
Pidgin term used by US servicemen for any older
Vietnamese woman, now considered offensive

Mike Boat
Flat-bottomed boat used for river traffic and
military assaults from ship to shore

Mortars
Rounds that are dropped into a tube to
launch into the air toward the enemy

MP
Military Police

Napalm
Highly flammable, thick, jelly-like substance that
explodes with the intensity of a volcano

North Vietnamese
People who lived north of the Ben Hai River

NTA
Northern Training Area located on the
Japanese island of Okinawa

NVA
North Vietnamese Army, soldiers of the
north lead by Ho Chi Minh

On line
Walking or standing side-by-side in the same direction

Papa-san
Pidgin term used by US servicemen for any older
Vietnamese man, now considered offensive

Private First Class (PFC)
One grade (stripe) up from private, which is the lowest rank

Platoon
Consists of a lieutenant, sergeant, and
three squads or 27 Marines

Poncho
A green plastic, waterproof liner, with a hood
to keep moisture away from the body

Puff
Puff the Magic Dragon, a DC-3 airplane converted
to a flying gun platform often used at night

Punji Stick
Sharpened bamboo stake placed in the ground to injure hostiles

R&R
Rest and relaxation, days during which the
Marines get a brief reprieve from the war

Recon
Reconnaissance patrol sent out to inspect an
area before larger forces are sent in

Regiment
Usually had a full colonel and three battalions, or 2,187 Marines

RPG Rockets
Rocket-propelled grenades shot from a tube
to neutralize armored vehicles

Sappers
Special NVA unit slipping through the lines
throwing grenades and charges

Seabees
Navy construction battalions for building
naval shore facilities in combat zones

Short-timer/getting short
A serviceman who was a short-timer or "getting
short" had less than 99 days left in his tour

Sit-rep
Situation report

SLF
Special Landing Force

Spooky
Another name for a flying minigun platform used
solely at night to destroy enemy units

Squad
Consists of a sergeant and three four-man
fire teams or thirteen Marines

Take point
To take point, walk point, be on point, or be a point man
is to assume the first and most exposed position in a
combat military formation, the leading soldier or unit
advancing through hostile or unsecured territory

USO
United Service Organizations

Ville
Small Vietnamese village

VC
Viet Cong, Southern Vietnamese sympathizers to the North Vietnamese Army

XO
Executive officer, second in command

ABOUT THE

AUTHOR

WHILE BILL TAYLOR'S FRIENDS were at home going to school and dating, he was fighting for his life.

At eighteen years old, Bill served in the First Battalion, Third Marine Regiment in Vietnam—a journey that seemed impossible to survive. For the battles they fought, Bill was awarded three Purple Hearts and his battalion earned two Presidential Unit Citations. World War II battles of that magnitude at Tarawa and Iwo Jima are well-known, yet few know of the hard-fought battles of the Vietnam War. Bill's battalion participated in twenty-five combat operations. In *On Full Automatic*, he brings to light the bravery and sacrifices of so many. His platoon was wiped out several times, once leaving only seven out of fifty men standing. Every platoon lieutenant, sergeant, and squad leader was killed, wounded, or relieved of command. Staying alive became Bill's full-time job.

CONNECT WITH THE AUTHOR

CONTACT THE AUTHOR,
find combat photos, and additional information at:

williamvtaylor.com

William V. Taylor, Jr. (Bill) is available for interviews, speaking engagements, and book readings, in person or remote via web meetings. If you are involved with a book club, podcast, museum, library, school, church, military association, or historical organization that is interested in hearing more, you can reach Bill directly through the Contact form on his author website.

Photographs from Bill's 1967-68 tour of duty featuring the events, places, and people in this book can be found on the Photos page of the website named above.

Made in United States
Orlando, FL
15 August 2022

21055749R00211